A SHORT HISTORY OF THE
MODERN
MEDIA

A SHORT HISTORY OF THE
MODERN MEDIA

JIM CULLEN

WILEY Blackwell

This edition first published 2014
© 2014 Jim Cullen

Registered Office
John Wiley & Sons Ltd, The Atrium, Southern Gate, Chichester, West Sussex,
PO19 8SQ, UK

Editorial Offices
350 Main Street, Malden, MA 02148-5020, USA
9600 Garsington Road, Oxford, OX4 2DQ, UK
The Atrium, Southern Gate, Chichester, West Sussex, PO19 8SQ, UK

For details of our global editorial offices, for customer services, and for information
about how to apply for permission to reuse the copyright material in this book please
see our website at www.wiley.com/wiley-blackwell.

The right of Jim Cullen to be identified as the author of this work has been asserted in
accordance with the UK Copyright, Designs and Patents Act 1988.

Library of Congress Cataloging-in-Publication Data is available for this title

HB: 9781444351415
PB: 9781444351422

A catalogue record for this book is available from the British Library.

Cover image: © clu / Getty Images
Cover design by Simon Levy.

Set in 10.5/13.5pt Palatino by Laserwords Private Limited, Chennai, India
Printed in Malaysia by Ho Printing (M) Sdn Bhd

1   2014

For Nancy,
a little girl
a little longer

Contents

List of Figures

Acknowledgments

Some projects gestate for a long time before they suddenly snap into place. Others stubbornly resist you every step of the way. This one did neither. It began during a conversation with my editor, Peter Coveney, about a new edition of my 2001 anthology *Popular Culture in American History* (which has since been reissued). At one point in our discussion, I made an offhand observation that what the publishing marketplace could really use is a brief, student-centered history of the media, segmented into homework-sized chunks and adaptable for classroom use. Peter suggested I write a proposal for such a book. A few weeks later, we were in business. Eighteen months after that, I had a manuscript.

But I didn't finish this book alone. A talented array of collaborators joined the dance. The first included a circle of friends and colleagues. Among the most important was my colleague William Norman, an exceptionally knowledgeable musician and pop-culture maven who caught multiple embarrassing errors, made numerous useful observations, and gave me steady encouragement. Another colleague, Andy Meyers, also critiqued parts of the manuscript. My best friend, Gordon Sterling, and my brother-in-law, Tod Sizer, drew on their vast knowledge of technology to keep me straight on matters like television broadcasting and computer hardware.

I'm also grateful to the anonymous readers of the manuscript who made many valuable suggestions for further revision and research. I doubt the collective efforts of these people entirely prevented me from making mistakes. But they did their best.

In addition to his editorial wisdom, I was the beneficiary of Peter Coveney's team at Wiley-Blackwell. This includes his editorial assistant Elizabeth Saucier; project manager Leah Morin, who also copy-edited the manuscript; and Jane Taylor, who did photo research.

This is the seventh book I've completed while working for the Ethical Culture Fieldston School. It's been a wonderful place to work. In addition to my students and colleagues – especially the members of Fieldston's History Department – I'd like to thank Principal Laura Danforth and Head of School Damien Fernandez for their support. I don't think there are many educational institutions on the planet that can match ECFS as a conducive home for the life of the mind.

A final word of thanks to my family, especially my wife, Lyde Cullen Sizer. I think by now they understand – perhaps they always did – that indulging my addiction to words has kept me out of worse trouble. No matter where I go when I'm at my desk (or hunkered down at Starbucks), they're always with me.

Jim Cullen
Hastings-on-Hudson, New York
June 2013

Introduction
Medium Message

Figure 0.1 EXHIBITING CURIOSITY Image of the exterior of Barnum's American Museum (above) and its lecture room (below), from *Frank Leslie's Illustrated Newspaper*, 1865. The first great impresario in the history of American popular culture, P.T. Barnum was uniquely gifted in figuring out what his fellow citizens wanted to see – and making entertainment seem educational. (Barnum's American Museum; Library of Congress, Prints and Photographs Division)

A Short History of the Modern Media, First Edition. Jim Cullen.
© 2014 Jim Cullen. Published 2014 by John Wiley & Sons, Ltd.

Overview

IN THE BEGINNING, there was no medium, literally no in-between. Communication took the form of live sound and visible gesture. Information was delivered in person, whether to an individual or to a crowd. Time and space were shared; to participate in an exchange, you had to be there. And if person A wished to contact person C without doing so directly, it had to be another human being, person B, who delivered the message in person. The means of communication was flesh and blood.

And yet, very early on – long before such an event was ever recorded – somebody figured out how to convey a message that *wasn't* delivered in person. A picture on a cave wall, some lines made in clay. Maybe a drum pattern that served as a warning to listeners in the distance. The chalk used for the picture, the stick pressed into soft stone, the stretched skin of the conga: each of these was a means by which individuals were connected. In these cases, the tool in question was an early technology, a medium, for communication in which you *didn't* have to be there for the message to go through.

Picture, word, music: each was a different medium. The plural of "medium" is *media*. From the earliest days of human civilization, there was always more than one way to communicate. We are instinctive pluralists.

We also seem to have an instinct to communicate widely, to reach many people across time and space, whether simultaneously or even after death. Our media are not only individual, but collective: *mass* media. Actually, this urge seems to transcend humanity. When Moses came down from Mount Sinai with the Ten Commandments on two tablets of stone, the word of God went out to all the children of Israel, then and forever forth. Other messengers mediated between creator and subjects in similar ways, the mission of spreading the news delegated to generations of successors who discharged their imperatives using the mass media of the day.

It's an open question whether human beings collectively get wiser over time; speaking as a historian, I have serious doubts about the degree to which one can really speak of progress when it comes to things like moral improvement or political equality. But there's little question that the history of civilization is one of gradual improvements in the speed and scope of communications technology. A series of refinements in the written word led to the replacement of tablets with scrolls, then scrolls with bound books, and then faster and cheaper ways of producing bound books through the miracle of the printing press, which in turn made possible variations like newspapers, magazines, and pamphlets. Meanwhile, even as publishing was evolving, entirely new media were emerging, making it possible to distribute sound and image in ways that would astound earlier generations.

This book looks at the modern mass media, i.e., those media that have emerged as everyday facts of life in the last two hundred years or so, a time of accelerating technological innovation. In the nineteenth century, cylindrical presses made it possible to blanket the world in print, and the age-old craft of theater became a form of mass entertainment. More recently, entirely new media – photography, sound recording, and broadcasting, to name three examples – have been invented and become widespread.

But the stories you'll find here are not solely tales of technological innovation. Indeed, they're intertwined – in some cases inextricably so – with economics, culture, and politics. Nor can the machines surveyed here and the people who invented them be considered separately from the audiences for their creations, because audiences drove innovation as much as innovators created audiences.

There's another important dimension to these stories as well: the relationship *between* media. This can be complicated. Sometimes, it seems that the arrival of a new medium displaces old ones: radio put a dent in newspaper readership, and television put a dent in radio listening. There's some truth to that, of course, but the reality is never that simple (newspapers hardly disappeared once radio came along). Sometimes new media don't so much cannibalize old media as repurpose them – it was only when television came along that radio became a medium for playing records, for example. And sometimes new media resurrect vanishing elements of old ones, as when the ghost of the nineteenth-century minstrel show hovers over a twenty-first-century late-night comedy act or hip-hop recording.

Before trying to spell out in more detail what you'll find in this book, I'd like to say a few words about some of the ambiguities involved in interpreting the history of the media. But first a suggestion for caution regarding definitive statements about what content providers in any given media really intend to make, and what definitive messages audiences really receive. In my experience, students tend to be a little too quick to think they can readily discern both. For example, they conflate what a character or narrator says with what an author actually thinks. Actually, I think it *is* possible to make persuasive assertions about what the creators of works of popular culture are saying through any number of means: the frequency with which a message is conveyed, the fates of the characters who carry that message, the way a story ends, and so on. But this usually requires a fair amount of attention to detail. And there are no fixed rules about such matters.

Far more complicated is gauging audience reaction. All works of popular culture have a reasonably specific audience: no document can speak to everyone (unless perhaps it is bland to the point of irrelevance). That said, an audience of more than one is never homogeneous. As has long been recognized, factors like race, class, and gender can decisively shape responses, and sometimes lead to diametrically opposite ones. So can region, religion, and history. Audience response has been a subject of growing attention among scholars in recent decades, addressed by means that range from cultural theory to statistical data. I'm less interested in arguing for a particular approach to the question than in simply posing it *as a* question, inviting students and classes to keep it in mind as they engage and discuss the various topics in this book and the culture they find outside it.

In addition to considering questions like intention and reception, I'd also like to pose one at the outset about the role market capitalism plays in the mass media. This was something that was well understood very early on by people like Benjamin Franklin, who made a fortune in the printing business (see Chapter 1). This understanding was refined, and maybe even perfected, by the entrepreneur P.T. Barnum, who made hucksterism itself part of his marketing appeal. Was Joice Heth, the subject of one of his most successful exhibitions, *really* a 161-year-old woman who had been the childhood nursemaid of George Washington, as Barnum claimed in 1835? Maybe you would pay to find out, at least as much to see how he made the claim as to ascertain whether Barnum was telling the truth. In a career that included starting a museum, promoting the wildly successful tour of opera singer Jenny Lind, and serving as a founding father of the American circus, Barnum demonstrated that the marketplace was the central arena of American culture.

It would be hard to overstate its influence in the two centuries since. There are all kinds of reasons this is true. For one thing, we often consider the sales of a particular work of popular culture as an index of assent to what it says – something that may be valid in some cases but deeply misleading in others. (The box office may really be a kind of voting booth, but both are subject to corruption of various kinds.) We also tend to overlook the degree to which our notions of choice are shaped by unseen, and often unknown, forces that play a very big role in our notions of "personal" taste. Program directors at radio networks who determine what songs get played on the airwaves; studio executives who decide which pictures get green-lighted; publicity directors who decide which books will get advertising: all these people serve as gatekeepers and, while there are a lot of them (and lots of alternative pathways to new content), they plainly have more power and access than you do in channeling the media in a particular direction.

We do recognize that there are structural factors that determine the possibilities of any given medium: few people *watch* radio broadcasts. But sometimes students have a harder time recognizing that there are many aspects of radio broadcasting that are *not* intrinsic to the medium, that are in fact highly contingent and might have been resolved in any number of ways. Radio networks, for example, were not ordained. Nor was advertising. But once, after a complex process that was highly contested and never entirely complete, radio *did* end of up with networks that *did* have advertising, some pretty deep tracks were laid that shaped the fates of television and the Internet. History is certainly not the same thing as destiny (it is possible, for example, to listen to radio or watch television without ads). But history is a powerful force that can sometimes seem impervious to logic or popular will.

Because advertising has played such an enormous role in the history of the popular media, one might be surprised and chagrined to see that it does not get its own chapter in this book, even though its impact is considered throughout. That's a legitimate reaction. There are two reasons why that didn't happen, however. One is that in a book of this size – a book whose size was really the first parameter established at the time of its creation – it's simply not possible to do justice to all media. The other is that I finally regard advertising as an instrumental phenomenon: it does not exist for its own sake to communicate an idea, vision, or sense of beauty – though it may do all three – but rather for the purpose of selling something else.

My primary interest, by contrast, is the way in which the media present us with any number of propositions for our consideration that certainly don't exist outside the marketplace – indeed, getting rich is very often the goal – but that are not entirely (or necessarily) defined by that marketplace. I should point out, however, that my perspective has skeptics, and that this skepticism is old and varied. In the nineteenth century, critics of popular culture like the British poet and essayist Matthew Arnold lamented its coarseness, one rooted in a desire to pander to the lowest common denominator in the name of profit, and feared it would degrade the overall level of public discourse. A century ago, advertising and publicity executive Edward Bernays (a son-in-law of psychologist Sigmund Freud) pioneered techniques of mass manipulation that reflected a relatively dim view of the masses, as did journalist Vance Packard, whose 1957 book on advertising, *The Hidden Persuaders*, attracted widespread attention.

In the decades following World War II, scholars of the so-called Frankfurt School, influenced by Marxist theory, also critiqued the way they believed cultural expression could become an instrument of mob psychology. This critical tradition continues in the work of later scholars, among them the so-called Birmingham School (named after the university in England) clustered around Stuart Hall, which incorporated the insights of postmodern literary theory, and more contemporary figures such as Naomi Klein, who applies such insights in her analysis of corporate globalization. I recognize the value of such work, even if I don't embrace all of its conclusions.

My less critical stance regarding the dangers of collective manipulation and exploitation helps explain why I have always considered myself a scholar of *popular* culture rather than of *mass* culture, the preferred term among many scholars of my generation. At the very least the latter has the virtue of parallel structure: mass media, mass culture. Such scholars prefer "mass" because it calls attention to structures of power, and the way individuals are subject to forces beyond their control, particularly corporate ones. I have some sympathy for this view, more now than at any other time in my quarter-century in this business. But I continue to cling to a notion of popular culture rather than mass culture, because I continue to believe in the power of individuals, and the power of ordinary people, to shape imaginative worlds in ways that have a positive impact on real ones.

To a great extent, that belief in the power of the people stems from my identity as an American – and Americans, as I believe we all understand, have a particular predilection (some would say weakness) for the cluster of ideas surrounding freedom, individualism, and the like. It's also no coincidence that the period of time covered by this book loosely corresponds to the first two centuries of American national life. Actually, long before there was a place known as the United States, British North America was regarded as the cutting edge of modernity in all kinds of ways (though, as Chapter 1 makes plain, not cultural ones). The young nation was a locus of restless innovation economically as well as technologically, and by the late nineteenth century had emerged as a leading force in modern communications. Mass media long preceded the era of US global power, and they will probably long survive it. But the global media, as well as the messages of modernity they transmit, have been decisively shaped by the American experience.

I've explained *why* I use the term "popular culture" with reference to the mass media, but I haven't really *defined* it. Actually, the definition I've long used – one that appears in a number of my books – is not mine, but rather that of the late Lawrence Levine, one of the giants of modern cultural history. In a 1992 essay for the *American Historical Review* published the following year in his book *The Unpredictable Past*, Levine defined popular culture as "the folklore of industrial society." According to the now defunct Microsoft Encarta encyclopedia (a source I cite here because it resurfaces at the end of this book; see Chapter 7), folklore is a "general term for the verbal, spiritual, and material aspects of any culture that are transmitted orally, by observation, or by imitation." But in contrast to a folk culture, industrial societies convey these verbal, spiritual, and material aspects via the mass media, which reproduce and distribute information through the use of machines, the most important of which in our time are computers.

There is an important corollary to Levine's definition of popular culture that's worth spelling out here (or, perhaps more accurately, repeating). In the United States, among other nations, the folklore of industrial society is also capitalistic: it operates in an economic system that emphasizes private, rather than government, ownership of economic enterprises and the means of production. Not all industrial societies are capitalist – the now abolished Soviet Union, for example, was not; it's not quite clear to what degree China is – but for at least a century capitalist pop culture has been the norm, even when the media have been state owned. That doesn't mean this will always will be the case, however.

There's no presumption in this book that the media whose histories are rendered here represent a complete set, and no assumption that those histories themselves are anything resembling comprehensive. Some readers will lament omissions (shouldn't professional sports have a place here?); others will wonder about media that made the cut (is theater really a *mass* medium?). Whether or not my choices amount to defects, I hope they furnish the basis of a useful discussion. Indeed, even more than providing information, I regard my role here as a catalyst for further investigation, whether that investigation takes place in a classroom, in a coffee shop, or in the personal journey that results from writing a worthwhile essay.

A few words about organization. Each chapter of the book is divided into four parts. The first, an overview, surveys the history of the medium in question: its origins, trajectory, and current state. This is history at 30,000 feet, and as such favors breadth over depth. I also go light on statistical data, since it can clutter up a story.

The second part of each chapter consists of what I call a genre study. Though definitions tend to be loose and rules are made to be broken, genres are sets of conventions within the world of the mass media that are widely understood and durable over long periods of time – centuries, in some cases. The western is a *kind* of movie; the situation comedy is a specific *type* of television; the e-newsletter is *variety* of e-mail. Genres can leap across media (westerns were novels before they were movies) and coexist simultaneously in multiple media (as in Broadway musicals inspired by movies). While there are other genres that I don't discuss here (the detective story comes to mind), it's my hope that learning about one will prompt readers to make forays into others. I also hope to invite conversation about the boundaries and utility of the very term "genre," which I arguably stretch to include the Internet phenomenon of the social network as a specific subvariety of the World Wide Web.

The third section of each chapter consists of one or two document studies that look at a particular work of popular culture as it surfaced in a particular medium and genre. To some extent, these brief essays are meant to compensate for the general tenor of the overview sections, providing a level of detail not otherwise available in the book. It's my hope that these pieces can serve as an accompaniment for a class discussion or assignment involving the work in question – all are available in some form online – offering context and questions that can deepen a student's appreciation for the accomplishments of particular artists and the work they produced.

The final section of each chapter, "Further Reading," offers a point of departure for a student embarking on research or simply seeking to sate personal curiosity. New scholarship on the mass media is appearing all the time, and search engines and scholarly databases are inevitably more up-to-date than print bibliographies. Since this is a textbook and not a piece of academic scholarship, these brief bibliographic essays included here are limited to highlighting recent major books on the topic in question. They also indicate the sources that most informed my thinking in writing this book, and as such afford the acute reader a means to assess the quality of my research.

One last point of explanation. My goal in these chapters is to offer a series of compact narratives, along with a few illustrations, of the main trunk lines of media history. I'm less interested in making an overt argument, or offering novel perspectives, than I am in providing a series of coordinates whereby teachers and students can situate more analytic writings or less mainstream culture and thus gain a fuller appreciation of what it means to be truly alternative. Readers seeking examples of such work may wish to consult my book *The Art of Democracy*, or my anthology of scholarship, *Popular Culture in American History*, cited below.

I am a student of the mass media generally, but I am a child of print. Books have always been the source of my deepest wonder, and it's no accident that the primary way I have experienced the world and expressed myself has been through the written word. I say this recognizing that many, if not most, of the people whose eyes will scan these pages do not necessarily share this passion, and will only be reading them because a professor with some influence on their academic transcript has told them to do so. I have tried to keep this in mind, and have strived to avoid boring you (the major reason the book is relatively short). If, in the process of traversing these pages, you can sense why someone with a different set of priorities from you may make choices whose appeal you can understand – not endorse, much less emulate, just understand – you will accomplish something substantial: you will learn.

Have a good trip.

Questions to consider

1. What are some of the social relationships embedded in the word "media"?
2. How would you describe the interaction between older media and new ones?

3. What are some of the complexities involved in assessing the intentions of creators or audiences of media messages?
4. Describe the role of industrial capitalism in creating, and limiting, the possibilities of cultural expression in American life.
5. What kinds of priorities are revealed in the table of contents for this book?

Further Reading

There are lots of histories of the mass media in the marketplace, and a simple Google or Amazon.com search will yield titles and latest editions (one reason why all the bibliographies in this book will be short, calling attention to the most important, and perhaps least obvious, sources). It should be emphasized that my approach to the subject is decidedly that of the historian; communications studies is a large field, of which history is one component of a much broader, typically contemporary, discussion. In terms of manageably sized books meant to be read for pleasure as well as textbook instruction, two stand out. The first is Paul Starr's *The Creation of the Media: Political Origins of Modern Communication* (New York: Basic Books, 2004), which is exceptionally strong in covering the colonial period through World War II. Tim Wu's *The Master Switch: The Rise and Fall of Information Empires* (New York: Knopf, 2010), has more of a modern orientation.

The late Lawrence Levine was perhaps the greatest scholar in the field of pop-culture history. His important books include *Highbrow/Lowbrow: The Emergence of Cultural Hierarchy in America* (Cambridge, MA: Harvard University Press, 1988) and a collection of essays, *The Unpredictable Past: Explorations in American Cultural History* (New York: Oxford University Press, 1993). The best overarching one-volume treatment of popular culture is LeRoy Ashby's *With Entertainment for All: A History of Popular Culture since 1830* (2006; Lexington: University Press of Kentucky, 2012). Ashby's treatment is comprehensive and organized chronologically. This study, by contrast, is abbreviated and organized by medium.

In terms of reference sources, the most complete is the *St. James Encyclopedia of Popular Culture*, edited by Tom and Sara Pendergast (2000; Detroit, MI: St. James Press [Gale Group], 2013). (I wrote the introduction to this five-volume set.) It includes essays on media history and technology as well as on specific figures and works.

On audiences, perhaps the best overview is Richard Butsch's *The Making of American Audiences, from Stage to Television, 1750–1990* (Cambridge: Cambridge University Press, 2000). Tom Stempel offers an example of audience-based scholarship in *American Audiences on Movies and Moviegoing* (Lexington: University Press of Kentucky, 2001); see Stempel's notes in the introduction of his book for more citations on the scholarly field known as "reception theory."

In terms of cultural theory, the go-to source is John Storey's *Cultural Theory and Popular Culture: An Introduction*, now in its sixth edition (Harlow: Longman, 2012). The accompanying *Cultural Theory and Popular Culture: A Reader* (5th ed., Harlow: Longman, 2009) offers selections from some of the figures cited in the introduction, including Matthew Arnold, the Frankfurt School, and Stuart Hall.

Readers of this book may also be interested in my earlier, more ideologically pointed, *The Art of Democracy: A Concise History of Popular Culture in the United States* (1996; New York: Monthly Review Press, 2002). See also my anthology of two generations' worth of scholarship, *Popular Culture in American History* (2001; Malden, MA: Wiley-Blackwell, 2013). One other anthology worthy of note: *Major Problems in American Popular Culture: Documents and Essays*, edited by Kathleen Franz and Susan Smulyan (Boston, MA: Wadsworth, 2012).

1

Print's Run
Publishing as Popular Culture

Figure 1.1 PRESSING MATTERS   A cylindrical printing press from the mid-nineteenth century. A major advance from the hand-operated presses that only allowed one document to be produced at a time, cylindrical presses dramatically accelerated the pace and reach of the publishing business, establishing print as the dominant medium of popular culture in the United States. (© Stapleton Collection/Corbis)

A Short History of the Modern Media, First Edition. Jim Cullen.
© 2014 Jim Cullen. Published 2014 by John Wiley & Sons, Ltd.

Overview

READING? For fun? Seriously?

It's not exactly that you hate reading (not *all* reading, anyway). For a student, reading is a fact of life. But, notwithstanding the occasional *Harry Potter* novel or *ESPN* story, most of the reading you do – other than facebook or text messaging, which doesn't really count here – is a means to an end: good grade, good degree, good job. Not typically something you do for kicks.

You may be interested to know that, in this regard, you're like the overwhelming majority of the human beings who have ever lived. Most – the ones who actually *could* read, as mass literacy is a modern invention – didn't read for fun, either. They, too, typically saw reading as a means to an end, and in a great many cases it was largely a matter of education in some form or another. (Originally, what we think of as books were actually scrolls; they were gradually replaced by the codex – handwritten pages bound on one side – which only began to disperse widely with the advent of the printing press in the fifteenth century.) But there was a specific historical moment, in the early nineteenth century, when reading suddenly *did* become something you would do for fun. There are a number of technological, economic, and cultural reasons for that, which I'll get to shortly. But the important thing to make clear at the outset is that the arrival of reading as an entertainment activity was a transformative moment in the history of the mass media – in an important sense, it marked the *beginning* of the history of the mass media – and one whose reverberations continue to this very day.

You can thank God for that. I mean this literally: I've mentioned technology, economics, and culture as important factors in the rise of reading, but in a Western-civilization context, and more specifically in an American context, religion was crucial. For much of recorded history – which is to say history that could be read, as opposed to committed to memory and spoken – the written word served a variety of purposes, among them law, finance, and art. But religion is at the top of the list.

In any event, reading for most of humankind was a practice of the elite. Indeed, in many cases you weren't *allowed* to read unless you were a member of the elite. The Roman Catholic Church, for example, didn't want just anybody reading the Bible, because someone might get what the clergy regarded as the wrong idea. For about 1500 years, the primary everyday interpreter of Christianity was the priest, who stood between – which is to say mediated between – Christ on the altar and his people in the pews. The priest read the word of God, as it was recorded in the Gospels and other sacred scripture, and explained what it meant.

The Catholic Church was always a hierarchically managed institution, and at the top of the chain was the Lord's presiding representative on earth, the pope, who was the final arbiter of scriptural authority. But when Martin Luther nailed those famous 95 theses on that church door in 1517, kick-starting the Reformation, the pope ceased to be reader-in-chief of the Western world. Now, suddenly, a series of Protestant churches competed for followers, organizing themselves in ways that ranged from networks of bishops to self-contained congregations. In such an environment, individual worshippers experiencing the word of God for themselves became a new possibility – and, in many cases, a new imperative. Such a quest was greatly aided by technological innovations in publishing, among them the ability to recombine letters on a metal plate, a technique known as moveable type, pioneered by the German inventor Johannes Gutenberg in the half-century before 1500.

In the intensity of their rebellion from the Catholic Church, these new Protestant sects varied widely. Some, like the Church of England (which became the Episcopalian Church in the United States), were content to largely follow traditional practices. Others, like the people we have come to know as Puritans, made more fundamental demands on their followers, among them the expectation that they would teach their children to read so that those children could forge their own relationship with God. Whether they were looking for economic opportunities, seeking to escape religious oppression, or simply trying to find a home they could call their own, many of these people – most from the British Isles, but some from other parts of Europe – made their way to English North America and founded colonies which, unlike French Canada or Spanish Latin America, were largely Protestant.

The religious emphasis on reading in North America made much of this territory, particularly New England, one of the most literate places on the face of the earth a century before the American Revolution. The first printing press was established at Harvard College in 1638. They didn't have indoor plumbing. But they did have prayer books.

So reading was primarily about God. But it wasn't *solely* about God. It was also about making money, planting crops, and baking bread. Annual publications called almanacs (which are still published every year) were among the first places where one could find information about such things. Almanacs were effective from a market point of view because, while the information they contained, like seasonal weather forecasts, was reasonably current, they could also be sold for a while before going out of date. So they made sense economically from a publishing standpoint as well as from a reading standpoint.

The all-time genius of the almanac business was a fellow named Benjamin Franklin. Franklin was born in Boston in 1706 and, as a child, worked for his older brother James, who was in the printing business, and in fact founded one of the first newspapers in America. James Franklin got in trouble around the time he began running a series of articles in his paper criticizing the Boston authorities, among them pieces that were submitted anonymously by someone who wrote as an old woman under the name of Silence Dogood (which was a play on the titles of books by the famous Puritan minister Cotton Mather). What nobody, not even James himself, realized was that Silence Dogood was not, in fact, an old woman. He was an adolescent boy named Benjamin Franklin. In the furor that followed, young Ben decided he'd better leave town – fast. He went to the rapidly growing city of Philadelphia, on its way to becoming the largest in North America.

Franklin would later take on a few other projects in his long life, among them working as a world-famous scientist, diplomat, and revolutionary with a hand in the creation of documents like the Declaration of Independence and the US Constitution. But his *job*, one that made him rich enough to do all those other things in his spare time, was in the printing business, and he had a particularly clever idea when it came to publishing almanacs. For *his* almanacs, Franklin created a fictional character – he dubbed him "Poor Richard" – who became a kind of mascot whose wit and wisdom would pepper the books and create a distinctive brand. (Pithy lines like "There are no gains without pains," "Lost time is never found again," and "Great spenders, poor lenders" are among Poor Richard's greatest hits.) *Poor Richard's Almanac*, issued annually between 1732 and 1758, was hugely successful, and a widely reprinted collection of Poor Richard's sayings, *The Way to Wealth*, is among the most famous works of popular culture of all time.

Poor Richard could be funny, but his humor always had a point, and that point usually had a moral tinge (ironically, Franklin, long associated with the maxim "early to bed, early to rise makes a man healthy, wealthy, and wise," was a notoriously late sleeper). When it came to the lingering power of religion in public life, the rules of the game tended to get bent more than broken. Insofar as there was secular writing to be found in North America in the decades preceding and following the American Revolution, it was still mostly for elite consumption. Newspapers, for example, were relatively expensive and had to be paid for in advance by subscription. They were typically aimed at high-end merchants with some kind of stake in the shipping business. Books were increasingly available, but they too were costly and typically also had to be paid for in advance by subscription (another one of Franklin's innovations was the first lending library in North America).

The American Revolution, in which Benjamin Franklin played such a large role, was a military, political, and diplomatic struggle, but it was also a communications battle. Great Britain, of course, had developed a print-media culture before its colonies did, but by the mid-eighteenth century those colonies were catching up rapidly. A rich discourse of political pamphlets, written by men with names like Adams and Jefferson, fed the argument on both sides in the years leading up to 1776 as well as the years following. The pivotal document, by all accounts, was Thomas Paine's legendary manifesto *Common Sense*, published in January of that year. Paine, who came to the colonies in 1774 from England with a letter of introduction from Franklin, proved crucially important in crystallizing a belief that the issue was no longer colonists having their rights as British subjects protected, but rather that it was time to move on and found a new nation. Paine's passionate polemic, and the intensity with which it was embraced, illustrates the way in which politics is a matter of winning minds as well as hearts.

But even after American independence was secured, the nation's culture remained literally and figuratively imported, and thus all the more pricey. The United States may have achieved its political independence in 1776, but in many respects, among them cultural, it remained a British colony for decades afterward. "In the four quarters of the globe, who reads an American book?" asked the Reverend Sydney Smith, founder of the highbrow *Edinborough Review*, in 1820. It was a rhetorical question.

But even as Smith posed his sneering query, the United States was on the brink of a transformation. An important element in this transformation was technological; the early decades of the nineteenth century marked the beginning of the Industrial Revolution in the young nation. Nowhere was this more evident than in the publishing industry. Up until this point, printing presses were just that: devices with which an individual pushed ink onto paper. With the advent of the cylindrical machines, in which paper rolled off presses powered by steam, it now became possible to run a much larger volume at a much lower cost. Publishers could now sell newspapers, books, and other forms of print at a fraction of their former price.

Which is why the nation's relatively high literacy rates proved so important. The fact that so many Americans could already read for religious reasons – and the fact that the United States was a large market with a shared language, growing cities, and a rapidly expanding transportation infrastructure – made it possible to turn the printed word into something it had never really been before: a true mass medium.

Mass publishing, in turn, created the prospect for a dramatic change in the *way* people read. Until the early nineteenth century, most reading was *intensive*, which is to say that readers tended to know a few books really well. The self-educated Abraham Lincoln, for example, was deeply knowledgeable about the Bible and Shakespeare, but read little else beyond that which he needed for his career as a lawyer. But from about the 1830s on, reading became increasingly *extensive*, which is to say that readers absorbed lots of different kinds of writing. Extensive reading was generally perceived to be less demanding, and more fun, which is why it was sometimes condemned. But it also became the dominant mode of reading in modern life. Most people today are extensive readers, not intensive ones. (We tend to be more intensive when it comes to things like listening to music, though technologies like digital downloads have broadened our palates.)

A new class of entrepreneurs was able to take advantage of the new extensive order and turn reading into a highly profitable form of entertainment. One such pioneer was Benjamin Day, publisher of the *New York Sun*, the first in a great wave of so-called penny papers to be founded in the United States. Founded in 1833, and rapidly followed by competitors like New York's *Herald* (1835), *Tribune* (1841), and *Times* (1851), as well as other daily newspapers around the country, the *Sun* specialized in running sensational stories that ranged from murder trials to an elaborate 1844 hoax of "Moon Men" landing in South Africa that actually prompted Yale University to send researchers to investigate. The penny papers were sold by the then-new methodology of the "London Plan," which replaced paid subscription by having publishers sell batches of papers to so-called newsboys, who in turn sold them on the street to readers.

By the mid-nineteenth century, US cities were blanketed with newsprint that was passed from hand to hand. These papers varied in size; most were large "broadsheets," and for a brief period in the 1840s so-called "mammoth" papers were poster-sized publications that could be read by more than one person at a time. Until the advent of photography later in the century, newspapers were illustrated with woodcuts. The primary source of revenue in the business was advertising, not sales. That's pretty much been true ever since.

The penny press was part of a larger reorganization of American politics. The middle of the nineteenth century was a democratic era in more than one sense. Ordinary people became part of the electoral process on a new scale as voters and citizens, and even those who were excluded, among them women and African Americans, could find a voice in the public sphere, particularly in journalistic venues like *Freedom's Journal*, a New York paper founded by free black men in 1827. Many newspapers embraced the avowedly egalitarian values of the Democratic Party generally and the presidency of Andrew Jackson in particular (though there were exceptions, like Horace Greeley's *New York Tribune*, which reflected the views of the opposition Whig Party). Democracy was not always pretty. Celebrations of freedom for some rested on a belief in the necessity of enslaving others; in many states, teaching slaves to read was banned. Mass opinion also often involved all manner of mockery of women, immigrants, or anyone who held unconventional views. This is one reason why respectable opinion often tried to avoid popular journalism, if not control it. Both proved impossible.

News and politics, in any case, were not the only kinds of writing that flourished in this golden age of print as popular culture. Gift books, forerunners of today's coffee-table books in their emphasis on arresting images and writing meant more for browsing than sustained reading, became common by the 1840s. So were women's magazines like *Godey's Lady's Book*, whose line illustrations of women in the latest couture – the term "fashion plate," used to describe someone who looks great in the latest clothes, lingers to this day – made it the *Vogue* of its time. Some of the images in *Godey's Lady's Book* were printed with colored ink, using a process known as lithography, which was also quite common in the creation of cheap, colorful prints published by firms like Currier & Ives. Such prints became fixtures of middle-class homes.

But *Godey's* was more than just a fashion magazine. Under the editorship of Sarah Josepha Hale, who had a distinguished literary career before taking over as editor, it became a leading voice on education, morals, and the role of women in US society. It also became a showcase venue for major writers like Nathaniel Hawthorne and Edgar Allan Poe, as well as for women writers who otherwise might lack an outlet for their work, whether in the form of essays or short stories.

Indeed, this was an era when fiction – and the novel in particular – came into its own as a commercial mass medium. Historians typically date the literary form of the novel back to the work of Spaniard Miguel Cervantes in his seventeenth-century work *Don Quixote* (1605–1615), though such writing can really be said to have come into its own in eighteenth-century England in the work of writers like Daniel Defoe and Samuel Richardson. In the nineteenth century, British novelists Sir Walter Scott and Charles Dickens enjoyed tremendous popularity in America, the diffusion of their work at least partially attributable to the fact that the US government did not observe international copyright until 1891, and thus most publishers did not have to pay for the right to sell their work.

Then as now, novelists typically had their work appear in the form of hardcover books. Then as now, too, other print formats proliferated, among them rag-paper pamphlets known as "chapbooks" that were common as early as the seventeenth century. One of the more effective ways of building an audience for fiction in particular was publishing it in serial form in newspapers and magazines; Dickens is the best example of a writer who became internationally famous by having his work appear in installments on a weekly or monthly basis. By the mid-nineteenth century there was a whole journalistic genre of so-called storypapers, which looked like newspapers but were dominated by the fiction of multiple writers. Around the time of the Civil War, another new format, the dime novel, made its debut. As its name suggests, a dime novel was an inexpensive work in a paperback format that had particular appeal for the young (especially boys). Dime novels would remain popular for the rest of the century until gradually replaced by "the pulps," magazines named for the cheap paper on which they were printed.

The emergence of a broad publishing infrastructure in the United States made authorship possible as a professional career. The first American writers to make something approximating a living from their fiction were Washington Irving (now best known for his tales of Rip Van Winkle and the Headless Horseman) and James Fenimore Cooper, whose five "Leatherstocking" (1826–1841) novels about frontiersman Natty Bumppo was the *Star Wars* of its day. (One of those books, *Last of the Mohicans*, has repeatedly been made into successful movies.) While many of the writers of this period that are now studied in college courses, like Nathaniel Hawthorne and Herman Melville, never became rich from their work, they did achieve some degree of fame and lived much of their lives plausibly believing their writing could allow them financial security, even if it didn't actually do so.

Actually, the most financially successful, and even influential, writers of the mid-nineteenth century were women. Though the names Maria Cummins, Mrs. E.D.E.N. Southworth, and Susan Warner are known today mostly to feminist literary historians, they were bona fide celebrities of their time on the basis of their writing, as was the tart-tongued newspaper columnist Fanny Fern. Hawthorne famously wrote with jealousy of the "damned female scribblers" whose fame he never matched; Melville's attempt to explore the sentimental style of such writers, *Pierre* (1852), was a critical and commercial disaster that effectively ended his career as a novelist. (Generally not a good idea to try and write a bestseller about incest.)

The most famous novel of this era – and still one of the greatest publishing phenomena of all time – was Harriet Beecher Stowe's *Uncle Tom's Cabin*. The daughter, sister, and wife of church ministers, Stowe was a little-known short-story writer in 1851, when her saga of a good-hearted slave began appearing in monthly installments in *The National Era*, one of a number of antislavery newspapers published in the northern United States. Stowe wrote *Uncle Tom's Cabin* in response to the Fugitive Slave Act, an 1850 law requiring Northerners to return escaped slaves to their owners. Though *Uncle Tom's Cabin* purveyed a clear political message, it also captured the nation's imagination through its vivid characters, many of whom became household names for the next 100 years: Little Eva, the angelic child whose death scene was the ultimate tearjerker in American fiction; Augustus St. Clare, the Southern intellectual who recognizes that slavery is wrong but fails to oppose it; Simon Legree, the Northern-born slave trader, whose very name became a synonym for heartless evil; and, above all, the patient, benevolent black Uncle Tom, whose life stands as an indictment of the slave system. While the novel has been subject to varying, and at times conflicting, interpretations in the century and a half since its publication, its success illustrates the power of fiction to dramatize public issues, as well as to offer a venue for people and ideas that would otherwise be neglected or silenced. Abraham Lincoln could only have been half joking when, at a White House reception during the Civil War, he reputedly greeted Stowe as "the little woman who made this great war."

While the Civil War's impact on the publishing industry was not direct, it was nevertheless important and lasting. Certainly the war created a demand for regular news updates in the form of "extras," or additional editions, that kept newspaper readers apprised of the outcome of battles in between regular issues. Perhaps the most important dimension of the war's influence was in the realm of photography, though its effect was not immediate because of the technical barriers involved in the rapid reproduction of images. Important milestones in the advent of photography date back to the 1820s in France, but it wasn't until two decades later that a process developed by French chemist L.J.M. Daguerre led to images known as daguerreotypes. When Englishman William Henry Fox developed a method for making such images reproducible, this led to a vibrant culture of *cartes de visites*, business-card-sized photographs people made of themselves to distribute among friends and family, something particularly common for soldiers to distribute to loved ones before going off to war. Photography also received a major boost in the work of people like Matthew Brady, who exhibited images from the battlefield at his Washington, DC gallery during the war.

Photography became a common feature of journalism in the 1880s with the development of the halftone process, which involves using black-and-white dots of varying size and intensity to create images. (The modern pixel, arranged in dots per inch, is a direct heir of the halftone process.) This newfound ability to present vivid pictures on a daily basis injected fresh energy into the penny press, which flourished under the direction of a new generation of editors like Joseph Pulitzer and William Randolph Hearst, famed for his role in whipping up public sentiment to provoke the Spanish–American War in 1898. ("You furnish the pictures and I'll furnish the war," he famously told a photographer who reported back that he didn't see much that would justify one.) Such "yellow journalism" was both roundly condemned and eagerly read. The term appears to refer to a comic strip called "The Yellow Kid" that was popular at the turn of the century and which ran in Hearst and Pulitzer newspapers. Comic strips, often part of considerably fatter Sunday newspapers, became a feature of turn-of-the-century life, their color lithography giving a festive air to what remained a largely black-and-white medium.

Newspapers also evolved in response to other changes in everyday life. The arrival of ever growing numbers of immigrants led to the growth of a vibrant foreign-language press in many cities, typified by the success of the *Jewish Daily Forward*, which remains alive and well to this day. Newspapers were also important instruments of activism for labor unions and African Americans; the *Chicago Defender* and *Pittsburgh Courier* were influential, and effectively national, black publications.

In addition to responding to these demographic developments, newspaper publishers adapted to changes in the urban landscape such as the emergence of subways and streetcars. To make papers easier to read, another format, known as the tabloid, rose to prominence, in large measure because it could be managed while strapholding on a subway or sitting on a train. Tabloids retained the same emphasis on sensation and corruption as the *New York Sun* had a century before (as indeed they do today). But they were sleeker and more visually appealing than the old broadsheet or mammoth papers.

By 1900, however, print culture faced challenges from new media – film and radio – that posed a threat to their dominance. In the short term, neither could compete very effectively, because both required a series of technological and cultural refinements before they could become mass media. Radio, for instance, was originally developed for nautical and commercial applications; film was little more than an arcade novelty until projection became a possibility and a whole host of legal and technical issues were worked out. By the 1920s, however, both were on track to become sources of news as well as entertainment. After a series of experimental approaches, radio adopted an advertiser-supported model in the United States comparable to that of print (which was different from Great Britain, where the government controlled airwaves and content). Movies, by contrast, were consumer-supported, but, like penny papers and dime novels, were priced low enough so that working-class people could afford to see them on a virtually daily basis. Radio broadcasts eventually became significant sources of information, as did newsreels – brief documentaries on current events – which became part of a typical movie-going experience in the first half of the twentieth century.

Print hardly disappeared. Indeed, in certain respects it acquired a prestige that it previously lacked. For example, magazine publishers responded to the challenge of up-to-the-minute radio broadcasting by developing newsweeklies like *Time* and *Life* that took a more reflective and analytic approach, both visually and in terms of their writing. Novels, which had been at least vaguely disreputable for much of the nineteenth century, were now widely seen as vehicles for the highest forms of artistic expression. Young men and women strived to become novelists the way later generations hoped to be rock stars or video-game designers. While few achieved the wealth and glamour of an F. Scott Fitzgerald or Ernest Hemingway, a life that was somehow bound up in the written word attracted the talent and loyalty of generations of young people.

At the same time, a countercurrent also emerged in the form of an array of pulps with an air of disrepute surrounding them – precisely the thing many of their adherents loved about them. They were a fixture of the publishing scene from the late nineteenth into the mid-twentieth centuries, featuring science fiction, detective stories, horror, and other kinds of genre fiction.

Other varieties in this "low-class" – a term which carried economic and/or social connotations – tier of publications included (illustration-driven) comic books and (photography-driven) pornography. A more reputable tier, though barely so, was gossip or celebrity magazines; there were also attempts to confer a sense of prestige on some of these publications, as with publisher Hugh Hefner's successful launch of *Playboy* as a sex-oriented lifestyle magazine in the 1950s. Yet another very popular, but widely disdained – when not ignored – genre was religious publishing, which proliferated in multiple subgenres. In the first decade of the twenty-first century, the apocalyptic "Left Behind" series of twelve novels by Jerry Jenkins and Tim LaHaye sold tens of millions of copies.

Meanwhile, new formats continued to emerge to meet evolving conditions. One of the more important innovations of the twentieth century was the modern rack-sized paperback, which generated a new wave in the democratization of literature. Publishers like Simon & Schuster and Random House, founded between the World Wars, produced cheap books, both new and classics, which could be sent to soldiers overseas during World War II, where at one point they were consuming 250,000 a month. When those soldiers came home, the GI Bill of 1944 paid for their college educations, which in turn stimulated a significant new demand for books. By the 1970s, the trade paperback, a hybrid between the rack-sized paperback and traditional hardcover with a price in between the two, had become common. By this point, it was a well-established cultural convention that a book would be issued in hardcover first, to be followed a year later in paperback. This model would also be adopted in other media, like home-video versions of Hollywood movies, in the 1980s, another way in which print influenced other media. It's also worth noting that home video, like music recorded on compact discs, was packaged in ways that resembled books – yet one more illustration of how books continued to shape popular culture.

The *social* environment in which print has been read has also been one of change over time. Back in the day when reading was a largely elite activity, it was typically conducted in secluded environments: the monastery, the office, the private library. To some extent, reading was a social event in the family circle, as reading to children, very often by women, was widespread and celebrated both as an enlightening activity and as one that built familial bonds. But the penny press made reading a truly *public* ritual; perusing and discussing the contents of books and newspapers in places like coffee houses became a new – and, to some, dispiriting – fact of life. (Workers in factories would sometimes chip in to hire someone to read to them as they labored.) Well into the nineteenth century, bookselling was a slow, expensive proposition; even a writer as popular as Mark Twain sold his novel *The Adventures of Huckleberry Finn* (1885) by subscription, which required buyers to pay in advance. But, over time, books became an increasingly inexpensive and available commodity, and bookstores themselves became important cultural institutions. Until the 1980s, they were largely the domain of small entrepreneurs, or independents, who ran their own stores. But the advent of large chains like Barnes & Noble increasingly displaced these independents, because they offered both better amenities (like baked goods) and the wider selection and discount prices made possible by economies of scale.

For a while, it seemed like chain bookstores, which also sold magazines, would swallow everything in their path. But they have increasingly become dinosaurs themselves, and a number have gone out of business. That's because an entirely new, electronic mode of expression, namely the Internet, revolutionized the publishing business more than any development of the last two centuries. (For more on the impact of the Internet on print culture, see Chapter 7.)

For the moment, you should note two important components of the Internet's impact on the publishing business. The first concerns the movement of information. The birth of Internet retailing, typified by the explosive growth of Amazon.com, founded in 1995, has fundamentally changed the way books (and other merchandise) are sold. In effect, online commerce took two of the biggest advantages of the chains, selection and price, and took both to an entirely new level, so much so that consumers were willing to defer gratification by getting their goods by mail. Meanwhile Web sites, which quickly absorbed traditional print media like newspapers and magazines, also became an important venue for adding or updating "content" – a word that became newly important in an era when information could morph and jump across media. Today news and entertainment organizations like CNN or *Rolling Stone* maintain active sites that have become an increasingly important part of their overall operations.

But the Internet has also become more than an important means of information *delivery*. It is now also an important *source* of content. Words like "Web site" and "blog" scarcely existed when you were born, but are now considered commonplace venues for the written word. Much of the content one finds at such sites resembles earlier forms of print culture, but nevertheless has distinctive accents or conventions. The blog post, for example, might resemble a diary entry, a review, or even an essay. But elements like interactivity, the frequency with which it can be updated, and the ease with which individuals can create as well as read them are unique to this time.

The first decade of the twenty-first century also witnessed one of the more stunning developments of human history: the moment when the very word "book" ceased solely to be a physical object and instead became a metaphor for an electronic file. The potential for e-books was recognized long before they became widespread, and it took a while for culture to catch up with technology (it's taking longer still for the economics of e-book publishing to make much sense, as pricing and availability still vary widely). But the obvious utility of e-books is now too strong to be ignored, even for those who might want to disregard them – and as a book lover myself, I will report more than a few pangs of fear and regret at the prospect of physical books' disappearance.

Amid all this change, at a pace that rivals – but does not nec-essarily exceed – that of two centuries ago, a fact that may seem more obvious to you than it does to your teachers must also be noted: relatively speaking, print is a lot less important than it used to be. I would not be shocked to learn that you've read a book for fun recently, or that your gaze has recently crossed a newspaper. I *would* be shocked to learn that this was your primary form of entertainment. Audio and (especially) video are the two main axes of communication in the modern world. Practically speaking, it might be hard to drive a car to the beach, order a pizza, or install software on your desktop without the ability to read. But you could still be a well-informed citizen without reading, by relying on radio, television, and Internet streaming. (Well, maybe not *well* informed. But *adequately* informed. Fortunately, you are still reading.)

And yet, in a very important sense, print remains of decisive importance, and in all kinds of ways. Most other forms of popular culture, from television shows to video games, would be impossible without good writing. Print remains an extremely important source of content in other media; without the free programming provided by authors discussing their work on talk shows or Web sites, for example, lots of news organizations would probably go out of business. And a great many of the most beloved movies of our time began their lives as books. Such wizardry is hardly limited to Harry Potter.

So yes: reading really does remain a way to have fun. Seriously.

Questions to consider

1. How did religion shape the emergence of print culture in the Western world?
2. What factors promoted literacy in British colonial America and the young United States?
3. What are some of the forms published words have taken in the last 200 years? What marketplace or cultural factors made some

of these forms particularly appealing at a given moment or to a
given audience?
4. Describe the role of print as an influence on other media. What
    is its place in the landscape of contemporary popular culture?
5. What do you see as the effects of e-books on print culture? How,
    if at all, do they – or reading devices like tablets – affect the way
    you read?

Genre Study

Terrifying pleasures: Horror

Figure 1.2   MONSTER SUCCESS   Celebrated horror actor Lon Chaney Jr. in *The Ghost of Frankenstein* (1942). First imagined by British writer Mary Shelley in her 1818 novel *Frankenstein*, the character became a fixture across media in the horror genre over the ensuing two centuries. (*The Ghost of Frankenstein*, 1942, Lon Chaney Jr., director Erle C. Kenton. © Photos 12/Alamy)

Go figure: some people just like to be scared.

Strictly speaking, this is something you *can't* figure: a desire to be scared is irrational. Fear is an emotion of anticipated harm; harm by definition is a negative outcome one wants to avoid. But approaching the appeal of horror – a media genre that stretches across print, radio, film, music, television, and gaming – as a rational matter misses the point. For hundreds of years, horror has been cherished precisely because it *is* irrational and deals with situations that are outside the realm of ordinary life. By imaginatively immersing themselves in the unfamiliar – or in seeing the familiar in a new, darker light – horror fans satisfy an urge for novelty, confront fears that might otherwise be difficult to articulate, or affirm the (relatively safe) choices they've made.

Besides, it's only a book/movie/show/video game. The nightmares go away (eventually).

Though horror is not a genre one typically associates with reason, it makes a fair amount of sense to consider its emergence against such a backdrop. That's because its origins date from a specific historical moment – the late eighteenth century – and a specific intellectual movement: the Enlightenment. Horror happened as a reaction to the Enlightenment. So you can't really understand the former unless you have at least an idea of the latter.

Of course, the Enlightenment was itself a reaction. The preceding era in the Western world was one of superstition, conflict, and violence, much of it stemming from the Reformation, which pitted the old-line Catholic Church against a series of Protestant challengers, struggles that in many cases took on nationalistic dimensions. But after a century of almost continuous warfare, a growing number of people began to wonder if people killing each other in the name of Jesus Christ really made all that much sense. Such questions took on new relevance, even urgency, as an emerging scientific revolution unlocked secrets of the universe that had heretofore seemed unknowable. Logic, science, reason: is there anything we *can't* figure out eventually? A large number of thinkers from Voltaire in France to Thomas Jefferson in America believed the answer was no.

But even at the height of the Enlightenment, there were doubters. And that doubt took multiple forms. Some worried that an excessive emphasis on order and logic would simply take the beauty out of life. Among the first to act on this concern were a group of eighteenth-century architects who looked back to an earlier time when faith inspired the gorgeous cathedrals of the medieval era. This movement, which came to be known as Gothic, remained important, not only because the style it spawned continued to influence builders impatient with the aesthetics, or lack thereof, in the Industrial Revolution (whose governing ideas can also be traced back to the Enlightenment), but also because the term "Gothic" would come into wide use in a variety of subcultural movements that challenged Enlightenment thinkers. (The Goths, by the way, were barbarian invaders of the Roman Empire – "barbarian" being a term which Romans applied to anyone they considered less civilized than themselves. Which is to say just about everyone. Until their conversion to Christianity, the Goths were also pagans, which is to say they had beliefs that others found repellent or frightening – precisely what appeals to adherents of contemporary Goth culture, with its strong emphasis on dark fashion and music.)

Other critics of the Enlightenment believed its followers were both arrogant and naïve in their belief that the world was a reasonable place. In his 1764 novel *The Castle of Otranto*, considered by many historians the first major work of Gothic literature, Horace Walpole describes an aristocratic family haunted by prophecies of doom, helmets falling from the sky, and painted portraits that can walk. But the most important work in the founding of horror, in terms of both its popularity at the time and its vast subsequent influence, is Mary Shelley's 1818 novel *Frankenstein*. A signature document of Romanticism, the cultural movement that followed the Enlightenment, *Frankenstein* is a cautionary tale about a scientist, confident he understands the secret of life itself, who should have been careful about what he wished for. (Frankenstein, by the way, is the name of the creator of the monster, not the monster itself, which never actually gets a name.)

Gothic fiction was relatively easy to imagine in Europe, a place where decaying castles and monasteries, decadent old family lines, and lingering suspicion over the power of the Catholic Church – all fixtures of the genre – were common. Such features were a little more difficult to situate in the infant United States, where they could not be taken for granted. But that didn't stop some writers from trying. The most successful in this era was Charles Brockden Brown, who in novels like *Wieland* (1798), *Arthur Mervyn* (1793), and *Edgar Huntly* (1799) described murder, disease, and events that appeared to have supernatural origin. The tale that really put American horror on the map, though, was Washington Irving's 1820 short story "The Legend of Sleepy Hollow," with its unforgettable figure of Headless Horseman, who would go on to have a durable life in popular culture (most recently in the 1999 Tim Burton film *Sleepy Hollow*, starring Johnny Depp). Brown and Irving were gentleman writers who probably had a bigger following in Europe than they did in their native United States. But in the 1830s and 1840s a new generation of writers, among them George Lippard and Edgar Allan Poe, were making money, and making waves, by telling scary stories to an increasingly eager public. (See profile of Poe in this chapter.)

By the middle of the nineteenth century, Gothic fiction had established itself as a discrete branch of literature, and began to branch into specific subgenres. In a famous 1826 essay, English writer and Gothic pioneer Ann Radcliffe made a useful distinction between *terror*, which she defined as that which focused on anticipatory dread of bad things, and *horror*, which was more about their discovery or realization. One can also see an emerging divide between stories whose action is explained by supernatural events, like *The Exorcist*, a 1971 novel and 1973 movie that focused on demonic possession, and stories such as *The Silence of the Lambs* and its prequels/sequels (1986–2006), whose principal character, the brilliantly diabolical Hannibal Lecter, is terrifying in the sheer clarity with which he pursues his cannibalism. There is also overlap between the Gothic and other genres like science fiction; the 1938 Orson Welles radio broadcast of *War of the Worlds* – which began as an 1898 Jules Verne novel and was resurrected most recently in 2005 as a Steven Spielberg movie – combined futurism and fear into a compelling hybrid (see Chapter 4).

In the minds of many observers, the late Victorian era was the golden age of Gothic literature. Stories like Scotsman Robert Louis Stevenson's *Dr. Jekyll and Mr. Hyde* (1886) and Irishman Bram Stoker's *Dracula* (1897) became enduring classics and the basis of countless adaptations in other media. (*Dracula* in particular was important for injecting the folkloric figure of the vampire into pop culture, and establishing the Eastern European region of Transylvania as ground zero of horror tales.) One reason for the vitality of the genre was new currents in psychology – these were the years Sigmund Freud was laying the foundations for psychoanalysis – that emphasized the role of unconscious and forbidden impulses that lurked beneath the surface of polite society. These currents would be picked up and carried forward by American writers such as H.P. Lovecraft, who followed in the Poe tradition of writing cheap fiction in so-called pulp magazines, which thrived in the first half of the century.

By this point, though, the locus of the genre had begun shifting from print to new media, particularly radio and film. Crucially, however, these and later media relied heavily on print antecedents for their source material. Indeed, the great horror impresario of our time, novelist Stephen King, whose critical reputation has risen steadily in recent decades, has been a one-man industry across media platforms (see "Document Study / *Carrie*: Princess of blood, King of horror"). At the same time, a distinctly cinematic approach to the genre took shape, and film remains the dominant medium of horror. When one considers some of the landmark horror movies of the last century – F.W. Murnau's adaptation of *Dracula* in *Nosferatu* (1922); Alfred Hitchcock's *Psycho* (1960); Brian DePalma's film version of King's *Carrie* (1976) – it's easy to see that their power derives from their sense of visual spectacle (one reason why horror movies tend to be scarier in a movie theater than on home video). The iconic image of Janet Leigh's character being stabbed in a shower in *Psycho*, or the blood-drenched Sissy Spacek about to wreak havoc on her high-school classmates in *Carrie*, has long since become part of our collective memory. Sometimes, the fear such movies evoke can be all the more striking in the way they make the innocuous suddenly seem dreadful, as when Hitchcock shows us innocent-looking birds going collectively berserk in *The Birds* (1963). Other times, it's a matter of shockingly subverting our expectations for what a movie is supposed to do, as when he kills off the character we're led to believe is the protagonist early on in *Psycho*. In many cases the power of horror is augmented when almost unbearable suspense is broken by (uneasy) humor, a tactic Jack Nicholson executes brilliantly in playing a demonically possessed psychopath in Stanley Kubrick's film version of King's *The Shining* (1980), remembered today for the ironic signature line of the axe-wielding Nicholson singing "come out come out wherever you are!"

One of the more striking creative frictions in horror is that its power rests on the unknown, and yet the most cherished classics of the genre have often been recurring series that make the supernatural seem almost routine. The most important and beloved example of this phenomenon is the horror episodes that were a core component of *The Twilight Zone* (1959–1964), a television series created, produced, and often written by Rod Serling, who also appeared as a master of ceremonies to deliver monologues at the beginnings and ends of episodes. *The Twilight Zone* did not have recurring characters or fixed settings, but cohered around Serling's unique sensibility, which fused creepy occurrences and pointed moral messages in single-episode segments. This "anthology" approach was quite popular in radio and television. It was harder to make shows with a regular cast of monstrous characters, as familiarity is usually the antidote to fear. Indeed, two of the more successful situation comedies in TV history, *The Munsters* and *The Addams Family*, which ran simultaneously between 1964 and 1966, were based on this ironic premise.

In recent years, however, there has been an effort to create horror franchises with a recurrent cast, setting, and situations, notably in the subgenre of vampire stories, which have undergone a remarkable renaissance in the twenty-first century. The queen of the modern vampire tale is Anne Rice, whose "Vampire Chronicles" date back to her hugely successful 1976 novel *Interview with a Vampire*, which was made into a blockbuster movie starring heartthrobs Tom Cruise and Brad Pitt in 1994. *Buffy the Vampire Slayer* (1997–2003), which featured Sarah Michelle Gellar as the title character, focused on a young woman dedicated to preventing chaos in the ironically named town of Sunnydale, California. In 2008, the cable television network Home Box Office followed up the success of *The Sopranos* (1999–2007), a series about the not-quite oxymoron of everyday gangster life, by launching *True Blood* (2008–), a show about modern-day vampires in small-town Louisiana, based on the novels of Charlaine Harris. Among other things, the series functions as an allegory of gay rights; certainly vampire stories – and the overlapping subgenre of werewolf stories – have long functioned as surrogate means for exploring sexuality (werewolves also surface in *True Blood*). This is also true for another vampire saga, *Twilight*, which began with a quartet of novels by Stephanie Meyer (2005–2008) and continued as a movie franchise (2008–2012). But while *True Blood* works as a surrogate means of promoting gay identity, *Twilight* is more a parable of abstinence, as the vampire Edward Cullen (no relation – that I know of) struggles to restrain his bloodlust for his beloved, Isabella Swan. *Twilight* too has a werewolf dimension in the third character of the love triangle, Jacob Black.

Horror, meanwhile, continues to thrive in other media. "Goth," subgenre of heavy-metal rock that emerged in the 1980s in bands like The Damned and The Cure, continues to have adherents. The Goth look has also become perennial in youth fashion. And horror video games are among the most widely played, complete with an active online community. Ghosts remain alive in machines.

I'm afraid horror is here to stay. Are you relieved?

Questions to consider

1. What are some of the reasons people like to be scared?
2. Explain how the genre of horror emerged from the Enlightenment.
3. How did the migration of horror to other media change its impact?
4. How do you account for the recent popularity of vampire culture, from *Buffy the Vampire Slayer* to *Abraham Lincoln: Vampire Hunter*?

Document Study

The ravenous imagination of Edgar Allan Poe

Figure 1.3   MOURNING BIRD   Illustration of Edgar Allen Poe's grave, featuring the ominous creature from his celebrated 1845 poem "The Raven." Poe had one of the most fertile imaginations in the history of popular culture, and his celebrated poem eventually became the inspiration for a National Football League team. (© Illustration Works/Alamy)

Imagine, if you will, a not wholly implausible scenario: a Pop Culture Hall of Fame, modeled on those for professional sports (or the Rock & Roll Hall of Fame in Cleveland). Each year, experts would vote on new inductees who would be judged on the basis of a large and lasting body of work. But, as with other halls of fame, there would also be charter members for this one, a set of people who formed the core membership at the very outset. One of those people would surely be Edgar Allan Poe. I'd put a bust of him right out in the lobby. With a big black raven sitting on his shoulder.

Poe was a bona fide celebrity in his own time. He wasn't exactly Lady Gaga famous; he was more like Amy Winehouse famous: a name many people would recognize, some would know and admire (even if they knew there was something vaguely scandalous about him, partly involving addiction), and a few would follow with devotion and intensity. What makes Poe so special – really so important – is the breadth and depth of his impact in the century and a half following his death. His influence can be traced in an extraordinarily wide range of literary directions, among them the poems of Charles Baudelaire, the novels of Fyodor Dostoevsky, and the short stories of Flannery O'Connor. But even more than as a literary figure, Poe looms large as a founding father of popular culture, a writer who helped lay the foundations for a series of genres across media, among them detective stories, science fiction, and, our focus here, horror.

In some respects, his life was a horror show in its own right. Born Edgar Poe in Boston in 1809, his father abandoned his family, which included an older brother and younger sister, when he was an infant. When Poe's mother died the following year, he was essentially an orphan. He did have the good fortune of becoming the foster child of John and Frances Allan of Richmond, Virginia, who raised him as their own (hence his name Edgar *Allan* Poe). But, despite the fact that the Allans educated Poe well – his schools included the University of Virginia and West Point – he had a falling-out with his surrogate father that led to him being disinherited from what would have been a large fortune. Poe struggled financially for his entire adult life. He also endured tragedy when his wife – who was actually his cousin, and 13 years old when he married her – died of tuberculosis as a young woman (the theme of lost love is particularly prominent in his poetry). Perhaps not coincidentally, Poe struggled with alcoholism, a problem that probably contributed, directly or indirectly, to his death under never entirely explained circumstances in 1849 at the tragically young age of 40.

It didn't help matters any that Poe was determined to support himself as a writer, a precarious business in any era. He held – and lost – a series of writing and editing positions at a number of prominent magazines of the early nineteenth century, moving between Richmond, Baltimore, Philadelphia and New York over the course of his career. Though he boosted circulation for the periodicals for which he worked, he never held a job for more than a couple of years. At the time of his death he was planning to launch a magazine of his own in Philadelphia.

In literary terms, Poe was a sprinter, not a long-distance runner: many of his tales run to fewer than 10 pages. He published books of short stories and poems, and his only novel, a seafaring tale called *The Narrative of Gordon Pym* (1838), was also brief. But Poe packed a tremendous punch. One of his most famous characters, an elegant Parisian of simple – and nocturnal – tastes, C. Auguste Dupin, appeared in a mere three stories, among them Poe's masterpieces "The Murders at the Rue Morgue" (1841) and "The Purloined Letter" (1844), which laid the foundations for the modern detective story. (Each year the Mystery Writers of America hand out awards for achievement in their field known as "Edgars.") Poe's work was also important in the origins of modern science fiction; his 1835 story "The Unparalleled Adventure of One Hans Pfaall" tells the tale of a trip to the moon using a balloon and special technology that allows him to create breathable air from the vacuum of space.

Poe made his greatest impact as a writer of Gothic fiction. "The Fall of the House of Usher" (1839) is a masterpiece of gloomy atmosphere; "The Masque of Red Death" (1845) is a classic of feverish foreboding that has been alluded to many times by subsequent writers, among them Stephen King. Poe is particularly celebrated as a writer ahead of his time in the depth of his psychological insight. In "The Tell-Tale Heart" and "The Black Cat" (both 1843), he gives us unreliable narrators driven by guilt, insanity, or some combination of the two who confess to horrible crimes. A critic of science and the feel-good mentality of transcendentalists like Ralph Waldo Emerson, Poe crafted tales that were pointedly ambiguous about supernatural forces that may lurk below the veneer of placid everyday life.

During his lifetime, Poe was best known for his poem "The Raven," which turned him into a household name. You may find this a little surprising: today poetry (with the possible exception of hip-hop lyrics) is not really considered popular culture. But in the nineteenth century, poems were widely published, recited, memorized, and even parodied, and for no poem was this more true than "The Raven." From the time of its appearance in a New York newspaper in 1845, the poem became an inescapable presence. Like gangsta rap or Harry Potter in our time, it's something you know about whether you want to or not.

Part of the reason is that it's so catchy. "The Raven" is like a song that you get into your head and find yourself singing without even realizing it. Here's how it begins:

> Once upon a midnight dreary, while I pondered weak and weary,
> Over many a quaint and curious volume of forgotten lore –
> While I nodded, nearly napping, suddenly there came a tapping,
> As some one gently rapping, rapping at my chamber door.
> "'tis some visitor," I muttered, "tapping at my chamber door –
>   Only this and nothing more."

Poe sets the scene with economy: a melancholy scholar is struggling to stay awake while poring over books (sound familiar?). But his sadness is more than casual: he is mourning the death of his true love, Lenore, and had vainly hoped his studies would afford him distraction from his sorrow. Now, however, someone appears to be knocking on the door of his apartment. Someone – or some thing. But when the narrator opens that door, there's no one there: darkness and "nothing more." Wait: could it be that in the December gloom he heard the name "Lenore"? Apparently not. He closes the door.

But then our scholar hears tapping at his window. So he opens the shutter – and in flies a raven, which lands on a pale marble statue of Pallas, also known as Athena, the Greek god of wisdom.

Is this a coincidence? At first the scholar is amused, and he begins talking to the big black bird, asking its name. He's a bit startled when the bird replies in a single word that constitutes its entire vocabulary – and the last word in every subsequent stanza of the poem: "Nevermore."

Funny name: Nevermore. The scholar guesses that the Raven was trained to say this by a missing master. Initially glad for the company, he speculates aloud that the bird will soon leave him, just as Lenore has. But the Raven responds to this suggestion by parroting its trademark expression. Sitting down, the narrator begins to ponder the Raven and its disconcertingly fiery eyes. As he sinks deeper into brooding, he senses spirits lurking in the room, and asks the fowl to provide some reassurance and relief from his grief over Lenore. Not a great question: you can guess what the bird says. Indeed, one way of reading the poem is as an illustration of self-sabotage: why on earth would a person ask a one-trick bird whether he and Lenore will be reunited in heaven when he knows what the answer will inevitably be? And what does he think that bird will say when he insists that it fly away? He's got to be crazy.

But that doesn't explain everything. For there *is* something creepy about the way the bird flew in, and the way it just sits there as the poem ends:

> And the Raven, never flitting, still is sitting, still is sitting
> On the pallid bust of Pallas just above my chamber door;
> And his eyes have all the seeming of a demon's that is dreaming
> And the lamp-light o'er him streaming throws his shadow on the floor;
> And my soul from out that shadow that lies floating on the floor
> > Shall be lifted – nevermore!

It's not clear from the way the poem ends whether the narrator has literally killed himself, or whether it's simply his soul that he imagines floating, but not rising, off the floor. Either way, the raven – and the uncertainty as well as possible malice it represents – remains to haunt the rest of us.

"The Raven" has had an afterlife in popular culture that has been nothing less than phenomenal. It has appeared, directly or by allusion, in countless books, movies, and television shows straight into the twenty-first century. Among the references you might recognize are those to "the Nevermore Tree" in *The Vile Village* (2001), the seventh volume of Lemony Snicket's *A Series of Unfortunate Events*; a 1990 episode of *The Simpsons* in which James Earl Jones (of Darth Vader fame) recites the poem; and the Seattle-based heavy-metal band Nevermore.

There's one more reference that's worth mentioning, and one that brings us back to our sports analogy. In 1995, the owner of Cleveland Browns National Football franchise, Art Modell, moved his team to Baltimore. The city's hometown newspaper, the *Sun*, which dates back to Poe's day – Poe is buried in Baltimore – conducted a poll to determine the team's new name. The winner, as you probably guessed, was the Ravens, whose colors are purple and black (the team wear black pants as well as jerseys on special occasions). Over 150 years after the poem was first published, "The Raven" had yet another new lease on life. Not even black cats have this many.

Questions to consider

1. How would you describe Edgar Allan Poe's place in American culture? With whom might you compare him in contemporary popular culture?
2. Poe is known for straddling across many pop-culture genres, like the detective story, science fiction, and horror. What qualities mark these genres? Do they have anything in common?
3. What do you think is actually happening in "The Raven?" Do you see it as a psychological tale, a supernatural tale, or something else altogether?

Document Study

Carrie: Princess of blood, King of horror

Figure 1.4 *CARRIED* AWAY One of many paperback editions of Stephen King's 1974 novel *Carrie*, which was also made into a highly successful 1976 movie. There was a feminist subtext to the story that helped propel the horror genre into the twenty-first century. (© CBW/Alamy)

When Stephen King was in college at the University of Maine in the late 1960s, he had a summer job as a janitor at his old high school. King was intrigued by the girls' locker room, in particular by two metal boxes on the walls, which he learned contained tampons. He filed the image away in what was already a vivid imagination.

By this point, King had already been writing stories for many years. They were, to be sure, amateur efforts; he had placed a couple in fanzines. But he worked steadily on them even as he held a series of other jobs after he finished college, among them at a laundry, where he routinely handled dirty (and bloody) linen. It was there that a scenario began to take shape: of an unpopular girl belatedly and unexpectedly experiencing her first menstrual period in a locker room, and her alarm that she was bleeding to death provoking scorn among classmates, who pelt her with tampons ("Plug it up! Plug it up!" they chant). King filed *that* image away – along with some information he had gleaned about telekinesis, a reputed ability to mentally move physical objects, one often attributed to children – until he began his first real job as a high-school English teacher, whereupon he finally tried to turn it into a short story.

And whereupon he threw it away. King wasn't sure he liked his characters, especially a protagonist he based on two high-school classmates of his own who were both outsiders and who both died young. He also realized that the piece had to be a good deal longer than a short story if it was going to work, making it difficult to sell. He also felt out of his comfort zone. "I had landed on Planet Female," he mused in his lively 2000 book *On Writing*. "One sortie into the girls' locker room at Brunswick High School years before wasn't much help in navigating there." It was King's wife, Tabitha, herself a novelist, who fished King's manuscript out of the trash. She coaxed him through the nuances of girl culture, even as King left plenty of narrative room for "those pictures of cheerleaders who had somehow forgotten to put on their underpants," which would appeal to a male audience.

He also tapped a vein of universal dread. "Nobody was really surprised when it happened, not really, not on the subconscious level where savage things grow," reads a sentence on the first page. We don't know at the outset what "it" is, but we're drawn to find out even as we know it can't be good. Such skillful language, combined with an uncanny gift for storytelling, allowed King to sell the manuscript for what became a short novel – simply called *Carrie* – which was published in 1974. The book launched one of the great careers in American literary history, and one of the great characters of the horror genre.

Though one can't make such a case with any precision, the fact that the main character in King's debut novel happens to be a female seems at least fitting, if not culturally determined. The early 1970s were the golden age of what historians call "Second Wave" feminism (the first, early in the twentieth century, culminated in the 19th amendment to the Constitution, which gave women the vote). Second Wave feminism is often typically associated with workplace and family issues, along with those surrounding reproductive rights. But in its broadest formulations, feminism has always been an imaginative construct, too, involving the effort to engage aspects of women's lives that were ignored or disparaged in terms of their propriety as a matter of public discourse. An important measure of this movement was the degree to which it affected men; one of the great anthems of rock music in this period, for example, was Tom Petty's classic song "American Girl" (1976), which attributed some of the same longings and restlessness that had long been considered male prerogatives to females as well. Though it's a slight stretch to consider King a feminist writer, the success of *Carrie* can plausibly be attributed to the way he rode the zeitgeist even as he was situated squarely within the genre of horror fiction. In this regard, it's striking that the most important, and gendered, trope in the novel is blood: the menstrual blood of the opening scene is bookended by the menstrual blood of another at the end of the novel; in between are a series of other references to blood of other kinds, notably in the climax of the story.

Carrie is a somewhat unusual tale within the horror genre in other ways as well. King narrates the novel in documentary fashion, constructing it from a series of excerpts from fake newspaper, memoir, and scholarly accounts, all of which were "published" years after *Carrie* itself was, giving the story a slight futuristic overlay. It's also striking that the title character is, for most of the story, a victim.

The novel opens with the title character, Carrie White, in the scenario King had imagined years before. In the pages that follow, she suffers at the hands of multiple antagonists – not only vicious classmates, but also an inept principal and a fundamentalist Christian mother whose severely puritanical notions of sin and sexuality lead her to lock Carrie in a closet with a macabre crucifix at the slightest hint of independence. It's not that her community is devoid of goodwill; after thoughtless behavior early in the story, Carrie's gym teacher tries to help her and punish those who abused her, and her classmate, Sue Snell, arranges for her boyfriend to take Carrie as his date to the prom. But their efforts are finally fruitless in the face of the malignant Chris Hargensen, who retaliates for getting barred from the prom by hatching a scheme with her boyfriend to humiliate Carrie at the very moment of her triumph.

What no one – except, gradually, Carrie herself – realizes is that she is endowed with telekinetic powers that express themselves in moments of high anxiety. For a while it seems like the bizarre rain of stones on her house (or the blowing of a bulb in the locker room, or the toppling of the principal's ashtray) are isolated phenomena. But Carrie comes to understand and direct her submerged anger. When finally confronted by the unremitting hatred of Chris and her allies, she lashes out in cataclysmic fashion. The literal and figurative explosions that follow represent both satisfying comeuppance and dismaying tragedy, one of a number of ambiguities in the novel that are confusing, but which also give the tale its haunting power.

Like much popular fiction of its time, *Carrie* made its real impact not upon publication in hardcover, but rather when it appeared the following year in a paperback edition. The paperback rights for the novel sold for $400,000, a sum King found staggering, but would soon seem paltry for a man who became one of the most prolific and successful writers of modern times. By the early 1990s, there were 90 million copies of his books in print. Many subsequent King novels – *The Shining* (1977), *The Stand* (1978), and *Misery* (1987) – are widely regarded as classics. King has also been an innovator in the way he presents his work; he published his 1996 novel *The Green Mile* in six serialized paperback installments, and was among the first writers to experiment with e-book fiction, some of which he issued for free. For most of his career King was not considered a serious literary figure, in large measure because genre fiction of all kinds was considered less serious than more self-consciously artistic novels. But that has begun to change in recent years, as narrative craft (as opposed to, say, complex language) has received more critical recognition.

King has also become a one-man cottage industry in Hollywood, where his work is routinely adapted for movies and television.

But perhaps no screen version of his work has the charm (if that's the right word) of the 1976 film version of *Carrie*. It was the break-through commercial film for the noted Hollywood director Brian DePalma, who brought a highly stylized (and famously gruesome) sensibility to the project. *Carrie* was also notable for the breadth of its acting talent, which included veterans like Piper Laurie and Betty Buckley as well as newer faces, among them John Travolta as Chris Hargensen's boyfriend and Sissy Spacek as Carrie. Unusually for a horror film, Laurie and Spacek were each nominated for Academy Awards on the strength of their mother–daughter performances. The movie still routinely makes various best-of lists.

Carrie has also been the subject of multiple remakes. Most of these have been flops, among them a 1988 Broadway musical (there was an off-Broadway revival in 2012), a 1999 sequel (*The Rage: Carrie 2*), and a 2002 made-for-television movie. A 2013 film version, starring Chloe Grace Moretz and directed by Kimberly Peirce, took advantage of new technology to give the movie a more spectacular climax that reflected the novel better than DePalma wanted to and/or could 37 years earlier.

But the heart of *Carrie* remains a tormented teenage girl. As long as we have those, the story will have a certain resonance.

Questions to consider

1. How did Stephen King's experiences shape his abilities as a storyteller? What were the limits of those experiences? How did he overcome them?
2. Do you think *Carrie* is a feminist story? Why or why not?
3. What are some of the most important elements in the making of a successful novel? Memorable characters? A good storyline? Vivid language? Do any of these count more than others?
4. What is it about *Carrie* that has proven so resonant across multiple generations? How would you compare it with other horror stories you know?

Further Reading

The scope of print culture is so vast that it's almost never discussed, as it has been in this chapter, in terms of the medium as a whole. Typically people who write, research, and read about publishing choose a particular form of print: journalism (segmented in terms of newspapers, magazines, online publications, and so on), fiction (of various genres), and then non-fiction by subject. Given the intensifying specialization of modern times, one has to go pretty far back for general surveys even within a particular genre. Important examples include Frank Luther Mott, *A History of Newspapers in the United States through 250 Years, 1690–1940* (New York: Macmillan, 1940), and Mott's *A History of American Magazines, vol.1: 1741–1850* (Cambridge, MA: Harvard University Press, 1938). On books, see James D. Hart, *The Popular Book: A History of America's Literary Taste* (New York: Oxford University Press, 1950).

For more recent surveys, see John Tebbel's distillation of his multi-volume history of book publishing, *Between Covers: The Rise and Transformation of Book Publishing* (New York: Oxford University Press, 1987). Tebbel is also the author of *The Magazine in America, 1741–1990* (New York: Oxford University Press, 1991). Recent surveys of newspapers include Michael Schudson, *Discovering the News: A Social History of Newspapers* (New York: Oxford University Press, 1987), and George H. Douglas, *The Golden Age of the Newspaper* (Westport, CT: Greenwood Press, 1999). For a very good analysis of print culture in a specific historical moment, see Isabelle Lehuu, *Carnival on the Page: Print Media in Antebellum America* (Chapel Hill: University of North Carolina Press, 2000).

One important angle of approach to print shifts the subject away from the producers to consumers. A pivotal figure here was Raymond Williams. See *The Long Revolution* (1961; Cardigan: Parthian Press, 2012). See also Alberto Manguel, *A History of Reading* (New York: Penguin, 1997). Two anthologies are of note: Cathy Davidson's *Reading in America: Literature and Social History* (Baltimore, MD: Johns

Hopkins University Press, 1989), and the more general *History of Reading in the West*, edited by Gulielmo Cavallo and Roger Chartier (Amherst: University of Massachusetts Press, 2003). On the future of print and reading, see Dennis Baron, *A Better Pencil: Readers, Writers, and the Digital Revolution* (New York: Oxford University Press, 2009).

On the genre of horror, see David J. Skal, *The Monster Show: A Cultural History of Horror* (1993; New York: Faber & Faber 2001), and Wheeler Winston Dixon, *A History of Horror* (New Brunswick, NJ: Rutgers University Press, 2010). See also the anthology *The Philosophy of Horror*, edited by Richard Fahy (Lexington: University of Kentucky Press, 2010).

Edgar Allan Poe's work has been widely anthologized, and much is available online. He has also been the subject of numerous biographical studies. For a brief point of departure, see Peter Ackroyd's *Poe: A Life Cut Short* (New York: Doubleday, 2009). Stephen King's 1974 novel *Carrie* is available in multiple editions, the most recent of which was published by Anchor Books in 2011. See also King's combination of advice and autobiography in *On Writing: A Memoir of the Craft*, now in its second edition (2000; New York: Scribner, 2010).

2

Dramatic Developments
The World of the Stage

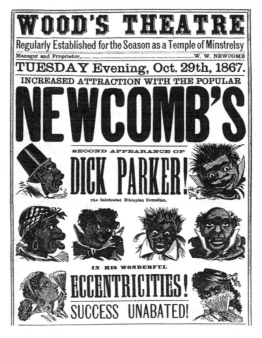

Figure 2.1 COLOR LINES   A poster for the Newcomb minstrel troupe, which appeared at Wood's Theater in Cincinnati (a crucial juncture between North and South in the years prior to the Civil War) in 1867–1868. Minstrels were almost always white men portraying black men and women in highly exaggerated, racist ways. Minstrelsy was probably the most popular form of stage entertainment in the United States in the middle third of the nineteenth century. (Wikimedia Commons: http://commons.wikimedia.org/wiki/File:Blackface_stereotypes_poster.jpg)

A Short History of the Modern Media, First Edition. Jim Cullen.
© 2014 Jim Cullen. Published 2014 by John Wiley & Sons, Ltd.

Overview

THOUGH NO ONE can prove it, and though it depends on how you define it, I suspect theater is the oldest art in human civilization. Unlike pictures on cave walls, or words chiseled on stone, the essence of a live performance – a premeditated speech, song, movement, or gesture performed by one or more people for the benefit of others – disappears immediately after it is executed (though it is typically executed repeatedly over a period of time as a commodified experience). The only audiences that can ever experience it must do so firsthand. In modern times, it has become possible to preserve aspects of such performances, whether in terms of scripts, scores, costumes, or modern technologies like sound and video recording. But none of these tools of performance can ever quite replicate the experience of a live show, one so palpable and exciting for some people that they will spend considerable sums of money, and travel considerable distances, to experience one. And do so because it is experienced with strangers in real time. Even in an age of instant entertainment at our fingertips on a laptop or tablet, going to the theater remains alive and well as a cherished experience, and a major art form.

And a *popular* art form. For much of recorded history, theater has been a variety of religious experience: rituals, reenactments, and pageants of various kinds that unfolded in ceremonial spaces like churches or temples. As such, they were important forms of social cohesion. At the time of the ancient Greeks, crowds of thousands would sit on benches in spaces known as amphitheaters, specially designed for their acoustics, where they would be regaled with comedies and tragedies – a cultural tradition (albeit with religious overtones) that they passed on to the Romans. With the fragmentation of the Western world in the wake of the Roman Empire's collapse, performance became a more episodic affair, with wandering troupes of performers known as minstrels (not to be confused with the American form of minstrelsy, discussed below) traveling between feudal estates.

Like other forms of art in an age dependent upon aristocratic and royal patronage, theater was often domesticated: something done in a home, albeit homes that were more like castles or estates than houses. But by the time of Shakespeare's England in the sixteenth century and Molière's France in the seventeenth, theatrical audiences achieved sufficient mass to once again sustain shows that could cross class and gender lines. (Men, however, were usually the only ones allowed on stage.)

In North America, however, the stage evolved slowly – more slowly, in many cases, than print culture did. There are a number of reasons for this. New England was dominated by Puritans who tended to take a dim view of any cultural practice they associated with Catholic idolatry like Christmas pageants. Up until (and also because of) the American Revolution, theatrical performance was banned in many New England communities. The middle and southern colonies were more favorably disposed toward plays and other forms of stage entertainment, but often lacked the infrastructure, from roads to theaters, to allow it to really take root.

By 1800, major cities like Philadelphia and New York had sufficient heft to support a theatrical culture, one highly dependent on British imports, Shakespeare in particular. But the 1787 play *The Contrast*, by Massachusetts jurist and writer Royall Tyler, is widely cited as an early example of a truly American production. (The title referred to a difference between effete and duplicitous Englishmen and the sturdy yeomen of the States, typified by Tyler's protagonist, who went by the not-so-subtle name of Colonel Manly.) Britain nevertheless remained an important source of theatrical culture. A good example is furnished by novelist Susanna Rowson, author of the wildly popular novel *Charlotte Temple* (1791), who was also a well-known actor and playwright who emigrated from England and spent much of her life in the United States. Ever since, the Anglo-American connection has been an axis upon which the theater world spins.

In one sense, theatrical performance cannot really be considered popular culture, because a live show can't be replicated and distributed in quite the way a book, a sound recording, or a movie can.

And yet in important respects the coming of the Industrial Revolution in the United States had profound implications for transforming stage entertainment and making it part of the fabric of everyday life in the same way that print and later media like film did. Better transportation systems – roads, canals, railroads – made it possible for touring companies to travel. Bigger cities made it possible to support a wider variety of shows for longer periods of time. And a burgeoning print culture made possible new forms of publicity for shows and performers who developed truly national reputations. A famous actor of the time like Edwin Forrest in effect became a brand, someone whose work a fan would come to know and experience whenever he came through town (or someone whose work you could catch if you yourself were traveling). When opera legend Jenny Lind came to the United States in 1851, her tour was promoted by entertainment impresario P.T. Barnum; thousands of people greeted her upon her arrival in New York with "Jenny Lind" gloves, hats, and other mass-market merchandise.

Then, as now, the capital of live performance in the United States was Manhattan. It was in nineteenth-century New York that a distinctively American theatrical culture emerged. A series of large, inexpensive theaters opened in downtown Manhattan over the first third of the century, catering to a new working-class clientele that was typically youthful. A night at the theater was a multi-hour affair that included a wide variety of acts – dances, skits, and music as well as traditional drama. Because this was an era before electric lighting, illumination was constant (provided by kerosene, whale oil, candles, or other means). Audiences were highly diverse, but segregated by race and class in terms of seating. The most expensive seats were elevated boxes; the middling classes milled around the pit near the stage; and the gallery in the back was typically the domain of African Americans, prostitutes, and their customers. Going to a show was no decorous affair, and audiences were quick to demonstrate their feelings, whether with cheers, jeers, or tossing rotten vegetables at the performers. At the same time, theatergoing was itself a kind of performance; young men, many of them immigrants from Ireland, wore the garb of so-called Bowery B'hoys (their girlfriends were known as Bowery G'hals). For them, a show was a place to see and be seen. By mid-century, more elite theatergoers were increasingly impatient with working-class antics, and began migrating to more exclusive establishments.

Such moves engendered resentment, apparent in the notorious Astor Place Riot of 1849, when working-class champions of a more street version of Shakespeare's *Macbeth* starring Forrest left their show and converged on another, more highbrow performance of the same play featuring Englishman William Macready that was taking place at the nearby Astor Place Opera House. In the fisticuffs that followed, more than 20 people died and over 150 people were wounded. Clearly, some people took their Shakespeare very seriously.

The nineteenth century was also an era when stage entertainment diversified, and solidified, into a series of discrete genres. Of course, traditional plays – whether comedies, tragedies, or hybrid forms like the History play – had been around since the time of the ancient Greeks. Shakespeare was a master of these genres, and indeed he remained a crowd-pleasing favorite all over the United States straight through the century – more so, in fact, than he was in the twentieth century, when Shakespearian drama was increasingly viewed as a pastime of the elite. The other major branch of theater was musical, namely the opera, in which all vocal parts were sung. Opera, too, was more of a mass entertainment than it would be later; a composer like Guiseppe Verdi was a household name in decades on either side of the Civil War, and his songs (sometimes translated into English) were what might today be called pop hits.

Perhaps inevitably, however, the line between drama and opera began to blur in this era. It first became obvious in light comic operas coming out of France that came to be known collectively as operetta. The genre was decisively musical, but had spoken as well as sung lines and would eventually evolve into what we have come to know as the musical. Companies performing this kind of theater crisscrossed the European and American continents.

But it was also at this moment that a uniquely American form of stage entertainment emerged: the minstrel show. Though now obscure, minstrelsy, as it came to be known, was arguably the single most popular form of entertainment in US history in the first half of the nineteenth century, and a tremendous influence on the evolution of pop music, stage entertainment, and stand-up comedy, among other media and genres within media. But minstrelsy had another distinctive characteristic that many Americans would perhaps like to forget: it was a deeply racist art form, and, while it could achieve a complexity that included moments of racial solidarity as well as revealing social commentary, minstrelsy rested on a foundation of white supremacy, one all the more notable because in many respects it was a genre that flourished not on the slave plantation but rather in the cities of Northern non-slaveholding states.

No one really knows how minstrelsy emerged. Some historians have traced its origins to the construction of the Erie Canal, when working-class whites mingled with free and enslaved blacks (who were only gradually emancipated in New York state). The famed stage performer Thomas D. Rice is sometimes cited as the inventor of the form. We do know that one night circa 1828, in a brief performance that was part of a larger evening's entertainment, Rice reputedly came up on stage in Lexington, Kentucky blacked up – he'd covered his hands and face in burned cork so as to look like a black man – and proceeded to perform a "Jim Crow" song and dance that he claimed was an authentic reproduction of one he had seen firsthand. ("Jim Crow" was once a denigrating term for a black man.) Over the course of the next few years, Rice and a host of other performers began to elaborate on such wildly popular routines, which became an increasingly prominent part of the American stage.

Though its racial dimensions were obvious to anyone who saw a minstrel show – minstrel characters were typically portrayed as objects of ridicule, whether because of their stupidity or because of their pretensions to gentility – the genre was also a vessel for expressing class conflict. To at least some extent, performers and audiences in minstrel shows reveled in expressions of racism because they knew it offended polite sensibilities. The archetypal minstrel character Zip Coon, who wore sharp attire, was a satire of white pretensions as well as black ones.

> I caution all the white dandies
> Not to come my way
> For if dey insult me
> Dey'll in the gutter lay

went one song Rice performed in 1832. Minstrel songs also mocked the presumably enlightened political views of the elite, particularly those who advocated antislavery.

> There is some folks called abolition
> Who want to mend de nigger condition

go the lyrics of the famous song "Old Dan Tucker."

> If dey would leave the niggers alone
> The niggers will always have a home.

   Other curious countercurrents also ran through the genre. A song in which the slave in the city pined for the good old days on the plantation could also express the sadness of the immigrant an ocean away from a beloved home. There were even moments – like in the song "Blue Tail Fly," in which a slave slyly exults in the death of his master – of solidarity among working people against an arrogant master class.

   Minstrelsy not only spread rapidly, but also evolved rapidly. At first a sideshow, it developed into a full-fledged form of entertainment in its own right: the minstrel show. (It also lost some of its class edge as it became a more popular form of entertainment.) By the 1840s, troupes of minstrel performers were traveling across the nation as well as across the Atlantic, turning figures like E.P Christy, founder of the legendary Christy's Minstrels, into international celebrities. Some of the greatest songwriters in American history, among them Stephen Foster (composer of "Oh! Susanna," "I Dream of Jeannie with the Light Brown Hair," and "Camptown Races"), came out of the minstrel tradition.

The typical minstrel show unfolded in three parts. In the first, introductory section, the blacked-up performers formed a semi-circle on the stage, bookended by a tambourine player and a drummer – Tambo and Bones, as these two figures were known. These people were dressed and behaved as exaggerated black caricatures like (dumb) Sambo, (lazy) Mose, and (foolishly dapper) Jim Dandy. The master of ceremonies for this section of the show was known as the Interlocutor. Unlike the rest of the crew, he did not black up, and was formally attired. Vestiges of this cultural practice survive in the late-night talk show, where a host will engage in casual comic patter with the audience as well as make jokes with (or on) sidekicks in the band.

The second section of the minstrel show was known as the olio, a term of Spanish/Portuguese origin referring to a mixture or medley. The olio consisted of songs, skits, or routines of various kinds. Once again, the primary purpose of this entertainment was to make fun of black people. Occasionally, the humor would go in different directions – puncturing the pretensions of the elite for example, or satirizing white women. Just as pre-Civil War minstrels were usually all white, they were also usually all male, though many masqueraded as women, which of course lent a bawdy (homoerotic) sexual subtext to the proceedings.

One reason for the olio is that it allowed the stagehands to work behind the curtain to set up the final part of the minstrel show. This final section, or finale, was typically a more elaborate performance lampooning stage life, where slapstick humor – pies in the face, whoopee cushions, an so on – prevailed. However, there were also moments in minstrel shows that were melodramatic, in which characters sang sad songs about the good old days. Those good old days, however, were slave days: these characters expressed regret that they had run away from home and the protective nurturance of their benevolent masters. The most famous example of this kind of song is Dan Emmet's "Dixie" (1859), whose lyrics begin with the lines

> I wish I was in the land of cotton
> Good times there are not forgotten.

(Like all such songs, it was usually sung in black dialect.) "Dixie" became the unofficial anthem of the Confederacy during the Civil War.

In the decades following the Civil War, minstrelsy continued to attract very talented people. In one of the stranger twists in American cultural history, these years also witnessed the entrance of *black* minstrels into the genre who *also* wore burned cork and managed to achieve substantial success. One such figure was the legendary Bert Williams, who went on to have a distinguished Broadway career. But success for such people was a complicated affair; Williams was lionized by some African Americans for beating white men at their own game, while he was criticized by others for exploiting black stereotypes. Williams himself struggled with such contradictions as an international celebrity who was not allowed to check into all-white hotels, for instance. A variant form of minstrelsy known as "yellowface" also emerged late in the century, in which performers, Chinese as well as Caucasian, played with stereotypes of Asians.

Minstrelsy proved to be an astonishingly durable art form. In the 1920s and 1930s, a radio minstrel show, *The Adventures of Amos 'n' Andy*, became the most popular program on the airwaves, and a film version was released in 1930. Remarkably, *Amos 'n' Andy* actually migrated to television and was shown in reruns into the mid-1960s before the ascendant Civil Rights movement simply made it too embarrassing to continue. One minstrel song, James M. Bland's "Carry Me Back to Old Virginny," in which a slave pines for plantation days, remained the Virginia state song until 1997, when the state legislature voted to retire it. (Bland was African American.) In 2000, the African American director Spike Lee made *Bamboozled*, an acidic satire about a wildly successful minstrel TV show. Among Lee's objectives was to dramatize the lack of cultural awareness on the part of both black and white Americans about their past.

In the second half of the nineteenth century, stage entertainment continued to diversify. An important transitional genre was that of the concert saloon, a venue in which men could drink alcohol as well as see stage entertainment (and in some cases buy entertainment of a more private kind). These establishments were disreputable and controversial. Their dim reputation led an entrepreneur named Tony Pastor – who first made a name for himself as a singer-songwriter of highly patriotic songs – to repackage the concert-saloon format and make it more acceptable as a form of family entertainment. He established a series of venues for shows featuring such acts and, while the term associated with this genre is French – "vaudeville," alternately understood as light comic song or the voice of the city (*voix de ville*) – the genre rapidly became distinctively American.

Vaudeville became the dominant form of stage entertainment in the last third of the nineteenth century, in large measure because it was a notably flexible stage genre on a number of levels. It was essentially a variety show in which a number of acts – singers, dancers, actors, musicians, novelty performers of all kinds – could function as interchangeable parts. Many shows ran continuously, so that someone could buy a ticket and enter at any point and experience the show as a cycle. Within this structure there were also different tiers. "Small time" vaudeville referred to neighborhood theaters, often with local acts. "Medium time" venues were bigger, and "big time" referred to large urban playhouses in major cities. (The terms 10–20–30, which referred to the price of admission in cents, were also used to designate the tier of the venue.) By the 1880s, some businessmen, notably the partnership of B.F. Keith and Edward Albee, acquired a continental chain of theaters known as a circuit so that they could book acts to perform in a variety of theaters over a period of time. Decisions about who to book and where were made on the basis of the perceived appeal of the act; the once-proverbial question "Will it play in Peoria?" referred to whether the performer would have mainstream appeal.

Vaudeville was a tough business. Performers traveled frequently, were poorly paid, and for the most part did not enjoy anywhere near the status we accord Hollywood movie stars. As such, they were part of a long tradition; eighteenth-century performers like Susanna Rowson may have been well-known, but that hardly meant they enjoyed riches. This remains true. There are probably thousands of people in the nation today who can say they are making a living as an actor. But for the overwhelming majority it's a marginal living at best, and in many cases a temporary one.

Yet another dimension of the vaudeville machine was the status of individual performers, who could move up and down the pecking order in terms of what particular slot they occupied in a show, and also in terms of moving from small time to the big time. Performers at the top of their game could become international celebrities. The famed stuntman Harry Houdini began his career in vaudeville before going off on his own to stage his own shows of ever more dazzling escapes from seemingly impossible situations.

Vaudeville was a theatrical genre with particular appeal for immigrant communities. Vaudeville theaters often catered to specific demographic groups, like Jews – performers would speak or sing in Yiddish, a working-class dialect – or the Irish. (African Americans also had their own vaudeville culture.) A highly successful local artist like Sophie Tucker or Fanny Brice could graduate to the big time and become a "goldbrick" act, introducing a specific ethnic culture to a broader audience.

Because they were so elastic, and capable of absorbing any number of stunts or fads, vaudeville shows remained popular in the United States until the 1930s. But, long before that, the genre underwent a steady decline. The major reason was competition from other, cheaper media. In the early twentieth century, shows began using a new "chaser," or closing segment, to indicate a show was ending: the motion picture. Eventually, of course, this novelty ceased being a fad and movies became a highly prized form of entertainment in their own right, so powerful it swallowed the vaudeville venues that then became known as movie palaces.

Yet even in its heyday, vaudeville was never the only game in town. Another important form of stage entertainment that arrived at roughly the same time as vaudeville was burlesque. The most distinctive aspect of the burlesque show was the people who performed in them: women. These highly stylized extravaganzas often featured large casts, outlandish costumes, and sly humor. Given the sheer novelty of female performers, there was inevitably an element of sex appeal, often accentuated in the posters for burlesque shows, which typically featured illustrations of attractive women who towered over male figures in the background. In many cases, burlesque shows were adapted versions of well-known plays that were parodied and/or augmented by incorporating elements of minstrel shows. At first, burlesque was considered a relatively highbrow affair for sophisticated urban audiences. Over time, however, the status as well as the content of burlesque declined to the point where it was little more than a striptease show. At the same time, however, a number of performers who got their start in burlesque shows, among them the comedy team of (Bud) Abbot and (Lou) Costello, W.C. Fields, and Mae West – known for her famous line, "Why don't you come up and see me sometime?" – performed in burlesque shows early in their career. Though the genre died out by the mid-twentieth century, in recent years there has been a burlesque revival in some American cities.

If the turn of the twentieth century was a time of considerable diversity within the world of the stage, it was also one of consolidation – and centralization. In New York, the entertainment industry began downtown, because most of the economic activity in the city was there. The main north–south thoroughfare of New York has always been Broadway, which moved up the island of Manhattan as the city expanded. By the mid-nineteenth century, the theater district had largely migrated toward midtown, but it was only at the turn of the twentieth century that the intersection known as Times Square – so named for the newspaper whose offices were located there – became the theatrical capital of the United States, comparable to the West End of London. Broadway became the ultimate big-time entertainment destination.

Then, as now, a Broadway locale in itself tended to confer prestige on the form of entertainment that was performed there. In the first decade of the twentieth century, entertainment impresario Florenz Ziegfeld began producing a lavish, vaudeville-inspired variety show known as the revue. The *Ziegfeld Follies*, which ran into the 1930s, featured only the most beautiful women, the most elaborate sets, and the most highly regarded talent. For the 1910 *Follies*, Ziegfeld made the controversial decision to hire Bert Williams as a featured performer, holding firm against cast members who said they would resign before sharing the stage with a black man. Over the course of the next decade Williams became a staple of the annual shows, consolidating his place as one of the leading lights of the American stage.

Broadway was also the home of a series of musical productions that had more of a storyline than the *Ziegfeld Follies* did. Many of these shows depicted the way the nation's melting pot – the term is actually the title of a 1908 Israel Zangwill play about an interfaith marriage between a Jew and a gentile – formed a pluralistic national identity. The writing and acting team of Edward Harrigan and Tony Hart – known collectively as Harrigan & Hart – made a series of comic shows that specialized in gently lampooning their own Irish ethnicity. The comic *A Trip to Chinatown* (1891) was a long-running Broadway show that also toured widely (a song that was incorporated into the show during its run, "After the Ball," became one of the all-time greatest hits in American history). Bert Williams teamed up with longtime partner George Walker in *Dahomey* (1903), a comedy about an attempt to found a black colony in Africa. At a time when class, ethnic, and religious divisions were rife in American society, the stage proved to be a cherished meeting ground where different groups of people could learn about each other and laugh, if in often stereotypical ways.

The tendency to indulge in stock characters was by no means limited to immigrant communities. All through the nineteenth century Americans were treated to stage characters with names like Solomon Swap, Industrious Doolittle, or Brother Jonathan, who embodied sturdy archetypes of the yeoman farmer, local mechanic, or urban tradesman. One of the most popular plays of the century, *The Old Homestead*, first mounted in 1876, sentimentally celebrated receding ways of life. Such shows mingled with showcases for more splashy personalities, like Davy Crockett – subject of an 1873 show titled with his famous slogan "Be sure you're right, then go ahead" – and Wild West shows featuring performers like Buffalo Bill Cody and Annie Oakley, who mixed their prowess with guns alongside their chops as entertainers. These and other real-life characters lived multiple lives in popular culture, in media that included print, television, and film.

Americans could also engage with more serious subjects rendered in more complex ways at the theater. Up until this point, I've had little to say about drama, in large measure because I've wanted to emphasize the sheer variety of stage entertainment, including some kinds that have largely disappeared from our collective memory. But traditional plays have always been a staple of the American stage. As noted, Shakespeare remained a popular favorite straight through the nineteenth century, though he tended to become more of a refined taste in the twentieth. Nineteenth-century drama inclined toward the emotionally extreme and moralistic, hence the subgenre of melodrama. Two of the most popular melodramas of the era were based on successful novels: stage versions of Harriet Beecher Stowe's 1851 antislavery saga *Uncle Tom's Cabin* (which was also played for laughs, particularly in minstrel shows), and T.S. Arthur's 1854 anti-drinking polemic *Ten Nights in a Barroom*. Both plays were fixtures of local and touring companies for half a century.

One key figure in endowing the American stage with a new sense of seriousness and realism was the producer, director, and playwright David Belasco. At the turn of the century Belasco became well-known for technological innovations, particularly those concerning the use of lighting on the stage. A vivid personality no less than an admired artist – Belasco was nicknamed "the bishop of Broadway" for his signature style of dress – he attracted some of the best talent known at the time, in a career that stretched from the 1880s until the 1930s. His best-known productions include *The Heart of Maryland* (1895), *Madame Butterfly* (1900), and *Lulu Belle* (1926).

Until about 1900, stage entertainment was so varied and widespread because, aside from the largely solitary act of reading, it was the most easily available form of diversion available to Americans both in cities and in the countryside (though rural folk also enjoyed fairs and traveling-circus shows). But with the advent of radio and film, the theater was faced with competition that was not only new, but in many ways more convenient and cost-efficient. While theater was too entrenched in the national imagination to ever entirely disappear – the annual school play alone guarantees at least some people will be coming to a show at least once a year – it was also increasingly clear that the survival of the medium would depend on its ability to really exploit the truly unique elements of its appeal. Broadway in particular responded to this challenge in a notably creative way that resulted in an era that many historians consider its golden age. The most notable example of this was the evolution – some would say the perfection – of the Broadway musical in the mid-twentieth century (see "Genre Study / Notes from the stage: The Broadway musical").

Perhaps reflecting the nation's preeminent economic and political status, American drama also enjoyed a golden age of its own in these decades. Playwrights like Eugene O'Neill became famous in the 1920s for hard-hitting plays that dealt with alcoholism, politics, and race (one production of his 1920 play *The Emperor Jones* starred the legendary African American actor Paul Robeson). Lillian Hellman explored taboo subjects like homosexuality and the seamier side of family life in *The Children's Hour* (1934) and *The Little Foxes* (1939) respectively. Arthur Miller dramatized the pathos of the American Dream in *Death of a Salesman* (1949), while Tennessee Williams thrilled audiences with his hard-hitting renditions of southern life in *Cat on a Hot Tin Roof* (1955). Many of these playwrights' works were later adapted for the screen, and immortalized by actors such as Marlin Brando and Vivien Leigh, who hopscotched between Broadway and Hollywood. So did director Elia Kazan. The Tony Awards, created in 1947 and named after actor-director Mary Antoinette Perry, were quickly recognized as the stage equivalent of the Oscars in film, and helped raise the profile of Broadway generally.

After World War II, however, structural changes in US society and the economy transformed Broadway. White flight to the suburbs and the dispersion of the national industrial base toward the south and west (and eventually overseas) depleted the city's population – and, especially, its theatergoing population. Times Square was increasingly afflicted by crime and urban squalor. At the same time, the need for theater to be a compelling alternative to other forms of entertainment meant that stage shows became more elaborate – and/or featured more star talent – which in turn required higher ticket prices. To what seems like an ever increasing degree, the audience for Broadway shows was suburban, and the theater district became at least as much a tourist attraction as native ground. This was particularly true after urban renewal gentrified the area beginning in the 1980s. By the turn of the twenty-first century, much of the serious drama on Broadway had been crowded out by glitzy musicals.

There were other signs of diminished vitality. It's a longstanding pattern in popular culture for the hits of one medium to become source material for hits in another. Many plays had their origins in novels, and many, in turn, became the basis for hit movies. One good illustration of this is Michael Morpurgo's 1982 children's novel *Warhorse*, which was adapted for the English stage in 2007 and came to New York shortly afterward before being turned into a 2011 movie by Steven Spielberg. But by the early twenty-first century, the traffic tended to move in the other direction, as a successful movie "pre-sold" an audience for a stage version. A typical example is the Walt Disney animated feature *The Lion King* (1994), which became the basis for a long-running Broadway musical three years later.

This is not to say that innovative work dried up entirely. But increasingly it came from the margins. By the second half of the twentieth century the phrase "off-Broadway" (as well as "off-off-Broadway") connoted smaller, more adventurous fare that was typically offered in lower-rent districts than Times Square. Though the scale of these productions was modest, and their audiences sometimes minute, this was often a vibrant theatrical culture. So was that of repertory companies – organizations that mounted seasons of shows that mixed old and new plays – which were fixtures of small cities like Providence, Rhode Island (though economic pressures were constant). Every once in a while, one such show would migrate to New York, and/or from off-Broadway to Broadway. New York's Public Theater, founded by impresario Joseph Papp, was an important conduit for such shows. One such production to make this journey was the wonderfully adventurous musical *Bloody Bloody Andrew Jackson*, which premiered in Los Angeles in 2008 before coming to the Public in 2009, where its success became the springboard for a brief run on Broadway in 2010. The Public has long been a beloved New York institution for its Shakespeare in the Park series, shows that are offered free to the public in Central Park each summer.

In short, by the twenty-first century, the American stage had completed an arc that began on the fringes of national life, became central to everyday experience for a great many people, and then retreated to the margins again – if margins are defined in terms of the numbers of people who go to see plays relative to the population as a whole. But, like the medium of print, the stage continues to exert considerable influence on popular culture as a whole even among people who don't think of themselves as readers or theatergoers. Each year the Tony Awards are broadcast on national television, giving exposure to work that would otherwise go unseen. More importantly, the theater continues to be a source of inspiration for new generations of artists, whether actors, writers, directors, musicians, or technicians who work in other media as well as ply their craft in theaters. Sets, domains, or studios notwithstanding, for most of us, the world remains best described as Shakespeare said it was: a stage.

Questions to consider

1. What were some of the social functions of theater in earlier civilizations?
2. Name some settings in which stage productions were mounted. What does the scale of those settings suggest about the nature of those societies? Consider in particular the United States in the colonial era versus the first half of the nineteenth century.

3. What does the genre of minstrelsy in the United States reveal about its race relations? What *forms* did racism take? How was class a factor?
4. What happened to theatrical culture in the second half of the twentieth century? How did the nature of audiences change?
5. What kinds of values and traditions do you associate with the theater today?

Genre Study

Notes from the stage: The Broadway musical

Figure 2.2 FOR KICKS *A Chorus Line* being performed at the 61st annual Tony Awards in New York, June 2007. The musical, which tells the story of a group of dancers auditioning for a show, became one of the longest-running productions after it opened on Broadway in 1975, and has since been revived a number of times. (Kevin Mazur/WireImage/Getty Images)

In the most general sense, you can't really consider the musical – if what you mean by the term is a play with songs – as an American invention. Even if you did, you'd be hard-pressed to say just when the genre emerged, since multiple pioneers, from minstrels to opera composers, could make plausible claims. Adding a geographic marker – Broadway – helps, though the location of New York's theater district moved (northward) over a period of a century. And yet both fans and historians have a rough clarity about what the term "Broadway musical" means: a golden age in the genre whose locus was roughly the two middle quarters of the twentieth century. It was, moreover, a golden age that many consider distinctively American in its diverse influences, its democratic ethos, and its optimistic spirit.

The concept of a hybrid form of stage entertainment that fuses drama and music goes back at least as far as *The Birds* (414 BCE), a comedy by the Greek playwright Aristophanes, which appears to have been performed with words accompanied by music. In the Middle Ages, the Roman Catholic Church actively fostered a series of variations on the acted/sung combination: mystery plays (dramatizations of Bible stories), miracle plays (lives of the saints), and morality plays (allegorical renditions of sin and virtue). Folk plays dramatizing real-life legends like Robin Hood or mythical ones involving dragons were also widespread. In addition to music, such performances included dancing and costumes, often in the form of masks. Such elements were further refined in the Renaissance-era *commedia dell'arte*, which first emerged in Italy and remained popular for hundreds of years.

More immediate roots of the musical can be found in the work of Briton John Gay, whose *Beggar's Opera* caused a sensation at the time of its premiere in 1728 for its combination of humor, political commentary, and use of tavern songs. The German- (and Jewish-) born Jacques Offenbach attained widespread acclaim on the European continent in the mid-nineteenth century for a series of works in the genre of operetta, an offshoot of opera that was a direct ancestor of the musical. Offenbach, in turn, was an influence on English composer Arthur Sullivan, who teamed up with British lyricist William Gilbert to form one of the most successful duos in the history of popular culture: Gilbert and Sullivan. Together they wrote over a dozen works, among them the much-beloved *Pirates of Penzance* (1879) and *The Mikado* (1885), works that made them internationally famous and continued to be staged a century later.

In one way or another, the artistry of all these people reached North American shores with the arrival of the earliest European immigrants; once in the United States, they interacted with more native elements like the minstrel show and vaudeville. One sees clear forerunners of what became the modern musical in the comic works of Irishmen Harrigan & Hart or the 1891 show *A Trip to Coontown*. Composer Victor Herbert, who was born in Ireland and trained as a cellist in Germany, came to the United States in the 1880s, going on to write a series of shows like *Babes in Toyland* (1903), which perfected an evolving formula that combined exotic settings, cross-class romance, and lots of sentiment – all of which would be core components of the emergent genre.

Not all the pivotal figures in the rise of the musical were people who thought of themselves solely as writing or performing for the theater. One key incubator for the talent, inspiration, and songs in this subculture at the turn of the century was the Tin Pan Alley, a group of publishers on West 28th street in Manhattan, where writers and musicians plied their wares. (Legend has it that the noise generated by this work gave the Tin Pan Alley its name, which became a shorthand reference for a certain kind of pop music that dominated mainstream tastes for at least 50 years.) Perhaps the greatest figure Tin Pan Alley produced was Irving Berlin (born Israel Baline), whose remarkably long career began in the late nineteenth century and extended through most of the twentieth. Many Berlin songs, which became beloved for generations, found their way into musicals. He also wrote musicals; one of his more famous productions, *Watch Your Step* (1914), featured the dancing of Vernon and Irene Castle, the most celebrated duo of the era. Another major performer in the first third of the twentieth century, Al Jolson, was renowned as "the world's greatest entertainer"; he straddled every major pop-culture medium of the time – vaudeville, musical recording, radio, movies – as well as appearing in a string of musical plays.

Most historians and musical devotees would agree, however, that the founding father of the modern musical, with its center of gravity on Broadway, was George M. Cohan. The phrase "founding father" seems particularly apt here, in that Cohan was avowedly – to modern ears comically – patriotic. A playwright, composer, actor, singer, dancer, and producer, Cohan was a tireless entertainer whose career stretched from the 1880s until the 1940s. His first show, *Little Johnnie Jones* (1904), about a jockey who feels unworthy of his wealthy fiancée unless he can win the British Derby, established Cohan as the quintessential American song-and-dance man. His heyday were the years on either side of the World War I, when hits like "Yankee Doodle Dandy," "You're a Grand Old Flag," and "Over There" made him a household name. Though many critics of the time found him impossibly corny – he belted out these songs without a trace of the irony that would be inescapable today – Cohan became an icon of the New York stage; "Give My Regards to Broadway" was one of his biggest hits.

It was in the 1920s and 1930s that musicals first came to maturity in a recognizably modern form, which is to say they became "integrated" or "book" musicals. Whereas earlier musicals strung songs together with little if any effort to sequence them or relate them to a storyline, these newer shows stitched the music into the fabric of the story, using it to advance plot or characterization. Perhaps not surprisingly, the more rigorous demands of such an approach generated a new set of collaborators in the form of composers, lyricists, and librettists (who wrote the script, or book, of a musical). Sometimes the same person performed more than one of these roles. When synergized with the talents of actors, singers, dancers, and directors – roles that sometimes overlapped – these people took the form to a new level of sophistication. One early example of this synergy is that of composer Jerome Kern and librettist Oscar Hammerstein II, who adapted Edna Ferber's 1926 novel to create *Show Boat* (1927), widely hailed as one of the greatest musicals ever made (see "Document Study / *Show Boat*: High tide of the American musical"). Another was the work of brothers (composer) George and (lyricist) Ira Gershwin, who teamed up with lyricist and librettist DuBose Heyward to write *Porgy and Bess* (1935), which bridged high and low as well as black and white cultures in a profoundly innovative way. George Gershwin's death in 1937 cut short one of the greatest musical careers in American culture. The success of musicals was not only a matter of writing great material; very often it was also a matter of having great performers to interpret it. Cole Porter's highly urbane, witty songs were animated by a variety of performers, from dancer Fred Astaire to singer Ethel Merman, who were able to bend Porter's work – which he sometimes wrote with them in mind – in directions that made them stars of the stage (and later the screen).

Another important composer of this era was Richard Rodgers. Rodgers teamed up with librettist Lorenz Hart to write a string of successful musicals that included *Babes in Arms* (1937) and *Pal Joey* (1940). After Hart's death in 1943, Rodgers began working with Hammerstein. Their first project, *Oklahoma!*, is considered by some to be the greatest musical ever written. One hit song from the show, "Oh, What a Beautiful Mornin'," set new standards for musical sophistication – it was also a daring step to have a show open with an old woman churning butter with an a cappella voice offstage, rather than having a line of chorus girls – even as the song is part of a musical with plenty of crowd-pleasing humor and romance. Rodgers and Hammerstein went on to have comparable success with a run of other hit musicals: *Carousel* (1945), *South Pacific* (1949), *The King and I* (1951), and *The Sound of Music* (1959). Many songs from these shows, all of which were made into movies, became part of a growing body of work popularly referred to as the "Great American Songbook." Generations of Americans grew up listening to these songs, singing them, and sometimes performing them in revivals that ranged from high-school to Broadway stages.

The post-World War II era was one of unprecedented prosperity and confidence in the nation's history, reflected in the unselfconscious optimism of many Broadway productions. Composers like Frank Loesser wrote catchy and sophisticated songs that appeared in satirically affectionate portraits of American life like *Guys and Dolls* (1950) and *How to Succeed in Business without Really Trying* (1961). At the same time, old-fashioned stories of romance across class lines remained popular, as attested by the adaptation of Irishman George Bernard Shaw's 1912 play *Pygmalion* into *My Fair Lady* (1956). The following year witnessed Meredith's Willson's *The Music Man*, the story of a turn-of-the-century con man seduced into honesty by the heart of a good Midwestern woman.

The social changes of the 1960s, however, posed a challenge for Broadway. The Civil Rights movement, the Vietnam War, and the rise of the counterculture challenged many longstanding assumptions and stereotypes in American life. Actually, musicals had never been relentlessly sunny; one of the most beloved works of the contemporary stage is *The Threepenny Opera*, an updated version of *The Beggar's Opera* that resulted from the collaboration of composer Kurt Weill and playwright/lyricist Bertold Brecht. It opened in 1928 and became a perennial favorite on stages around the world, though not in New York until the 1950s. (A song from the show, "Mack the Knife," about a stylish murderer, has become a pop perennial.) One of the longest-running musicals of all time, *The Fantasticks*, which opened off-Broadway in 1960 and ran continuously for over forty years, played with boy-meets-girl conventions central to the genre but bent them in a distinctly melancholy direction at the end.

Broadway grappled with new realities in a variety of ways. Sometimes those responses were demographic, as in a show like *Fiddler on the Roof* (1964), which incorporated a more ethnic flavor (specifically that of Russian Jews) into mainstream theater. Other times, they were a matter of adapting timeless themes in a more hip way, as in the religion-meets-rock-and-roll shows *Godspell* and *Jesus Christ Superstar* (both 1971). In still others, they depicted contemporary issues, as in the case of the countercultural *Hair* (1967), or *A Chorus Line* (1975), which in effect deconstructed musical theater by attempting to show aspects of life as it was lived behind and beyond the curtain.

Perhaps the most impressive and durable attempts to keep up with the times came from those who took the genre in new artistic directions. Among these were multitalented choreographers who also wrote or shaped long-lasting shows. Bob Fosse injected a jazz dimension and complex sexuality into a number of musicals, among them *Chicago* (1975). Jazz was also an important vector in *West Side Story* (1957), a modern interethnic version of Shakespeare's *Romeo and Juliet* choreographed by Jerome Robbins, with music written by the legendary conductor Leonard Bernstein. The lyrics for *West Side Story* were written by a Hammerstein protégé named Stephen Sondheim. Sondheim, in turn, has become one of the most widely admired artists in the history of the American stage with edgy, experimental, and yet highly popular shows like *A Little Night Music* (1973), *Sweeney Todd* (1979), and *Sunday in the Park with George* (1984). While some Sondheim shows such as *Pacific Overtures* (1976) and *Assassins* (1990) were not great popular hits, he nevertheless has a strong following among those who are most passionate about theater.

It was in the 1980s that Broadway musicals entered the era in which we now still appear to be living: one of glitzy extravaganzas that provide viewers with a sense of spectacle impossible to experience elsewhere (like their hometowns – the tourist trade is now central to the industry's survival). To a great extent this shift toward the grandiose reflects economic changes. After decades of urban decay, New York's theater district in and around Times Square underwent steady gentrification in the closing decades of the twentieth century. Sharply rising ticket prices reflected this upgrade, along with the imperatives of star power and visual pizzazz. The British composer Andrew Lloyd Webber, creator of shows like *Cats* (1981) and a stage adaptation of Gaston Leroux's 1910 novel *The Phantom of the Opera* (1986), continues to enjoy huge success on both sides of the Atlantic. Given the major capital investment required to stage such shows, there was increasing emphasis on "pre-sold" ideas or properties, as with hit movies, that promised safe box-office returns. Thus it was that Walt Disney studios effectively created a Broadway subsidiary for musical versions of big cinematic hits like *Beauty and the Beast* (1991 film/1994 musical) and *The Lion King* (1994 film/1997 musical). But the multiple woes afflicting the much-delayed *Spider-Man: Turn Off the Dark*, which finally opened in 2011 after cast injuries, cast replacements, and budget overruns, illustrated how the economics of such projects could backfire.

Certainly such shows pleased crowds that showed up for many years amid widespread laments that Broadway isn't what it used to be. At the same time, more demanding – and more rewarding – fare like *Rent* (1996), *Bring in 'da Noise, Bring in 'da Funk* (1996), and *Spring Awakening* (2007) showed the capacity for the Broadway musical to absorb newer musical genres like rock and hip-hop into the vast stream of popular song. The periodic and yet unpredictable arrival of such vitality suggests that for the moment, at least, the show will go on.

Questions to consider

1. What are some of the cultural forces that converged in the emergence of the musical?
2. What are some of the reasons New York emerged as the locus of the American musical?
3. What was the "golden age" of the Broadway musical? Why is it considered golden?
4. Describe the changes in Broadway musicals since the 1980s. What social changes do they reflect?

Document Study

Show Boat: *High tide of the American musical*

When the show was over, and they had clambered up the steep bank, and the music of the band had ceased, and there was left only the dying glow of the kerosene flares, you saw them stumble a little and blink, dazedly, like one rudely awakened to reality from a lovely dream.

Edna Ferber, *Show Boat* (1926)

Figure 2.3   DREAMBOAT   Paul Robeson sings "Ole Man River" as Joe in the 1936 film version of the Rodgers and Hart musical *Show Boat*. His performance in the role is widely regarded as definitive. (© Underwood and Underwood/Corbis)

The first highways in North America were rivers. The Hudson, which empties into New York Harbor, runs along the spine of the state, where it connects with Lake Champlain, the St. Lawrence River, the Great Lakes, and the vast American interior. Not surprisingly, it was fought over for hundreds of years before it finally became American (in no small part because of the US victory at the Battle of Saratoga). The same can be said of the Rio Grande, a crucial thoroughfare for Spain, Mexico, Texas, and the United States of America (and, for a brief period, the Confederate States of America, too).

But the mightiest of American rivers – "the father of waters" as it is sometimes known – is the Mississippi. It too has been a site of struggle. But the Mississippi has also been a uniquely rich vessel of American culture. Its fertile delta, for instance, was the birthplace of the blues. It was also the setting for Mark Twain's *Adventures of Huckleberry Finn*. And for about a century, the Mississippi and its tributaries – the Missouri and Ohio, among others – was the habitat of the distinctive culture of the showboat.

The name pretty much says it all: a showboat is a floating theater. The origins of the vessel date back to 1817, when an Albany-born actor named Noah Ludlow took a troupe down to Frankfort, Kentucky, mistakenly believing there was an audience there waiting to be entertained. So he bought a boat, named it *Noah's Ark*, and began traveling along the Mississippi, looking for customers. Before long, it became apparent that the best place for stage performances was on the boats themselves. By the 1840s, showboats became fixtures of the nation's cultural life from New Orleans to Chicago. The performances ranged from minstrel routines to lectures, but rapidly evolved into a distinctive style of sentimental melodrama. (The term "showboating," which refers to a person who is excessive in attention-getting, survives as a popular term.) By the late nineteenth century, showboat entertainment had become a uniquely American cultural experience that blended region, race, and genre. The coming of railroads gradually sapped the vitality of that culture as the towns that had once been thriving nodes along the river were replaced by rail-based cities like Atlanta and Omaha. But showboats lingered into the first decades of the twentieth century.

Enter Edna Ferber. Though not well-known today, this Wisconsin-born Hungarian Jew was one of the most popular writers in the first half of the twentieth century. A number of her books were made into Hollywood movies, among them *Cimarron* (which won an Academy Award for Best Picture in 1931) and *Giant* (which starred the legendary James Dean in 1956). Ferber began her career as a writer of short stories. In 1924, one of those stories, "Old Man Minick," was adapted into a play that opened in Connecticut. When the audience for the premiere of the show proved disappointing, its producer tried to cheer Ferber up by making an offhand remark that next time, he would mount the production on a showboat. Ferber, who knew nothing about showboats, was intrigued. She began researching showboats, interviewing people who worked on them and making trips down to North Carolina, where they were still plying local waters. Such efforts resulted in her 1926 novel *Show Boat*, which was an instant success. A featured selection of the then-popular Book-of-the-Month Club, it was translated into a dozen European languages and reputedly sold hundreds of thousands of copies.

Though its plot would get tweaked in its various iterations, the core storyline of *Show Boat* features a few sets of fictional characters whose lives get traced in a multigenerational saga that stretches from the 1870s to the 1920s. There's Captain Andy Hawks, the cheerful owner of the *Cotton Blossom*, and his wife Parthenia (or "Parthy"), a dour New Englander. Their daughter Magnolia marries the dashing but unreliable Gaylord (or "Gay") Ravenal – the two meet on the *Cotton Blossom*, perform together, and eventually move to Chicago. Their daughter Kim (whose name is formed from the first three letters of Kentucky, Illinois, and Missouri, on whose borders she was born) later becomes internationally famous as a star of the stage. Secondary characters include Julie Dozier, who is secretly African American but passes for white, and her husband Steve Baker. There's also the black dockworker Jo and his wife Queenie, who works as a cook on the showboat. As with many Ferber novels, *Show Boat* is rich with description of its historical setting, and features a strong female protagonist – in this case, Magnolia – who rises to meet adversity. Though contemporary readers would consider Ferber's depiction of minorities dated, the book is relatively liberal in its handling of race relations, among other subjects.

Indeed, it's precisely because the novel deals with taboo subjects like interracial sexuality, alcoholism, and matrimonial abandonment that Ferber herself did not imagine *Show Boat* could be adapted for the stage. But Jerome Kern did. Kern, a New York native who had trained in Europe, had already established himself as one of the leading composers on Broadway. He asked a mutual friend to introduce him to Ferber; by coincidence that friend was able to make the introduction at the premiere of a musical written by Kern that all three were attending. Kern explained that he had a young protégé, Oscar Hammerstein II, with whom he had worked on other shows and who he felt was now ready to write his first complete libretto. In relatively short order, Kern secured the rights to the show and cut a deal with the famous impresario Florenz Ziegfeld, who agreed to produce the musical in a new theater he was building. After a test run in Washington, DC, *Show Boat* opened on Broadway in December of 1927.

Kern and Hammerstein were committed to maintaining the novel's hard edges even as they translated them for the conventions of the Broadway stage. Thus the very first line audiences heard, amid a chorus of African Americans lugging cotton bales, was

> Niggers all work on de Mississippi
> Niggers all work while de white folks play.

While then, as now, such language was considered offensive, it served a useful purpose of evoking a gritty working-class milieu in which often backbreaking labor was performed amid white privilege. The challenges the show posed weren't only linguistic. Racial integration was a central component of *Show Boat*; in a way that was truly daring for its time, the musical featured black and white performers, onstage together, singing, talking, and interacting at the same time.

But *Show Boat* would not have won its way into the hearts of millions of Americans without other qualities that had long since been considered indispensable for a successful musical: humor, romance, and, especially, great songs. Among the most famous of these is "Ol' Man River," a gospel-influenced tune sung by Joe (now with an "e") that evokes the timeless flow of the Mississippi and the way it transcends mere human concerns.

> He must know sumpin'
> But don't say nuthin

he sings of the river. Another song, "Can't Help Lovin' Dat Man," is sung by Julie, who explains her feelings about Steve to the young Magnolia. Queenie, who hears Julie and expresses surprise that this presumably white person knows this black song, joins in, as does Joe. Much later in the story, when Magnolia is abandoned by her husband, she auditions as a performer in Chicago by singing so-called "coon songs." In so doing, she reflects the history of minstrelsy in the nineteenth century and anticipates a long line of white performers who appropriated and popularized black music in the twentieth. (Captain Andy eventually hears Magnolia sing "Can't Help Lovin' Dat Man" on the radio.) Kern also "interpolated," or integrated, an already existing song, the 1890s hit "After the Ball," which joined a series of tunes associated with the show, much in the way that successful movies have a number of older hits as part of their soundtrack.

But Kern and Hammerstein went beyond mere crowd-pleasing in their approach to music. In a manner that was unprecedented at the time, songs were truly integrated into the flow of the show. In the 1920s, a Cole Porter song always sounded like Cole Porter, and its interest to a great degree depended on how a particular performer interpreted the songwriter. But in *Show Boat*, songs were more truly a reflection of the character who sang them. Moreover, the songs of *Show Boat* reflect the more conditional, complex situations of the characters when they sing them. So, for example, when Gaylord sings "Make Believe" when he meets Magnolia, the comic friction derives from a stated premise that they aren't really in love even when everything else about their interaction suggests otherwise.

Show Boat enjoyed what at the time was considered a very long and successful six-month Broadway run before it went on the road to other cities, among them London, where the legendary singer Paul Robeson made the first of what became a number of appearances as Joe. It returned to Broadway in 1932, 1946, 1983, and 1994. In between these revivals and long after, *Show Boat* proliferated in countless productions and around the nation, taking its place in the standard repertory of the American musical.

Show Boat also became favorite fare in Hollywood. The first film version was released in 1929. The movie happened to be made in the transition between silent and sound film; first commissioned as a silent, it was partially converted to sound production in response to the success of *The Jazz Singer* (1927), the first "talkie." For many years, this version was lost. Most historians consider the 1936 black-and-white version of the film, which starred Irene Dunn as Magnolia and featured Paul Robeson as Joe, the best. (The cast also included Hattie McDaniel as Queenie, who would become the first African American to win an Academy Award for her performance as Mammy in *Gone with the Wind* three years later.) A third color version of *Show Boat* was released in 1951. Many viewers consider it the weakest of the three, particularly in the way it compresses the storyline and prettifies the settings.

Actually, such dilutions had long been part of the show's history. The phrase "niggers all work" was replaced with "darkies all work" in the 1936 film; then became "colored folk work" in the 1946 stage production; and was revised to "here we all work" in *Till the Clouds Roll By*, a 1946 musical on the life of Jerome Kern that included excerpts from *Show Boat*. Such evasions became silence altogether in a 1966 revival when the opening scene was removed from the show.

Certainly, it would be hard to call *Show Boat* a paragon of racial sensitivity, and the show has faded to some degree in recent collective memory because its artistic conventions – like that of the "tragic mulatto," in which interracial characters always come to some bad end – are considered antiquated at best (and may leave contemporary mixed-race young people scratching their heads as to why such an identity once seemed so fraught). *Show Boat* is nevertheless an important social document, and one that was progressive in its time, however limited that progress may seem in retrospect. At its best – principally in those songs, which transcend their immediate context and convey the broad sweep of American history – the musical still has the power to move those who experience it. Our primary highways are no longer rivers (nor, for that matter, rail lines). But memories of the time when they were are worth maintaining by experiencing this great piece of Americana.

Questions to consider

1. In what ways is *Show Boat* a quintessential piece of Americana?
2. Describe the racial dynamics of the show. How was it ahead of its time? How does it now seem dated? Which matters more to you?
3. Can you think of a contemporary work of popular culture you would compare with *Show Boat*? What's the basis of comparison? How is it different?

Further Reading

Overview works on American theater are hard to find. The best, though limited in its time frame, is David Grimsted's *Melodrama Unveiled: American Theater, 1800–1850* (1968; Berkeley: University of California Press, 1987). See also Robert Toll, *On with the Show: The First Century of American Show Business* (New York: Oxford University Press, 1976), and Howard Taubman, *The Making of American Theater* (New York: Coward McCann, 1965). Carl Bode's *The Anatomy of American Popular Culture, 1840–1861* (Berkeley: University of California Press, 1959) discusses many aspects of

American popular culture. For a superb treatment of Shakespeare in American culture, see Lawrence Levine's chapter on the subject in *Highbrow/Lowbrow: The Emergence of Cultural Hierarchy in America* (Cambridge, MA: Harvard University Press, 1988).

On minstrel shows, see Robert Toll, *Blacking Up: The Minstrel Show in Nineteenth-Century America* (New York: Oxford University Press, 1977); Eric Lott's theoretically dense *Love and Theft: Blackface Minstrelsy and the American Working Class* (New York: Oxford University Press, 1993); Dale Cockrell, *Demons of Disorder: Blackface Minstrels and Their World* (Cambridge: Cambridge University Press, 1997); Ken Emerson, *Doo-Dah! Stephen Foster and the Rise of American Popular Culture* (New York: Simon & Schuster, 1997); and W.T. Lhamon Jr., *Raising Cain: Blackface Performance from Jim Crow to Hip Hop* (Cambridge, MA: Harvard University Press, 1998). On burlesque shows, see Robert C. Allen, *Horrible Prettiness: Burlesque and American Culture* (Chapel Hill: University of North Carolina Press, 1991). David Freedland tours the geography of New York City to reveal now-vanished entertainment venues in *Automats, Taxi Dances and Vaudeville: Excavating Manhattan's Lost Places and Leisure* (New York: New York University Press, 2009).

Good recent histories of musicals include John Bush Jones, *Our Musicals, Our Selves: A Social History of the American Musical* (Hanover, NH: University Press of New England, 2003), and John Kendrick, *Musical Theatre: A History* (New York: Continuum, 2010). See also Larry Stempel, *Showtime: A History of the Broadway Musical Theater* (New York: W.W. Norton, 2011).

Since its first publication in 1926, Edna Ferber's *Show Boat* has been published in a variety of editions. The most accessible (available as an e-book) was published by G.K. Hall & Co. in 1981. The definitive study of *Show Boat*'s subsequent history as a musical and a movie is Miles Krueger's *Show Boat: The Story of a Classic American Musical* (1977; New York: Da Capo Press, 1990).

3

Reel Life
The Art of Motion Pictures

Figure 3.1   SCREEN SCENE   Thursday night shoppers outside a Baltimore movie theatre, 1943. By the time of World War II, film had become the dominant medium in US life, with many Americans typically going to theaters multiple times each week. (Library of Congress, Prints and Photographs Division, FSA/OWI Collection LC-USW3-022132-D)

A Short History of the Modern Media, First Edition. Jim Cullen.
© 2014 Jim Cullen. Published 2014 by John Wiley & Sons, Ltd.

Overview

LIFE ISN'T REALLY like the movies, we're often told. Movies give us an unrealistic idea of the way the world really works, attractive illusions that distort reality. This is true. But not necessarily in the way such comments suggest.

In fact, the multibillion-dollar global industry that has played such a dominant role in popular culture for the last century rests on a neural flaw in the ability of human beings to process visual images. When our brains register such images, our retinas continue to "see" them for a fraction of a second even after they've been removed. When presented with similar images in rapid succession, the neurological overload that results leads us to register a sense of motion even when none exists.

This reality of misperception has been noted, and manipulated, for thousands of years. The Roman philosopher Lucretius made references to "moving pictures" in the first century BCE. They were described by the ancient Greek scientist Claudius Ptolemy about 150 years after the birth of Christ. Artists in China, Java, and elsewhere created puppet shows and "magic lanterns" that also used shadows and screens to create the illusion of motion. By the late nineteenth century, toymakers were producing "zoetropes," in which a moving wheel with slits and mirrors allowed viewers to see illustrations "move," much in the way that cartoonists create such images through flipping similar images on each page of a book. Parallel innovations made it possible to manipulate the size of such images. In the eleventh century, Muslim scientist and inventor Al Hassan Ibn Al Haitham developed the camera obscura, in which an image viewed through a peephole could be projected on the wall of a darkened room, appearing upside down.

The modern motion-picture industry performed such manipulations with photographs rather than drawn illustrations. A key moment in its emergence occurred in 1878, when the California railroad executive Leland Stanford hired the British photographer Eadweard Muybridge to ascertain whether racehorses ever have all four legs off the ground. (They do.) Over the course of the next 20 years, a series of French inventors – Etienne-Jules Marey; Louis Aimé Augustin Le Prince; brothers Louis and Auguste Lumière – developed and refined camera and projection technology to a point that was recognizably modern. Le Prince, who was actually making movies in the 1880s, is an especially intriguing figure in this story, as he disappeared in mysterious circumstances in 1890 just as he was to present his work in Paris.

For all these people, the motion picture was a matter of science or a cultural curio. The man who understood and exploited – with notable ruthlessness – the commercial possibilities of the emerging medium was Thomas Edison. Edison was already a renowned inventor known for his work on electric lighting and sound recording when he and his partner William Dickson developed the kinetoscope, a device that allowed a single viewer to watch brief sequences, in 1892. This novelty rapidly became popular in kinetoscope parlors, where visitors could drop a coin into the machine and peer into presentations that typically involved human bodies working, playing, or preening.

The key technological innovation in the kinetoscope – one that would be central to the evolution of projected images that could be seen by multiple people – involved a series of punctured holes, or sprockets, on either side of a strip of film that allowed it to move seamlessly through a machine. Edison leveraged this crucial contribution, and through a series of business machinations that included collusion, lawsuits, and other tactics, cornered the early motion-picture industry. He required buyers and renters of his motion pictures to use only his equipment, which only used the film of his collaborating company, Kodak, to form an enterprise known as the Motion Picture Patents Company, known by the shorthand term of "the Trust." The films produced by the Trust, exhibited in often crowded and stuffy theaters known as nickelodeons, were little more than novelty acts. But they were compelling enough to attract large masses of viewers, many of them immigrants attracted to a form of (silent) entertainment where language was no barrier. By the end of the first decade of the twentieth century, there were thousands of nickelodeons in the United States, attracting millions of viewers. New York City alone had hundreds; concerns about their safety – and suspicions that their content wasn't entirely wholesome – led the city's mayor to shut them down entirely in 1908. They reopened again shortly thereafter, with social reformers moving away from condemning moviegoing entirely and toward focusing on the films they regarded as objectionable. Ever since, the content of films has been a subject of controversy and hand-wringing.

Meanwhile, even as Edison was building a cinematic financial empire, other innovators, far more attentive to providing mass entertainment than simply technological amusement, were focused on the artistic possibilities of the medium. In France, the former magician Georges Méliès developed a series of films that explored the literally fantastic dimensions of the medium, notably in the early science-fiction film *A Trip to the Moon* (1902, beautifully memorialized in the 2011 Martin Scorsese movie *Hugo*). Alice Guy, long overlooked as a pioneering figure in the history of cinema because she was a woman, made a series of films using deep-focus photography and elaborate sets. In the United States, Edwin S. Porter invented much of the visual grammar of the early motion pictures in his highly dramatic early western, *The Great Train Robbery* (1903).

Perhaps the truly catalytic figures in the emergence of film as a major form of popular culture, however, were neither the inventors nor the artists, but rather a remarkable group of Jewish immigrants who seized the vast opportunities created by the nascent industry. They did this by concentrating their efforts on the discrete, but often overlapping, domains of actually producing movies, distributing them (usually by rental, as films were rare and expensive objects), and exhibiting them in public venues. A number of these immigrants, including Adolph Zukor and Marcus Loew, got their start managing movie theaters. Others, like Carl Laemmle, were involved in making movies and making deals to disseminate them. By sidestepping – and, occasionally, violating – Edison's Trust (which was declared an illegal monopoly in 1915), they were able to start a series of companies with names like Paramount,

Fox, and Warner, which continue to dominate the film business to this day.

The second decade of the twentieth century proved to be the crucible of the movie business. It was during these years that the immigrant "moguls," as they became known, displaced Edison as the preeminent force in the industry. One means by which they did so involved paying much closer attention to the performers who appeared in their films, particularly those – Theda Bara, Clara Bow, and Douglas Fairbanks, among others – whom audiences wished to see repeatedly: they became known as "stars." Movie stars, in turn, increasingly appeared in movies that ran longer than a single reel of film, a development made possible by using two projectors, in which one reel would start as another ended. Such "feature" films became an increasingly prominent part of an outing that might include any number of shorter ones.

Meanwhile, other figures in the industry, like director D.W. Griffith and the uniquely talented writer-actor-director Charlie Chaplin, demonstrated that film was a bona fide medium for artistic distinction. Griffith's 1914 film *Birth of a Nation*, which chronicled with great visual innovation the era of the Civil War and Reconstruction – and, simultaneously, vicious racism, typified by a thrilling climax in which the Ku Klux Klan rides to the rescue of white people besieged by would-be black rapists – endowed the medium with a new degree of status. Chaplin amused and moved millions with a series of films involving his famous character of "The Tramp," which were notable for their deft critiques of industrial society. Movies like *The Immigrant* (1917), *The Gold Rush* (1925), and *Modern Times* (1931) turned Chaplin into an international celebrity. Though his unorthodox personal life and left-leaning politics later made him a controversial figure, Chaplin has always been considered among the greatest artists the medium has ever produced.

By 1920, major industry figures like Griffith, Chaplin, Fairbanks, and others migrated from New York to the obscure town of Hollywood, California, where good weather, cheap real estate, the absence of unions, and other factors led to the creation of an international media capital. Hollywood's importance was also intensified by World War I, which greatly reduced European film production. For the next century, the United States would be the primary producer and purveyor of motion pictures, even as other nations, from Russia to India, also developed distinctive cinematic cultures that remain part of a vibrant global cinematic community. Many such international figures, from German actor Marlene Dietrich to the contemporary Taiwanese-born director Ang Lee, would go on to have distinguished careers in the United States.

Over the course of the 1920s, Hollywood came to maturation by developing a series of industry norms that would structure moviemaking for the next thirty years. One manifestation of this emerging identity was the establishment of the Motion Picture Academy of Arts and Sciences, which hands out annual awards – the so-called "Oscars" – in 1927. (The statuette reputedly got its name because it resembled the uncle of the Academy's librarian at the time.) The core of this new Hollywood culture consisted of about half a dozen companies that comprised the so-called "studio system." In this system, the various workers whose occupations fell into the province of filmmaking – actors, writers, directors, and technicians of various kinds, from electricians to make-up artists – were salaried employees who were assigned to work on individual movies by studio executives. Occasionally, a studio could "loan" an actor or director to a rival at a premium price, and the studio would pocket the difference between that fee and the performer's salary. While this gave executives a good deal of power over their employees – power that would later be successfully challenged – it also gave those employees a sense of financial security (at least for the term of their contracts) and, in the case of stars, a degree of pampering that came with success.

This system also fostered the emergence of studio personalities. Universal, for example, became known for horror movies like *Frankenstein* and *Dracula* (both 1931). Paramount was associated with comedy, whether in the form of the anarchic Marx Brothers or the sly, entendre-rich jokes of Mae West. Metro-Goldwyn-Meyer (MGM) was the "Tiffany" studio, celebrated for its many classic musicals, ranging from *Broadway Melody* (1929) to the famed series of movies starring Fred Astaire and Ginger Rogers, such as *Top Hat* (1935). Warner Bros. specialized in hard-boiled crime dramas like *Angels with Dirty Faces* (1938) and *The Maltese Falcon* (1941).

One reason for the studio system's success was its capacity to adapt to emerging market conditions. When a 1921 sex scandal involving the death of a young woman at a party hosted by comedian Fatty Arbuckle generated national headlines, studio heads appointed a former federal official named Will Hays to monitor content, forestalling more formal government intervention. In the 1930s, this informal censorship was codified as the Motion Picture Production Code under the direction of former journalist Joseph Breen, who dictated what could and could not be said and shown onscreen. While many filmmakers chaffed under such strictures, studio bosses liked having a single standard (if it was safe for a staunch Catholic like Breen, it was generally considered safe for Protestants and Jews as well). Some believe that the Code fostered a sense of subtlety, even creativity, in the attempts of filmmakers to get around it. But it also severely circumscribed the careers of performers like West and scaled back the violence depicted in early gangster films like *Public Enemy* (1931). Films of this period rarely challenged the existing social order, though in this regard they probably reflected popular opinion rather than actively shaping it.

Other challenges the studios faced were technological. There were a series of experiments in sound recording to accompany that of visual filmmaking, but none was perfected before the proliferation of theaters in the early twentieth century. As a result, silent movies were often accompanied by live music (or live orchestras – so-called movie palaces conferred a sense of elegance and grandeur on those who could afford pricier tickets). By the time sound recording was sophisticated enough to be implemented on a mass scale, exhibitors were reluctant to make the costly investment in the new technology. But in 1927, the financially wobbly Warner Bros. introduced a few lines of speech into *The Jazz Singer*, featuring the great vaudeville star Al Jolson. The movie created a sensation, forcing the studios to follow suit. Holdouts like Chaplin notwithstanding, sound movies became the norm by the early 1930s.

The advent of sound was followed by the advent of color. Early experiments at the turn of the century involved dyeing film stock by hand, but technological refinements accelerated in the 1930s. Both the Kodak and the Technicolor corporations developed processes that were commonly used in cartoons and Disney features, as well as major productions like *The Wizard of Oz* (1939). Despite the success of color in terms of the increasing ease of production and the eager embrace of the public, black-and-white movies continued to be made, many quite successful. But, over time, color became the default option.

Ultimately, the success of the studio system rested on monopolistic practices that Edison, who had tried and failed to control the market, could only envy. Companies like Paramount not only made movies; they also distributed them through rental exchanges with theaters, many of which the studios owned directly. This power was augmented through a practice known as block booking, in which theaters were required to take movies they didn't particularly want as part of the price for ones they actively did. So, for example, they couldn't get a Clark Gable hit unless they also rented a "B" picture starring a lesser star like Ronald Reagan. Such practices would eventually be outlawed by the US Supreme Court, but until they worked their way through the legal system they gave the studios a sense of power and insulation from outside competition. It also gave them the resources to lure major foreign talent, like British director Alfred Hitchcock, and Swedish actor Ingrid Bergman, to Hollywood. Political upheaval in Germany in particular brought major directorial talents like Eric von Stroheim, Ernest Lubitsch, and Billy Wilder to the States, where they went on to have durable Hollywood careers.

The period from the onset of the Great Depression to the end of World War II is widely considered the golden age of the studio system. These were the years in which some of the most beloved works of cinematic art were created in its characteristic mode of assembly-line production. While this might not seem like a promising avenue of artistic achievement, it brought some of the most gifted figures in the business together in collaborative undertakings marked by a shared sense of style as well as occasional sparks of originality, much in the way the music of Motown would in the 1960s. This was the approach that resulted in the classic westerns of John Ford and Howard Hawks, the beloved comedies of Frank Capra and Preston Sturges, and the dark, stylish films collectively known as film noir. Even when the machinery broke down for various artistic, financial, or other reasons, it was often still possible for distinguished work to result. *Gone with the Wind* (1939) went through a series of directors swept aside by the fanatical producer David O. Selznick. *Casablanca* (1942) was filmed without a clear script and shot with multiple endings. Yet both films were eventually bolted into place, becoming the most beloved of all time. Hollywood's star-making machinery resulted in products that were global in appeal and built to last.

Moviegoing reached its peak in 1946, when most of the American public went to theaters multiple times a week. Though radio by this point had become a daily experience, movies were still the dominant form of entertainment, certainly as far as an outing was concerned. A trip to the cinema was typically a multi-hour activity that included viewing newsreels and cartoons along with the main feature (or two, in the case of a double bill). Though watching a film is in some respects a solitary experience, it was nevertheless a social one. Celebrity gossip, for example, became a topic of everyday conversation along with professional sports and the weather.

From this point on, however, moviegoing became steadily less popular, slowly but inexorably retreating from its central location in national media culture. A big part of the reason for this lay in legal challenges to the very foundations of the studio system. In 1944, actor Olivia de Havilland prevailed in a struggle with Warner Bros., which had extended her contract against her will after she refused to appear in a project demanded by the studio. The ruling was pivotal in the efforts of commercially successful actors to break out of the confines of corporate control. Meanwhile, after a long fight, the US Supreme Court ruled that block booking was unconstitutional in 1947. Around the same time, the government filed antitrust suits against Technicolor and Kodak, resulting in an agreement by Kodak, which by this point dominated the color-film business, to make its patents available to competitors. Then, in 1948, the studios made a legal settlement requiring them to divest themselves of their theater chains, ending this monopolistic practice. By the end of the decade, business as usual had effectively come to an end.

Hollywood was also increasingly ensnared in domestic politics. The so-called Red Scare of the late 1940s and early 1950s cast suspicions on those who were perceived to harbor sympathies for Communists at a time of great hostility toward the Soviet Union. Since Hollywood had by this point become a strong union town, and many of its stars were prominent liberals, there were widespread accusations that these people were trying to subvert the US government. A number of writers, directors, and actors were summoned by Congress to testify against their colleagues. Those who refused to do so were "blacklisted," unable to find work in their profession for many years, if at all. (The president of the Screen Actors Guild, Ronald Reagan, was cheered and vilified for his cooperation in these "witch hunts," establishing a reputation as a hard-core anticommunist that would later take him to the White House.) It was a time of bitterness and division before tensions finally subsided with the exposure of the fraudulent fearmongering of US Senator Joseph McCarthy in 1954.

If all this wasn't bad enough, the studios were also confronted by a powerful new medium: television. In the 1920s and 1930s, radio competed with the movie business for consumer dollars in that money spent on a ticket could be saved for a radio set, but the two media weren't really in direct conflict; indeed, radio proved to be a good promotional platform for the movie business. Television, by contrast, which was long in coming but began spreading rapidly in the 1950s, was widely perceived as providing comparable entertainment right in the comfort of one's own home. That's why the studios refused to allow movies to be shown on television for many years.

Studios tried to adapt to the new order by offering experiences that couldn't easily be replicated on TV. One such strategy was the 1950s fad for 3-D movies, which never really did catch on (until recently, though consumer resistance to higher 3-D ticket prices has limited their growth). Another was the production of big visual extravaganzas like *Ben-Hur* (1959) and *Lawrence of Arabia* (1962) that featured panoramic vistas and visually sumptuous sets. Sometimes this worked; other times (like the 1963 flop *Cleopatra*, featuring the superstar Elizabeth Taylor and her husband Richard Burton) it failed, or, in the slang of the time, "bombed."

Eventually, the movie business made its peace with the television business as it became clear the two could be symbiotic, given that television was voracious for content and was willing to pay for old films and B movies along with recent box-office successes. Actors and other performers could cross between the two media; as a term of shorthand, "Hollywood" soon encompassed both movies and television.

These emerging arrangements created new avenues to power for players in the entertainment industry like talent agencies, which could put together compelling packages of stars, studios, and distribution outlets. One such agency, the Music Corporation of America (MCA), ultimately bought Universal Studios (which in the decades since has gone through a series of corporate owners, most recently the National Broadcasting Company, or NBC). Eventually, the studios became pawns in multinational conglomerates; Paramount, for example, became a property in the stable of Gulf & Western, a corporation with holdings in the coffee and automotive industries. Warner Bros. was bought by Kinney, a company with interests in shoes and parking lots.

Even as the movie business struggled to recalibrate in economic terms by mid-century, it struggled to keep up with cultural developments such as the Civil Rights movement, the women's movement, and the Vietnam War. A series of films by young writers, actors, and directors in the late 1960s suggested that a new day was dawning. Many of these young American artists were influenced by foreign cinema, particularly the so-called French New Wave typified by the works of directors like Robert Bresson, Jean-Luc Godard, and François Truffaut. These directors, themselves influenced by post-World War II Italian neorealists like Robert Rossellini as well as generational successors like Federico Fellini, broke accepted conventions of cinema in emphasizing subjective points of view, informality in expression, and experiments in narrative pacing, lighting, and editing. Such influences were evident in the 1967 film *Bonnie and Clyde*, directed by Arthur Penn, in which a young Warren Beatty starred with Faye Dunaway. The film, which featured stylized violence new to American cinema, was based on a true-life tale of criminals on the run in the 1930s. A more directly countercultural sensibility emerged in movies like *The Graduate* (1967) and *Easy Rider* (1969), which defined the spirit of post-World War II baby boomers as well as proving immensely profitable.

A generation gap was opening up in terms of film content no less than film audiences. Ernest efforts to grapple with Civil Rights, like the interracial drama *Guess Who's Coming to Dinner?* (1967), became cringe-inducing in their conservatism within a few years, replaced by far more confrontational "blaxploitations" films like *Shaft* (1971) and *Super Fly* (1972), which explored African American life on more avowedly black (though still sexist) terms. With notable exceptions like Gordon Parks and his son Gordon Parks Jr., who directed *Shaft* and *Super Fly* respectively, African Americans and women continued to be underrepresented in power positions in the film industry, something that would only barely begin to change at the end of the century.

That such movies could be made at all reflected a Hollywood culture in transition. The old studio system had not only collapsed in terms of its structure; it had also lost its way in its ability to tell credible stories to the newer audiences of the late twentieth century (as attested by colossal flops like *Dr. Doolittle*, released the same year as *The Graduate* and *Bonnie and Clyde*). In part, that's because American society was changing so rapidly. One important indication of this was the death of the Production Code, replaced by a ratings system, which has continued in modified form to this day as G, PG, PG-13, R, and X ratings. Notwithstanding such classifications, American movies now exhibited an unprecedented level of frankness, reflected in the success of *Midnight Cowboy* (1969), the only X-rated film to ever win an Academy Award for Best Picture, and the sexually explicit *Last Tango in Paris* (1972), both of which are relatively tame compared to what came later.

An emerging group of young producers and directors was able to exploit this power vacuum in Hollywood and move the American film industry in new directions. Among the most important was Francis Ford Coppola, whose 1972 film *The Godfather*, followed by two sequels in 1974 and 1990, was pathbreaking in its cinematic virtuosity and its graphic depiction of violence. Another pioneering director of the era was Martin Scorsese, who in *Taxi Driver* (1976) and *Raging Bull* (1980) endowed brutal people and subjects with almost balletic visual grace. In a very different vein, the comedies of Woody Allen, typified by *Annie Hall* (1977) and *Manhattan* (1979), demonstrated the possibilities of pursuing deeply personal visions of filmmaking that could nevertheless reach broad audiences.

By the mid-1970s, however, the opening created by the Scorseses and Coppolas was closing. Ironically, this resulted from the success of two of their peers: Steven Spielberg and George Lucas. Spielberg created a national sensation in 1975 with *Jaws*, the story of a man-eating shark that made millions of Americans fearful of the beach for years. Lucas applied his considerable technical know-how to craft *Star Wars* (1977), a pioneering science-fiction franchise that made him an immensely rich man. The two teamed up (Spielberg directing, Lucas writing and producing) for the action-adventure film *Raiders of the Lost Ark* (1981). These and other Lucas and Spielberg projects were phenomenally lucrative, and led Hollywood studios to focus on blockbusters that would sell millions of tickets and spawn multiple sequels.

Power was reconcentrating in other ways as well. Once viewed as prized properties of individual studios, movie stars now became industry players in their own right on the basis of the box-office track records, typically referred to in terms of their ability to "open" a film with strong sales on its first weekend, a crucial factor in a film's eventual success. It was not uncommon for bankable talent like Tom Cruise, Julia Roberts, or Denzel Washington to command $20 million fees for a single movie. A shrewd star such as Arnold Schwarzenegger was able to originate signature characters (like his Terminator) and to receive not only a big payday, but also a share of gross receipts. Such income could be augmented still further by a panoply of tie-in merchandise like clothing, toys, and fast-food promotions.

Another major factor shaping the aggressive commercialization of the movie business was home video. The technological capacity to capture live performance on magnetic tape dates back to the 1950s, but it was not until the early 1980s that a relatively cheap and reliable means of doing so reached the consumer marketplace. There were a number of formats that competed for dominance, a struggle in which the Video Home Service (VHS) cassette finally prevailed. Once it did, video recordings of movies became a big business. Initially, Hollywood studios tried to stop home video, fearing that consumers would tape movies on broadcast television. But this never became a widespread practice. Instead, viewers turned to renting movies from local stores; the relatively high cost of tapes made this the most cost-effective approach. Later, as prices fell, consumer ownership of movies became increasingly common. The once widespread college film societies or repertory houses that had been the only practical way to see old movies were now replaced by a system that made it possible to acquire almost anything in modern film history. Eventually, the VHS tape would be replaced by the digital videodisc (DVD), which would itself be gradually replaced by the computer download.

In the closing decade of the twentieth century, Hollywood's obsession with blockbusters and sequels of established hits created an opening for entrepreneurs seeking to fill a niche for serious moviegoers looking for more artistically ambitious films. This effort spawned the so-called "indie" movement, whereby small-time producers made movies on a shoestring, which were then acquired by a bigger-name studio that distributed them. (This emphasis on film distribution, as opposed to film production, was increasingly common in studios that sought to finance or buy the rights to films rather than shoulder the risks of actually making them.) Some of these independent companies were foreign, such as Great Britain's television outfit Channel Four; others were little more than an individual maxing out multiple credit cards. A new generation of directors such as Steven Soderbergh, Spike Lee, and Kathryn Bigelow were able to prosper in this environment, as were established stars and directors such as Woody Allen and Martin Scorsese. The same could be said about emerging stars like Daniel Day-Lewis and Leonardo DiCaprio, who took their place alongside veterans such as Meryl Streep and Jodie Foster. These stars turned to independent productions when major studios showed less interest in their more adventurous projects (and when as women they were perceived as too old to function as vehicles of sexual fantasy). No people embodied the indie spirit more than the brash sibling team of Bob and Harvey Weinstein, founders of Miramax, the most successful of the indie studios. Miramax would eventually be acquired by Disney, before the brothers left the company to form the Weinstein Company. By the turn of the century, a number of major studios had bought or created indie-movie divisions, such as 20th Century Fox's subsidiary, Searchlight Pictures.

By the start of the twenty-first century, motion pictures had been around for over a hundred years. No medium in history had ever captured the collective imagination with quite the intensity movies did: they seemed as miraculous as life itself. Moreover, the movie business had become a multibillion-dollar global enterprise. Besides all the people who made their livelihoods in the industry, any given motion picture offered a wide array of revenue opportunities. In addition to theatrical exhibition – increasingly more a marketing strategy than a primary source of profit – a film could make money via home video, cable-TV rights, broadcast-TV rights, merchandising, and sequels. Movies were among the few things made in the United States (along with weaponry) for which there was steady international demand.

And yet, even as film gets enshrined as a major art form and film studies have been established as an academic discipline, it's also evident that movies are less central in American popular culture than ever. Moviegoing itself has been in steady decline, rising industry revenues a function of higher ticket prices rather than growth of the market. Once an art form noted for mass consumption – the five-cent admission of the nickelodeon a symbol of mass participation in cultural experience – movies have become an increasingly elite avocation for all but adolescents flocking to the latest glitzy extravaganza.

Technology continues to be a major factor. Innovations in computer graphics and animation have made possible visual spectacles that would simply be impossible to stage on a set. (The ability to situate simulated characters in those spectacles also threatens to make the very notion of the professional actor obsolete.) Refinements in 3-D technology have led to a revival of the format, one notable not only for its use in new movies like *Avatar* (2010), but also for new versions of classics such as *Star Wars*. And, in what might well be the most unsettling development of all, the advent of digital visual projection has made what was once the very essence of the medium – film – obsolete. Movies are no longer reels put on a projector; they're files that get downloaded on one.

And yet for this very reason, films are more accessible than ever. The rise of the personal computer has made it possible to download a movie in minutes without ever leaving your desk for the (now virtually extinct) video store, much less journeying to a theater. It's also easier than ever to find or navigate your way through a film, greatly aiding the work of scholars and teachers who may want to dissect the elements of style.

Computer technology is also altering the relationship between the creators and consumers of cinematic art. It's now possible to shoot footage with a cheap hand-held camera and edit the results on a laptop with software that would have been envied by a professional film editor a generation ago. Students today are probably better at reading films than they are at reading books. Teachers lament this reality, but it's one more indicator that the collective consciousness of the world is changing.

Still, there are other aspects of cinematic life that have not changed, and are unlikely to change anytime soon. Our brains are still as susceptible as they've ever been to the illusion of motion when shown images in rapid succession. Our eyes deceive us in narratives that rest on distortion, invention, fantasy, even when "based on a true story." But sometimes the best way to learn the truth takes the form of make-believe that you can see for yourself.

Questions to consider

1. Describe the role of Thomas Edison in the early film industry.
2. Name a few of the early technological innovations that helped popularize moviegoing.
3. How did the industry respond to the various social and cultural challenges of the 1960s?
4. What happened to the industry at the end of the twentieth century?
5. How important is actually seeing a movie at a theater? To what degree does the means of viewing affect the experience? Will it matter to you if a movie is no longer actually a film?

Genre Study

Horse sense: The logic of the western

Figure 3.2   SCENE STEALER   Still from the 1903 western *The Great Train Robbery*, directed by Edwin S. Porter. The film was pivotal in establishing many elements of the genre. (John Springer Collection/Corbis)

Ask any college student what a western is, and you'll probably get a slightly garbled but still largely coherent answer involving cowboys, Indians, horses, saloons, and gunfights (not necessarily in that order). That said, most college students have had exposure to the genre – albeit limited, especially compared with more popular ones like science fiction, horror, or romantic comedy. But for much of the twentieth century, westerns were a fixture of American popular culture, at times even dominant, across multiple media. In fact, the influential film historian Robert Ray has argued that a great many classic movies, from the gangster pictures of the 1930s straight through the *Star Wars* saga, are "disguised westerns." Where did the western come from – and where did it go?

As its name implies, the western is defined as a place. However, "west" is best understood as a relative, not fixed, location. Americans have always had a fascination with their frontier – an outer boundary of settlement that for a century and a half following the founding of Virginia in 1607 could be measured in dozens of miles from the Atlantic coast. Over time that line of settlement moved westward across the continent in an irregular pattern, jumping from the Mississippi River valley to California, and then filling in between. Beginning in 1790, the US census defined the frontier as a county with fewer than two people per square mile; by 1890 there was nowhere left within its continental boundaries that met this definition. Perhaps not coincidentally, this marked the beginning of the golden age of the genre.

The American Film Institute defines the western as "a genre of films set in the American West that embodies the spirit, the struggle, and the demise of the new frontier." That strikes me as about right, except that the roots of the western lay in print, not film. The woman who perhaps could best be described as the founding mother of the western was Mary Rowlandson, whose memoir of abduction by New England Indians during King Philip's War (1675–1676) led to *The Sovereignty and Goodness of God*, a 1682 memoir that became one of the most popular books of the colonial era. It spawned a whole subgenre of "captivity narratives" in the two centuries that followed, which became the theme of countless westerns in fiction, film, and other media.

The person who perhaps could best be described as the founding father of the western is James Fenimore Cooper. Drawing on the folklore surrounding pioneers like the legendary eighteenth-century frontiersman Daniel Boone, Cooper's frontier saga, sometimes referred to as "the Leatherstocking Tales," comprised five novels that can plausibly be considered the *Harry Potter* of the nineteenth century. The Leatherstocking in question was a protagonist who went by a series of other names, including "Natty Bumppo," "Hawkeye," "the Pathfinder," "La Longue Carabine," and "the trapper." Over the course of this multipart story, Cooper's ever restless protagonist keeps pushing to find open horizons, beginning in the northeast with *The Deerslayer* (1841; what we might today call the prequel was published last) and ending, as an old man on the Great Plains, with *The Prairie* (1827). From a modern standpoint, Cooper's fiction is almost unreadable in its stilted language and slack pacing. But the hallmarks of his style, among them gorgeous landscapes, a laconic hero, and a standard array of stock Indians (good as well as evil), proved vastly influential. In particular, *Last of the Mohicans* (1826) was made into a movie a number of times, most recently and most memorably in a 1992 version starring Daniel Day-Lewis. Cooper's Leatherstocking saga remained popular through the nineteenth century, as did western stories involving trappers, scouts, and other frontiersmen in the growing field of dime-novel fiction, much of it pitched to boys.

The genre took a new turn with the publication of Owen Wister's 1902 novel *The Virginian*. Subtitled *A Horseman of the Plains*, the book introduced or solidified a series of other conventions, among them tensions between east/west, domestication/nature, and order/violence (women representing the first half of these pairs and men the second). The unnamed narrator is forced to manage feelings for a friend who breaks the law; a hateful villain named Trampas – who is, as per the often racist convention of westerns, non-white; and an eastern schoolteacher who wants to domesticate him. Wister attended Harvard and was a friend of Theodore Roosevelt, who worked briefly as a cattleman and also became a bestselling writer on the strength of his multivolume history *The Winning of the West*, published between 1889 and 1896. Their masculine bravado continues to be a hallmark of the genre to this day.

But print culture wasn't the only fertile soil for the western. Soldier and bison hunter William F. Cody became famous as "Buffalo Bill," whose touring Wild West shows in the late nineteenth century featured real-life characters like the Native American chief Sitting Bull (who triumphed over George Custer at the Battle of Little Big Horn) and markswoman Annie Oakley. Illustrator Frederic Remington, who worked with Wister, became internationally famous for images that shaped the imagination of the region for generations to come.

With the arrival of film, the western got a new lease on life and lodged itself even more deeply into the nation's collective consciousness. Perhaps it's not surprising that the movie many historians consider the nation's first artistically significant piece of filmmaking was a western: *The Great Train Robbery* (1903). Written, directed, and produced by the cinematic pioneer Edwin S. Porter, the film was notable for a number of features that would soon become standard operating procedure in the movie business in terms of camera shots, editing techniques, and shooting on location. More specifically, the movie was a catalog of narrative elements that typified the western: railroads, horses, chase scenes, and gunfights. The final shot of the approximately 11-minute film features one of the bandits (played by Justus D. Barnes) firing directly into the camera. Though, like most movies dealing with this subject, *The Great Train Robbery* shows that crime doesn't pay, it certainly seems like a lot of fun.

One of the actors in *The Great Train Robbery* (who in fact plays three roles) is Gilbert M. Anderson, who later became famous as "Broncho Billy" Anderson, one of the first movie stars. Anderson became a fixture in a subgenre known as "series westerns," short films that were typically part of a longer bill of fare. Other early western stars included William S. Hart, who starred in dozens of serious feature-length westerns, and Tom Mix, whose varied career in lighter films lasted into the 1930s. In varying ways, these men offered an image of competent, attractive masculinity, of male figures comfortable with the rigors of nature but able to navigate the sometimes swift currents of human venality and corruption.

The arrival of sound in motion pictures in the late 1920s put westerns into temporary eclipse in the movie business. By this point, Hollywood had developed two tiers of films: so-called "A" pictures featuring the best studio talent, and "B" pictures that were made cheaply and quickly with rising (or falling) stars. Most westerns of the era were "B" pictures. The genre was strongly associated with boys, who comprised much of its audience.

Meanwhile, the genre was rapidly becoming a staple in radio broadcasting. Western serials became a fixture of the medium at the height of its power in the 1930s. To some degree, there was crossover potential in the genre; the character of Tom Mix got a new lease on life after his death as the basis of a radio show that lasted until the 1950s. The most famous radio star of the era, however, was the Lone Ranger, who, with his Native American sidekick, Tonto, dominated the airwaves for decades. The characters also became the basis of a film series and a television show (they were resurrected in a 2013 movie starring Armie Hammer and Johnny Depp in the Native American role).

In artistic terms, the turning point in the evolution of the western occurred at the end of the 1930s, when the fortunes of the genre turned sharply as a result of two key figures in the history of the cinematic western: John Ford and John Wayne. Ford's career dates back to the earliest days of the movie business, which he broke into as an actor (he has an uncredited appearance as a member of the Ku Klux Klan in the controversial 1915 D.W. Griffith epic *Birth of a Nation*). Ford began directing silent movies around this time; his 1924 western *The Iron Horse* is widely considered a landmark of the genre. He was also one of the first directors to make a foray into sound. Ford's favorite location for shooting his films, Monument Valley, on the Arizona/Utah border, became iconic in the history of the western. He worked with some of the best talent in the business, and cast Wayne (born Marion Robert Morrison) in a series of smaller parts. His decision to give Wayne a starring role in *Stagecoach* (1939) was pivotal not only for launching Wayne's career as one of the most successful actors of all time and cementing Ford's place as a leading Hollywood director, but also in establishing the western as a legitimate basis for A pictures. Over the course of the next 23 years, culminating in their classic elegy *The Man Who Shot Liberty Valance* (1962), Ford and Wayne would become among the most successful collaborators in the history of Hollywood (see "Document Study / *The Searchers*: Monumental western").

The 1940s and 1950s are regarded as the golden age of the western. In these years, the genre enjoyed its greatest prominence in terms of audience appeal, and developed a new sense of sophistication in terms of the themes it would tackle and its awareness of its own tradition. (It also showed a lyrical side in the so-called "singing westerns" starring Gene Autry, Tex Ritter, and Roy Rogers.) William Wyler's *The Oxbow Incident* (1943) explored the savagery that underlay even presumably "civilized" people; Howard Hawks's *Red River* (starring Wayne as a difficult cattle rancher) traced the love and hate that jostled between generations; Fred Zinnemann's *High Noon* (1952), starring Gary Cooper and a luminous Grace Kelly, was a compelling allegory about the dangers of giving in to anticommunist hysteria. The 1953 George Stevens western *Shane* (1953) was the quintessential embodiment of the genre, featuring Alan Ladd as a weary gunfighter who intervenes on behalf of a family fighting unscrupulous ranchers. Unable to settle down himself, he must ride into the sunset, leaving a little boy (Brandon De Wilde) calling "Shane! Shane!" after him as the movie ends. In terms of panoramic vision and unselfconscious confidence, the last great western of this era was probably *The Magnificent Seven* (1960), a John Sturges epic about a group of gunfighters who intervene on behalf of Mexican villagers besieged by bandits. The movie is an American remake of *The Seven Samurai* (1954), directed by the great Japanese filmmaker Akiro Kurosawa.

Large-scale movies like *The Magnificent Seven* became popular in the late 1950s and early 1960s because the movie industry was grappling with the challenge of a new medium that was stealing its audience: television. While TV could never compete with the sweeping cinematic power of a Hollywood movie, westerns quickly established themselves as a major, even dominant, force on the small screen even more than they did on radio. Some of the longest-running series of all time, among them *Gunsmoke* (1952–1961) and *Bonanza* (1959–1973), were westerns.

As they were in so many other ways, the 1960s were a time of dramatic change in the western. By this point the genre had developed to the point where some of its deepest adherents found themselves restless with its conventions. Perhaps the most significant form of innovation came from abroad. Foreign filmmakers had long been students of the genre; in particular a whole tradition of Italian "spaghetti westerns" were popular in Europe (many of these films were shot in Spain, where the landscape resembled that of the American west). The most famous director of spaghetti westerns, Sergio Leone, teamed up with a young star of the TV series *Rawhide* (1959–1966) named Clint Eastwood. The trilogy of films they made – *A Fistful of Dollars* (1964), *For a Few Dollars More* (1965), and *The Good, the Bad, and the Ugly* (1966) – helped infuse the western with a fresh sense of brashness and humor that loosened up the genre as a whole.

In an important sense, however, the most important legacy of the 1960s for the western was one of reappraisal, even a crisis of confidence. John Ford's late film *Cheyenne Autumn* (1964) reassessed Native American life far more sympathetically by portraying a tragic episode of US government aggression against Indians. A more avowedly countercultural spirit was at work in Arthur Penn's *Little Big Man* (1970), starring Dustin Hoffman as a boy adopted and raised as a Cheyenne. The western was pushed in a proto-feminist direction with Elliot Silverstein's 1965 film *Cat Ballou*, starring young Jane Fonda in an unusual case where a woman was the protagonist of a story. For the most part, however, the western remained a conservative, male-dominated genre.

This was a major factor in its decline. By the 1970s, the Civil Rights movement, feminism, and the war in Vietnam led many Americans to question long-held assumptions about US society. Such movements led them to reconsider the confident assumptions of the past as well, and in this period of self-doubt the serene confidence and/or nostalgia of the western began to seem suspect. The 1970 Best Picture winner, *Midnight Cowboy*, was not a western, but its main character, played by Jon Voigt, looked like a cowboy in a film that deconstructed such imagery as an illusion. In the Robert

Altman film *McCabe and Mrs. Miller* (1971), starring Warren Beatty and Julie Christie, the west comes off as a gritty, nihilistic place. The 1973 movie *Westworld* starred the iconographic Yul Brenner of *Magnificent Seven* fame as a cowboy robot gone amok in a dystopian theme park. John Wayne finished his career in 1976 with *The Shootist*, a western about a cowboy dying of cancer, as indeed Wayne was in real life.

There were nevertheless those who tried to keep the genre alive. Director Sam Peckinpah modernized the western by intensifying its violence in films like the graphic, fatalistic *The Wild Bunch* (1969). Clint Eastwood turned the Civil War into an allegory of Vietnam in westerns like *The Beguiled* (1971) and *The Outlaw Josey Wales* (1976). Veteran director Lawrence Kasdan wrote and directed the financially successful *Silverado* (1985); black director Mario Van Peebles launched an interesting experiment with *Posse* (1993), a western featuring a large cast of black actors.

In recent decades, important westerns have occasionally surfaced. The most notable example is Eastwood's *Unforgiven* (1992), which subjected the genre to a new sense of scrutiny by exposing some of its most cherished myths, like male virility, as largely fraudulent. The HBO miniseries *Deadwood* (2004–2006), set in a Dakota town with minimal territorial government, was marked by high production values and scripts that turned profanity into a kind of poetry (something possible thanks to the freer standards of cable television). The 2005 western *Brokeback Mountain*, helmed by the distinguished Taiwanese-born Ang Lee, took the genre in new directions by exploring homosexual love between two men. Such films suggest that the western continues to have possibilities as a form of artistic expression in the twenty-first century.

Which seems both inevitable and surprising. The primary setting for most exemplars of the genre – the trans-Mississippi west in the last third of the nineteenth century – was, in the larger scheme of American history, a remarkably brief chapter. And yet there's something about it that nevertheless seems emblematic of national experience as a whole, at no time more so than when it appears distant, even irretrievable. The frontier will never be fully closed until the United States is. And then, one suspects, it will go on fascinating anyone who cares to pay attention.

Questions to consider

1. Explain some of the ways "the west" has been understood in American history.
2. What are some of the most important themes in the western tradition?
3. How did figures like John Ford and John Wayne revitalize the genre?
4. Why do you think the western is less prominent today than it used to be?

Document Study

The Searchers: *Monumental western*

Figure 3.3 WAYNE'S WORLD   John Wayne as Ethan Edwards in the 1956 John Ford western *The Searchers*. The role ratified Wayne's status as the premier actor in the genre. (© Photos 12/Alamy)

There's a general consensus among American film historians that *The Searchers*, a 1956 western directed by John Ford, is the greatest western ever made, and indeed among the finest works of cinematic art ever to come out of Hollywood. For the casual observer, however, that may be hard to see, at least at first. For such a viewer, the most potent perception likely to take hold is the avowed racism of the film's protagonist, Ethan Edwards, played by John Wayne. We learn early in the film, which is set in post-Civil War Texas, that Edwards is a former Confederate soldier – or not-so-former Confederate, given his avowed refusal to pledge his allegiance to the United States.

He makes very clear upon meeting his adopted nephew, Martin Pawley (Jeffrey Hunter), who is one-eighth Cherokee, that he regards the young man as racially inferior – a point he brings up repeatedly over the course of the next two hours. And when, upon learning that the niece he spends years trying to find following her abduction by Comanche Indians has voluntarily adopted Native American ways, he pulls out his gun to shoot her, an intention that goes unrealized when Martin shields her with his own body and Edwards gets shot by an arrow fired by a member of the tribe. What's even more disorienting than his utterly unselfconscious racism is that Edwards appears to be the hero of this story: he's played by screen legend John Wayne, after all, who dominates every scene in which he appears (which is just about all of them). Are the filmmakers endorsing white supremacy?

It's hard to say – one major reason why *The Searchers* is so fascinating. Certainly, there are reasons to think the film is fairly conventional in its outlook of the time; Native American characters – who are mostly played by white actors, many of them unconvincing at face value – are not especially nuanced. Nor is Edwards the only character to believe that a white woman is better off dead than having sexual contact, consensual or not, with a person of another race. (This sentiment, expressed by Martin's betrothed, is surprising given that she wants to marry a mixed-race man herself.) But of course a writer, actor, or director who depicts a point of view is not necessarily advocating it. In any case, Ethan's hatred of the Comanche is all the more striking given his command of the language and knowledge of tribal folkways, knowledge he uses to hateful effect, as when he shoots a dead Comanche in the eyes, knowing that his people believe his spirit will then be condemned to wander the earth (like Edwards himself). While Edwards is undeniably the dominant force in the picture, the character who proves to have the most level head in the story is multiracial Martin. Critics have long argued over these and other elements of the movie, which continues to have its champions as well as its skeptics.

In large measure, the power of the film is the result of an ensemble working together at the height of their powers. Director John Ford had already been making movies for forty years by the time he decided to make *The Searchers*. He and Wayne had collaborated on a series of westerns that were recognized as instant classics, among them *Stagecoach* (1939) and *She Wore a Yellow Ribbon* (1949). But Ford also had a stable of other collaborators upon whom he depended, ranging from producer Merian C. Cooper to great character actors like Ward Bond (who plays a preacher and captain of the local volunteer militia, the Texas Rangers), Vera Miles (who plays Martin's girlfriend), and Olive Carey (who plays her Norwegian immigrant mother). Ford films were family affairs in a literal sense as well; Wayne's son Patrick has a small part in the film, as does Ford's son-in-law, and Olive Carey was married to Harry Carey, another great favorite of Ford's before Carey's death in 1947. The final image of the movie, in which Wayne clutches his elbow, is an act of homage to his old friend.

Ford's most important collaborator, however, might not have been a person, but rather a place: Monument Valley, a visually gorgeous, if austere, swath of land on the border between Utah and Arizona, where Ford shot many of his pictures. In *The Searchers* no less than in other Ford movies, the landscape functions as a character.

The source material for *The Searchers* derived from a 1954 novel by Alan LeMay, which grew out of a story he wrote for the *Saturday Evening Post*. LeMay's novel was a captivity story closely patterned on real events, notably the battles between white settlers and Comanche and other Indians that culminated in the Red River War of 1874–1875, which finally destroyed Comanche strength in the region. (Native Americans had already fought a series of wars with the Spanish, Mexicans, and Texans before Texas joined the Union in 1845.) The screenplay for the movie, which was written by Ford regular Frank S. Nugent, changed some of the plot details but kept the core story – virulent racist in postwar Texas determined to find his captive niece – intact.

Much of the film version's appeal, however, rests on a purely cinematic level – and, more specifically, a visual level. Ford began his career making silent movies, a background he continued to draw upon even when he moved into sound. The opening sequence of the movie shows Martha Edwards (Dorothy Jordan), wife of Ethan's brother Aaron (Walter Coy), gazing out her front door at the horizon, where Wayne's character slowly comes into view on a horse. (Doorways and entrances of various kinds function as a powerful motif in the movie.) Though no words are ever exchanged to this effect, it becomes clear that Martha and Ethan were – are? – deeply in love. Ethan greets Martha and Aaron's three children, Lucy, Debbie, and Ben. Could it be that one or more of these children are actually Ethan's – perhaps little Debbie, given what will come to seem like his obsession with her? (The adult Debbie is played by Natalie Wood, who appeared in *Rebel without a Cause*, also released in 1956, and would go on to even greater fame in *West Side Story* five years later.) Ethan is considerably cooler toward the couple's adopted young adult son Martin – "a man could mistake you for a half-breed," Ethan says with jarring contempt upon seeing him. Though we're told that Ethan fought with the Confederacy, the way he's spent his time in the three years since the war ended is unclear; when he presents his brother with a stash of gold coins, Aaron notes that they're freshly minted, implying that Ethan stole them.

There is in any case little time for the brothers to catch up. The next morning a group of deputized Texas Rangers arrives at the Edwards cabin announcing that cattle rustlers are in the neighborhood. Ethan tells his brother to stay home: he'll join the posse, as will Martin. This proves to be a tragic mistake: the stolen cattle were simply a ruse on the part of a band of Comanche to lure the Texans away so their homes could be raided. Ethan returns to his brother's house to find it in ruins; calling for Martha he apparently comes upon her violated body (which we're never shown – much of the violence in the film takes place offscreen, which has the effect of enhancing its horror). While his brother, sister-in-law, and nephew are dead, the Indians have apparently made off with his nieces, Lucy and Debbie. Crazed with grief and bloodthirsty for vengeance, Edwards joins the Rangers, among whose members is Lucy's bereaved fiancé, in a search for the girls.

As its title implies, *The Searchers* is an odyssey. The Rangers pursue the Comanche for a while, and actually succeed in finding them. But in the battle that follows they're outnumbered, and it's clear that in order to prevail in a direct confrontation they'll need many more men than are available. The only real possibility to rescue the girls, as improbable as it seems, would be a covert surgical strike, assuming they can be found. Ethan announces his intention to pursue this approach; Martin and Lucy's fiancé announce they're going to join him. Before long, Ethan comes upon Lucy's ravaged body (again, something we don't actually witness). He waits to tell her fiancé until the young man insists Ethan's seen her. When he learns of her actual fate from Ethan, he runs at the Comanche, getting himself killed. From this point on, Ethan and Martin are on their own.

Though the passage of time is vague, it's clear Ethan and Martin's quest goes on for years (we see seasons change repeatedly). The geography is similarly hazy yet vast; the landscape has an imposing grandeur that's meant to be understood as west Texas, though at one point the two men cross the border into New Mexico territory. Their journey includes episodes involving an unscrupulous merchant with murderous intentions, a comic interlude in which Martin inadvertently buys an Indian wife (which is played for laughs until she's found dead), and an encounter with regular US army troops who have custody of former Indian captive women and children, their emotional trauma a sobering indication of frontier violence.

Toward the end of the film, the two men actually find Debbie. Their encounter, brokered by a kindly Mexican, is a tense standoff. It turns out that the Comanche chieftain, Scar, has his own grievances, principally in the form of two sons who were killed by white men. The thin veneer of civility between the two sides will crumble, but not before Ethan learns that Debbie apparently wishes to remain Comanche – at which point she becomes dead to him figuratively, after he fails to kill her literally.

This is not the end of the story, about which I will reveal little, except to say that there it includes a big final gunfight of the kind on which the genre of the western so heavily depended. (Significantly, the regular US army, which enters the plot, ends up playing a minor role – Ford and Wayne were skeptics of Big Government of any sort.) Edwards proves himself to be savage in his thirst for revenge against Scar, even as he retreats from the most virulent expressions of his hatred and rage. The movie ends with a kind of order restored, but with Ethan unable to cross the threshold into civilized life. Like the brother of Aaron in the Old Testament, this Moses will lead his (reconstituted) people, but is unable to enter the promised land himself.

The Searchers was greeted with critical acclaim immediately upon its release in May of 1956. No film did more to legitimate the western as a vehicle for serious artistry. In the decades that followed, a chorus of voices, not all of them positive, would weigh in on the movie. Perhaps more importantly, it became a pivotal influence on a whole generation of subsequent filmmakers, among them Martin Scorsese and George Lucas. Ford and Wayne would go on to other successes, alone and together, perhaps most notably in The Man Who Shot Liberty Valance, in which Wayne once again played a flawed man who nevertheless paved the way for a stable future. But The Searchers remains their signature work, and a fine point of departure for anyone seeking to begin to understand the appeal of the western – however ambiguous it may be.

Questions to consider

1. Describe the racism of The Searchers. What forms does it take? How do you think viewers are meant to feel about it?
2. What are some of the reasons why the movie is considered one of the great westerns of all time?
3. What does the film seem to be saying about the Texas of the 1860s that remains true today?

Further Reading

There is now a tremendous amount of information available about films online. The best place to start is the International Movie

Database (IMDb.com). Certainly you can verify all kinds of factual information this way. Good analysis, though, is harder to come by.

The book that has long been regarded as the best single-volume history of US film is the late Robert Sklar's *Movie-Made America: A Cultural History of American Movies*. First published in 1975, it was reissued by Random House in 1994. The book that may well replace it as the standard work is Wheeler Winston Dixon and Gwendolyn Audrey Foster, *A Short History of Film* (New Brunswick, NJ: Rutgers University Press, 2010), which does a particularly good job of examining world cinema and the oft-overlooked work of women and racial minorities. For an excellent overview that includes more technical and theoretical approaches, see James Monaco's now-classic *How to Read a Film: Movies, Media, and Beyond* (1977; New York: Oxford University Press, 2009).

Good histories of Hollywood and the rise of the studio system include Neil Gabler, *An Empire of Their Own: How the Jews Invented Hollywood* (New York: Crown, 1988), and Thomas Schatz, *The Genius of the System: Hollywood Filmmaking in the Studio Era* (New York: Pantheon, 1989). Schatz is also the author of *Hollywood Genres: Formulas, Filmmaking and the Studio System* (New York: McGraw-Hill, 1981). For a lively account of the collapse of the studio order, see Mark Harris, *Pictures at a Revolution: Five Movies and the Birth of the New Hollywood* (New York: Penguin, 2008). The foremost chronicler of the independent movement is Peter Biskind. See *Easy Riders, Raging Bulls: How the Sex-and-Drugs Rock 'n' Roll Generation Saved Hollywood* (New York: Simon & Schuster 1998) and *Down and Dirty Pictures: Miramax, Sundance, and the Rise of Independent Film* (New York: Simon & Schuster, 2004).

A foundational text in the study of the western as a literary genre is Henry Nash Smith's *Virgin Land: The American West as Symbol and Myth* (New York: Knopf, 1950). The preeminent cultural historian of the genre is Richard Slotkin. See his famous trilogy tracing the mythology of the frontier from colonial time through the twentieth century: *Regeneration through Violence* (1973), *The Fatal Environment* (1985), and *Gunfighter Nation* (1992), all of which have been recently reissued by the University of Oklahoma Press. For a compelling feminist take on westerns, see literary historian Jane Tompkins, *West of Everything: The Inner Life of Westerns* (New York: Oxford University Press, 1992). For a good taxonomy of various western subgenres, see David Lusted, *The Western* (Harlow: Pearson/Longman, 2003).

The Searchers is among the most widely written-about films of all time, though much of the commentary is in the form of essays or part of larger discussions about westerns or film as a whole. For a very good point of departure, see Edward Buscombe's *The Searchers* (London: Palgrave, 2000), part of the British Film Institute's fine collection of brief studies of individual movies, of which Buscombe, a major scholar of the genre, is a series consultant.

4

Making Waves

Radio in American Life

Figure 4.1 TUNING IN   Radio hams operating early radio equipment, 1919. The early industry was dominated by hobbyists comparable to computer geeks. (© Bettmann Archive/Corbis)

A Short History of the Modern Media, First Edition. Jim Cullen.
© 2014 Jim Cullen. Published 2014 by John Wiley & Sons, Ltd.

Overview

ON AUGUST 1, 1981, at 12:01 a.m., Music Television (MTV) was launched from a cable satellite control room in Smithtown, Long Island. Though the broadcast could only be seen by a few thousand people in northern New Jersey that night, MTV grew rapidly into a major force in the modern media, reshaping the music, television, and film industries in the 1980s and long afterward. It also made huge stars of musicians like Michael Jackson and Madonna.

To mark what its founders considered a historic occasion, the first music video broadcast on MTV was "Video Killed the Radio Star," a 1979 song by the British pop band the Buggles. This synthesizer-rich tune, laden with futuristic imagery that now seems cheap and dated, was saturated in nostalgia for the lost world of radio. "Pictures came and broke your heart," the singer laments. "We can't rewind, we've gone too far."

More than three decades later, however, radio remains alive and well. (MTV, by contrast, no longer broadcasts music videos; most people watch them online.) Moreover, radio remains a home for stars, just like it was for decades before MTV came along. To be sure, the *kinds* of stars have changed; once a home for actors, for example, radio is now more commonly a home for talk-show hosts. But music has always been a staple of radio, from the live performances of Louis Armstrong to the latest recording from Rihanna. Among the oldest and perhaps the least glamorous of the modern media, radio nevertheless remains important, whether as a wellspring of popular culture in its own right or as a model for the organization and development of others, notably the Internet.

But if radio has proven to be a hearty survivor, the medium was also a long time coming, evolving over many decades in unpredictable ways. The direct ancestor of radio was the telegraph. A gigantic leap forward in the history of communication, the telegraph allowed humans to conquer time and space by sending instantaneous messages via electrical signals carried by wire in coded form in which letters of the alphabet were sent as long and short pulses that were transcribed as dots and dashes. This process was perfected by American inventor Samuel Morse in 1837 in the code that bears his name.

In the half century that followed, a series of scientists and entrepreneurs explored ways of achieving the results of wired communication without the wire. (The term "wireless" remains commonplace in our everyday language to describe a form of Internet access.) By 1900, the Italian inventor Guglielmo Marconi, building on the work of Scottish physicist James Clerk Maxwell, German physicist Heinrich Hertz, and American inventor Thomas Edison, had developed a system of wireless radio communication with practical applications.

Those applications were industrial. Radio was particularly valuable for the shipping industry, where navigation between sea and shore had long been challenging, if not dangerous. Radio's utility was still limited by the necessity to send messages in the dots and dashes of Morse code. But by 1910 it was possible to transmit the human voice, which marked a new chapter in the history of communications. Nevertheless, it would still be many more years and a good deal of corporate jockeying would occur among companies like American Telephone and Telegraph (AT&T), General Electric (GE), and the Radio Corporation of America (RCA) before the medium assumed anything like a recognizable form. During World War I, radio played an increasingly important role in naval communication, and the US government took control of the nation's radio stations.

Insofar as radio had any popular appeal, it was among groups of people, mostly men, who built and/or acquired radio equipment and used it to convey messages to each other. This was a culture of so-called ham operators. (The term "ham," as in "ham-handed," was a synonym for clumsiness, which radio mavens adopted as a badge of honor, much in the way early Internet enthusiasts were known as "hackers" or "geeks.") Hams prided themselves on their ability to connect with each other over vast distances, though what they had to talk about was often nothing more consequential than nice weather. The radio business for such people was thus hardware-driven, an industry for hobbyists.

That orientation began to change, however, in the early 1920s. Industry observers noticed that many more people were interested in listening rather than speaking, and in buying radio receivers for the former without acquiring radio transmitters for the latter. The idea of compelling information or entertainment going out to many listeners simultaneously – what we've come to know as broadcasting – emerged and became the dominant practice in the medium. Increasingly powerful transmitters based at individual radio stations, often operated by a panoply of interests that included schools, churches, unions, and retailers, gradually gave way to corporate professionals who owned multiple stations connected by telephone wire to form networks. The most important of these networks were National Broadcasting Company (NBC) and the Columbia Broadcasting System (CBS), both of which were up and running by the mid-1920s.

The growing commercialization of radio was reflected in other ways, too. Early radio programming was often an improvised, amateurish affair featuring local talent. But to attract larger numbers of listeners, station owners had to provide more compelling news and entertainment. And in order to do that, they had to pay for it. And in order to do *that*, they needed sources of revenue. In the UK, the government owned the airwaves, and used tax revenue from the sale of radio receivers to pay for content provided by the British Broadcasting Corporation (BBC). In the United States, however, the government had turned the airwaves back over to private interests after World War I, and during the 1920s became increasingly friendly to corporate interests. Those interests sought to pay for programming via advertising. At first, a particular company like Eveready, a battery manufacturer, would sponsor an entire program. Later, sponsorship would be carved up and sold by advertising agencies to create the modern commercial format we all know (and, for the most part, dislike). The point of radio broadcasting, then, was not to give listeners what they wanted to hear, but rather to give advertisers a market for their products. Insofar as there was any conflict there, the priority would be the advertiser, not the listener. This approach to funding radio content would have significant consequences for future media.

One form of entertainment that was *not* common in the early life of radio was recorded music. There are a number of reasons for this. In part, it reflected the poor fidelity of recording technology, still in its infancy (see Chapter 6), which got even worse when broadcast. But the music industry itself was a big part of the reason: it feared no one would buy music if it could be heard free over the airwaves. There's some reason to believe this fear was justified: the record business struggled to survive the ascendance of radio. The American Society of Composers, Authors and Publishers (ASCAP) demanded licensing fees for record broadcasts, which led many stations to avoid them altogether. It would be decades before radio and records achieved a sense of symbiosis.

So most early radio programming was live. But what form did it take? The answer is many kinds. Among the most important was news. Until the twentieth century, the primary means by which Americans kept abreast of current events was newspapers. But the dominance of print steadily eroded over the course of the last century. Film newsreels were one early alternative; television later became the dominant one. But for much of the twentieth century – and beyond – radio was the preferred medium through which a great many people got their news. At first, broadcasters simply read newspaper copy. But over time they developed their own sources of newsgathering, which became increasingly sophisticated. Among the most celebrated radio journalists of the twentieth century was Edward R. Murrow, whose reporting from Europe before and during World War II was legendary.

One of the reasons radio was such a popular source of news derived from its unique sense of immediacy. Journalists exploited this "you are there" quality to their reportage in ways that gave the medium unique power. Consider, for instance, the way the same 1939 news story, generated by the same news agency (United Press) that supplied content for both media, treated it. Here's the print version:

London, April 26 – (UP) – Prime Minister Neville Chamberlain announced today that Great Britain had decided to conscript all men between the ages of 20 and 21 for six months of compulsory training.

Conscription, he said, would be provided in a bill to be introduced in the House of Commons. In addition, he said, the bill would empower the government to call up any and all reserves.

Now here's the radio version:

Great Britain cast off centuries of tradition today in a desperate move to preserve the delicately balanced peace of Europe.

Prime Minister Neville Chamberlain announced England will expand her army by compulsory military service. A bill would be introduced to conscript all men between 20 and 21 years for six months of military training.

The radio version is clearly more dramatic. It also tilts more in the direction of approving Great Britain's decision to draft young men as a means to check the rise of Adolf Hitler; on the whole, radio had a more interventionist and politically liberal slant than newspapers of the time did, in part because it was less well established and thus less inclined toward tradition.

But radio was prized at least as much for entertainment as it was for news. Comedy was particularly popular, and took a variety of forms. As with journalism, radio comedy had roots in earlier media, in this case the stage, more specifically vaudeville. In the 1920s, many vaudeville acts migrated to radio, which presented them in the form of the variety show, among the best-known of which were *The Fleischmann's Yeast Hour* (1929–1936) and *The Chase and Sanborn Hour* (1929–1948). (Chase and Sanborn was, and remains, a coffee company.) These shows featured a variety of musical acts – pop star Rudy Vallee was the longtime host of *The Fleischmann's Yeast Hour*, which was sometimes actually called *The Rudy Vallee Show* – but their core was stand-up comedy. A number of acts that appeared on these shows ended up with programs of their own, notably Eddie Cantor, Jack Benny, and the married team of George Burns and Gracie Allen, all of whom became household names in the second quarter of the twentieth century. Their rapid-fire patter, often in the form of good-natured put-downs, entertained generations of Americans who repeated their best bits to each other in the days, weeks, and even years after their original broadcast.

By far the most popular comedy program in the history of radio – possibly the most popular entertainment program of all time – was *The Amos 'n' Andy Show*, which ran from the 1920s until the 1950s (at which point it migrated to television, where it continued to be broadcast until the mid-1960s). It's remarkable that any show would prove so durable; what's even more remarkable was the nature of this particular one, rooted in the racist history of the minstrel show (see Chapter 2). Charles Correll and Freeman Gosden were two white men with a background in minstrelsy when they first developed their radio show in Chicago. Gosden played Amos, a stereotypically dull-witted black man of the kind often labeled "Sambo." Correll was Andy, a sly, sharp-dressed black man of the kind often labeled as "Zip Coon." These two formed the core of the show, but there was also a gallery of similarly typed African Americans who also appeared, always played to comic effect. As with minstrel shows, *Amos 'n' Andy* allowed its largely white audience to experience a sense of superiority over the characters of the show, whose foibles and malapropisms – "Sho' sho," "Holy Mackerel!" and "I's regusted" – became daily conversation fodder for millions of Americans. At its height, the show was heard by about a third of the US population multiple times a week. Movie theaters played the show in lobbies; utility companies reported drops in water pressure after it was over, when listeners would make deferred trips to the bathroom. Rarely has popular culture been more popular.

As a recurring program with stable characters and ongoing storylines, *Amos 'n' Andy* belonged to a broader type of programming, known generically as a "serial," that became distinctive to the medium of radio and later influenced other kinds of popular culture.

Radio serials evolved in different genres – westerns and crime dramas were common – but the most durable genre was one that focused on everyday life, pitched specifically to female audiences. Because companies like Proctor & Gamble and Colgate-Palmolive often sponsored these shows, they came to be known as "soap operas." The most long-running of these, *The Guiding Light*, began its life on radio in 1937 before moving to television; it ran continuously until 2009.

Radio remained the dominant communications medium in the United States well into the 1950s. Yet just as its ascent was long in coming, its descent was also long anticipated. That's because the core technological components for the Next Big Thing – television – were in place as early as the 1920s. Indeed, a company like RCA was investing its considerable profits from the radio business to subsidize television's development long before TV broadcasting, and TV ownership, became widespread. The main radio networks, CBS and NBC – augmented by the arrival of the American Broadcasting Company (ABC) in the 1940s, carved out of NBC by government order to prevent that network from becoming too powerful – also positioned themselves to dominate the much-anticipated new medium. Its arrival took longer than planned, largely because of World War II (see Chapter 5).

Once TV was finally ready for prime time its impact was swift and dramatic, and it shook radio to its foundations. Listening habits quickly became viewing habits, and the leading lights of radio stardom – Benny, Burns and Allen, emerging talents like Desi Arnaz and Lucille Ball – migrated to television. Radio network budgets were cut dramatically. If the medium was to survive, it would have to be on a different basis.

The outlines of the new order were already apparent by the end of the 1950s. In the golden age of the medium, radio receivers were large objects that occupied substantial space in family homes. By the mid-1950s, listening to radio broadcasts was no longer the locus of shared domestic experience – television sets displaced radio sets from living rooms – but listening increasingly became mobile, thanks to the spread of radios in cars. A crucial innovation was the advent of transistors (see Chapter 7), which made it possible to manufacture ever smaller and cheaper radios that could be carried around with battery power. And devices called earphones made listening to music, whether at the beach or in a bedroom, a private experience.

The medium decentralized in other ways as well. Early radio had once been defined by an urge for distance on the part of individual hams, who gave way to radio stations and then to national networks. Now, however, the tendency moved back the other way to local stations, whose numbers proliferated as the networks reduced their holdings and/or focused their talent and capital on television. Programming also had to change, as those stations lacked the financial resources to support expensive shows. Instead of paying large casts or musical ensembles to perform, the idea now was to find individuals who could preside over cheaper forms of entertainment.

Among the cheapest was one previously largely banished to the sidelines: records. As we've seen, the record and radio industries did not mesh well in the early decades of the twentieth century. But times had changed for both. Though there had been reason to think hearing songs on the radio would decrease record sales, it later became increasingly apparent the opposite was true. Broadcast Music Incorporated (BMI), a licensing service that emerged in the 1940s to compete with ASCAP, took a more radio-friendly approach that allowed certain kinds of musicians, like country artists, to gain exposure that had previously been difficult to attain. While radio stations typically paid music publishers (not record companies) and songwriters of those songs (not performers) to broadcast individual songs, the fees were relatively small, typically measured in fractions of a penny per use, which could become substantial when multiplied many times over hundreds of stations. And regular radio broadcast of a song very often translated into higher record sales, with benefits for record companies as well as for artists (typically in that order).

Another important factor in the new music–radio alliance was more socioeconomic. The rising prosperity of the post-World War II decades – and, in particular, the demographic bulge of young people known as the baby boom (1946–1964), whose members entered adolescence with an unprecedented amount of disposable income on their hands – transformed American society. It has long been accepted as a truism that young adults have a unique receptiveness to music. Now such people were able to indulge that passion on an enormous scale. And the way these privileged people chose to do so – by embracing the musical legacy of slavery, refined and extended by generations of marginalized Americans – represents one of the most ironic dimensions of American history.

But also one of the more inspiring ones. With mid-century major record labels based in New York and largely focused on classical music, the pop-music industry, like radio, focused on local scenes, especially in the South. To a great degree, this meant circulating African American music, which found new audiences among white youth, particularly in the rapidly evolving musical genre of rock and roll. In many cases, the people who brokered an introduction between black musicians and white radio listeners were so-called disc jockeys, who interjected spirited commentary between songs and created a distinctive brand for a radio station. (Some of them also took bribes to play particular songs, a practice known as "payola," which became a national scandal in the late 1950s.) Among the most famous of these disc jockeys were the legendary "Wolfman Jack" in Los Angeles, Alan Freed of Cleveland, and Dewey Phillips of Memphis, who helped break Elvis Presley into stardom. Though there was no obvious political dimension to these figures or the music they played, the fact that they were fostering interracial communication in the heat of the Civil Rights movement gave them, and the medium in which they worked, significant liberal overtones. Indeed, radio was to a great degree *the* communications medium of counterculture as the 1950s gave way to the 1960s. Teenagers had no special claim on television; indeed many were actively hostile toward it. Radio, however, was another story.

A big part of the reason why was technological. Beginning in the mid-1960s, a new form of broadcasting, frequency modulation, or FM, became widespread. Until this point, most radio stations used amplitude modulation, or AM. As its name suggested, AM radio signals were measured in wavelength. By contrast, FM was measured in the frequency with which waves were generated. Though the geographic reach of AM was typically farther, FM allowed for significantly higher fidelity. It had originally been developed for use in television by a scientific engineer named Edwin Armstrong, who had close ties to NBC founder David Sarnoff before the two quarreled. Armstrong eventually committed suicide in despair over the way he had been pushed aside, but his innovations proved to be culturally important.

In the 1960s and 1970s, FM radio was a communications frontier. While AM typically focused on short pop songs, FM moved toward album-oriented rock (AOR) format, in which longer, often artistically ambitious, work by musicians like the Beatles and Bob Dylan received airplay. College radio stations in particular were sites of free-form formats – or, perhaps more accurately *anti*-formats – in which experimentation was prized. As was so often the case in popular culture, such anarchic freedom was eventually tamed into formats like contemporary hit radio (CHR). By the 1980s, playlists of songs were increasingly segmented and segregated. At the same time, music virtually disappeared from AM, which became the locus of another important broadcasting genre: talk radio.

Like recorded music, talk radio had the advantage of being relatively cheap, as it only took a single host to carry a show for hours at a time. To be sure, there were additional costs, whether they took the form of support staff, a sidekick, or the cost of phone bills (once a considerable expense) necessary for the practice of taking calls from the audience and having listeners appear live on the airwaves. But talk shows could be enormously popular and profitable.

By the late twentieth century, talk radio evolved into a series of formats. Most major cities, for instance, had a sports radio station, in which the exploits or mishaps of local teams were dissected in the aftermath of the big game, or sized up in pre-game shows. The games themselves were also a fixture of sports broadcasting. While radio could not compete directly with television in terms of literally offering a picture of the action, it was effective in locales like cars, parks, and other locations where television was not typically accessible. Radio was particularly well adapted for the rhythms of professional baseball, whose slow pace invited mental imagery in a way more frenetic sports like football or basketball didn't as easily.

In recent decades, the political talk radio has become a prominent, even dominant, format. In mid-century, political discussion was a comparatively temperate affair, in part because government rules required stations to broadcast multiple points of view. But this "fairness doctrine" was repealed in 1987 as part of the larger trend toward deregulation in American life. Actually, even before this happened, talk-show hosts explored increasingly assertive, even controversial, points of view as part of a competitive quest for ratings, in programming that was broadcast by local stations across the country, a practice known as syndication. Hosts such as Bob Grant, Don Imus, and Howard Stern found large and durable followings, often by stretching the bounds of propriety with language and themes that some found vulgar, even offensive.

For reasons that aren't entirely clear, talk radio was largely the domain of the political right. By far the most prominent right-wing talk-show host was Rush Limbaugh, who first emerged as a political force in the 1980s with an "army" of "dittoheads" who tuned into his show religiously for his daily attacks on political correctness and other forms of what he regarded as mindless liberalism. By the early twenty-first century, some observers considered Limbaugh the de facto head of the Republican Party, though even many conservatives found his bombastic style and personal foibles (which included multiple divorces and drug addiction) distasteful, if not hypocritical.

One important factor in Limbaugh's success was the next major technological innovation in the medium: satellite transmission. The ability to beam programming directly to stations from the sky rather than relying on telephone lines made it easier and cheaper to once again nationalize audiences with programs whose reach resembled that of radio's twentieth-century heyday. This capacity proceeded in tandem with a new wave of consolidation and mergers among broadcasting companies, leading to mega-broadcasters like Clear Channel – derided as "robot radio" for its tendency to provide taped programming to the over 1200 stations it owned by the turn of the twenty-first century – that controlled ever larger segments of the industry. Given that these firms also had holdings in the TV and newspaper business, there were increasingly free-speech concerns among industry observers, though the prevailing emphasis on free enterprise allowed these companies to maintain a relatively free hand in the marketplace.

Perhaps ironically, the most important source of alternative programming came not from small-time mavericks, but rather from the US government in the form of public broadcasting. National Public Radio (NPR) has proven to be one of the major legacies of the Great Society, a cluster of social programs signed into law by President Lyndon Johnson in the 1960s. One such initiative was the creation of the Corporation for Public Broadcasting (CPB), most of whose resources were devoted to television in the form of the Public Broadcasting System (PBS). But at the insistence of Johnson, who had owned radio stations before he became president, NPR was tacked onto the mission of the CPB. The radio network first began to emerge as a cultural force in the 1970s with the creation of programs like *All Things Considered*, which grew steadily in the 1980s and became a serious player in radio by the 1990s. Today, this and other NPR programs are among the most popular on the airwaves, along with locally produced, but nationally syndicated, content such as *Fresh Air*, an interview show hosted by the now legendary Terry Gross, which originated at an NPR affiliate in Philadelphia.

One reason for NPR's popularity is that, in marked contrast to commercial radio, the network was launched without the advertising that in effect has been the price listeners have paid for "free" content. In recent years, NPR has increasingly relied on paid promotion, though less frequently and overtly than most radio stations. Government funding has steadily been reduced, balanced by listener contributions that have made NPR a vibrant experiment in cultural democracy.

Meanwhile, technological developments in the twenty-first century are resulting in some of the most significant changes in the medium in a century, changes that are altering the very significance and meaning of words like "airwaves" and "broadcasting." To a great degree, these changes derive from the growing impact of the Internet on American life in general and radio in particular. Actually, many of the most important aspects of the modern Internet's character – its importance to the government before it became commercialized, the debate about whether it *should* commercialize, the role of advertising in paying for content, the commentary about its transformational role in modern society – were all anticipated in radio. Indeed, collective memory of radio's development proved to be a highly influential precedent for the way both television and the Internet would evolve.

Yet perhaps even more dramatic than radio's influence on the Internet has been the Internet's influence on radio. The World Wide Web has allowed radio stations to reach listeners through Web sites. It has also fostered the growth of tools like podcasting, which allows those listeners to hear stories they like on their own schedule. Strictly speaking, a podcast is a form of broadcasting, in that its content is available to anyone who visits a radio station. But the time-shifting element involved has changed radio from a shared experience in time to an always available recorded one. In that regard, a radio program is now a bit more like a book that you pick up rather than a show that you turn on.

More broadly, radio has come to resemble print culture in another sense as well: its surprising resilience in an era of rapid technological and cultural change. It's been a very long time since radio was at the cutting edge of popular culture, and in some quarters of US society it's been largely forgotten. But, as with books and newspapers, radio continues to have its partisans – not all of them geezers – and those partisans have been passionate. Moreover, radio has proven to be highly adaptable, not only in terms of the way it has been used, but for the varied agendas, ideological and artistic, to which it has been deployed.

So, no, video did *not* kill the radio star. It remains sound.

Questions to consider

1. What were the forerunners, and early applications of, radio? Who had the most interest in taking advantage of the new technology?
2. Describe the concept of broadcasting, how it emerged, and how it's different from other models of mass communication.
3. What factors prevented recorded music from becoming a factor in early radio? Why did that change?
4. Describe the relationship between radio and other media at the end of the twentieth century.
5. What role does radio play in your life today? How is it different from the role it played for previous generations?

Genre Study

Worlds away: Science fiction

Figure 4.2 SPACE RACE Still from *The Empire Strikes Back* (1980), the second installment of the *Star Wars* saga. Over the course of the last four decades, the films have spawned versions across media platforms and become one of the most beloved works of science fiction in US history. (*Star Wars: The Empire Strikes Back*, episode 5, 1980, director Irvin Kershner. Film Co, Lucas Film AF archive/Alamy)

As we've seen, there are certain patterns in storytelling in the history of popular culture that recur over time and across media, patterns that we call genres. Genres require no expertise to recognize; for the most part, you know a horror movie, a western, or a situation comedy when you see one. And that's true for the genre of science fiction (or sci-fi, or simply SF), too. It's been around for a long time, and it's probably more popular now than ever.

All genres have their wrinkles, ambiguities, or points of overlap with other genres, but sci-fi is a little trickier than most to define. A series of succinct descriptions are a mere search engine away, but, by way of an overview, I'll offer this one: sci-fi is a form of narrative extrapolation. Extrapolation involves using existing knowledge – usually scientific knowledge, which is to say knowledge rooted in empirically verifiable information – as a basis for imagining alternative or future scenarios. To an incomplete but substantial degree, sci-fi is a *rational* form of storytelling. This distinguishes it from more irrational ones, whether the story takes the form of unexplained supernatural phenomena (a staple of horror) or of unprovable assertions of mystical realities typically found in the realm of religion (like the series of Gospels that have Jesus Christ rising from the dead). Sci-fi stories are almost always about different worlds from the one we're purported to inhabit, but worlds that have a certain logical plausibility to them. If those worlds do not in fact rest on known physical laws, Newtonian or otherwise, the story may cross the line into what many of its fans would call the separate genre of fantasy, embodied most famously in works like the *Lord of the Rings* trilogy or the durably popular novels of Anne McCaffrey. Connoisseurs also distinguish between "hard" science fiction, which emphasizes technical elements, and "soft" sci-fi, which has more of a sociological focus. But that line is notoriously porous; indeed, for purposes of classifying books or videos, one often encounters the hybrid term of "sci-fi/fantasy." Perhaps the most obvious example of this straddle would be the *Star Wars* saga, where one can find Jedi Knights like Yoda speaking of "The Force" while wielding light sabers and traveling on imperial cruisers to other planets. The faraway galaxy those movies posit seems to have rules – or, at any rate, technologies – of its own. This may be one reason why the term "speculative fiction" has become a competing term for sci-fi and hybrid genres that cross over into horror (though it raises the question of whether all fiction by definition is speculative).

For all its variety, science fiction has characteristic icons and preoccupations. To some degree, they parallel those of other genres. The horses, frontiers, and Indians of westerns have their analogue in the spaceships, planets, and aliens of sci-fi. Westerns are usually stories set in the past that comment on the present. Not all sci-fi is set in the future – time travel is a perennial theme – but its characteristic preoccupations with societies that are either much better (utopian) or much worse (dystopian) suggest a desire to make a statement about which way the world is headed.

As for many genres of popular culture, the origins of sci-fi are in print. One can trace its antecedents at least as far back as the Roman Empire, when Lucian of Samosota wrote tales of space travel. There are also elements of space travel, alien contact, and other elements of what would become sci-fi in several of the stories comprising the Islamic collection of folk tales *A Thousand and One Nights*. Thomas More's *Utopia* (1516), Jonathan Swift's *Gulliver's Travels* (1726), and Mary Shelley's *Frankenstein* (1818) are all texts that can plausibly be considered part of sci-fi's lineage, though all of these belong at least as much to other literary traditions (as we've seen, *Frankenstein* is a touchstone of the horror genre). The remarkably protean Edgar Allan Poe can also be considered a founding father of SF; his story "The Unparalleled Adventure of One Hans Pfall" (1835) describes a trip to the moon by way of balloon.

Most sci-fi historians, however, really focus on the latter part of the nineteenth century as marking the modern emergence of the genre. Not coincidentally, this was a moment in which the impact of science was more evident than it had ever been in world civilization, in ways that ranged from the construction of railroads to the refinement of a germ theory of disease – and, particularly, the development of powerful new military weapons. In the fiction of Frenchman Jules Verne, science was relatively benign, making it possible, as much early science fiction did, to imagine the interior of the planet in works such as *A Journey to the Center of the Earth* (1864) and *Twenty Thousand Leagues Under the Sea* (1870), as well as to permit space travel in *From the Earth to the Moon* (1865). Verne is often paired with an English counterpart, H.G. Wells, who was more overtly Darwinian in his outlook, and who in books like *The War of the Worlds* (1898) provoked his readers to consider that malign forces from outer space might yet impose on Great Britain the kind of ruthless imperialism it imposed on Tasmania, whose native population had been largely wiped out.

As this very brief survey indicates, one can find forerunners of science fiction all over the world, and in Britain in particular it has always been an important part of the popular literary landscape. But as a place that was long regarded as the site of the future, the capital of science fiction in the twentieth century was the United States. This is not only because the US was a hothouse of technological innovation, but also because it had a huge literary marketplace that could support a relatively specialized genre (many of Verne's "scientific romances," as such works were called until the late 1920s, were set in the States). All accounts of the form agree that a major turning point arrived in 1926 when publisher Hugo Gernsback founded the magazine *Amazing Stories*. (A major science-fiction award, the Hugo, is named after Gernsback.) *Amazing Stories* and competitors such as *Astounding Science Fiction* were quintessential examples of a kind of publication collectively known as "the pulps," which referred to the cheap paper on which they were printed. The pulps were repositories of rapidly produced, sensational works of fiction, in the form of either self-contained or ongoing stories. Pulp fiction was typically aimed at a youth market, and for a long time it was puckishly said that the golden age of science fiction is 12, a reference to its (largely male) audience. It was in *Amazing Stories* that readers first heard tales of Buck Rogers, a time-traveling hero who later spawned a comic strip, a radio show, Hollywood movies, a TV series, and video games (see "Document Study / *Buck Rogers*: Finding time (in space)").

Indeed, the key to sci-fi's success was its ability to leap across media, even as print in general and the novel in particular remained its wellspring. Flash Gordon, a comic-strip character developed to compete with Buck Rogers for audience loyalty, also appeared in a variety of formats. More sophisticated adult fare also got a new life when it was adapted for other media. The 1920 play *R.U.R.* (*Rossum's Universal Robots*), by Czech writer Karel Capek – notable for coining the term "robot," which he derived from the Czech term that loosely translates as slave – was first broadcast over the radio a number of times in the 1920s and 1930s.

The true golden age of sci-fi is considered to be the middle third of the twentieth century. It was in these decades that the figures considered giants of the medium – Ray Bradbury, Robert Heinlein, Philip K. Dick, and Isaac Asimov – were in their prime. These and other writers were notable for the prescience with which they grappled with topics like the threat of fascism, the Holocaust, nuclear destruction, the Cold War, and other issues, usually in allegorical form. (As the great TV impresario Rod Serling, whose classic TV show *The Twilight Zone* ran on television from 1959 to 1964, once explained, "Things that couldn't be said by a Republican or a Democrat could be said by a Martian.") Science fiction also functioned as a platform for other agendas, perhaps most notably in the career of World War II veteran L. Ron Hubbard, who began writing for the pulps in the 1940s, and went on to found the Church of Scientology, a controversial sect promoting unorthodox views on the mind–body connection.

One reason why SF was so thoroughly anchored in print (and, to a lesser degree, radio) is that its imaginative constructs were difficult to credibly translate to visual media. Film-history lore is rich with examples of tinny, unintentionally comic movies like *Plan Nine from Outer Space* (1959) and a series of Japanese movies about huge creatures like the dinosaur Godzilla – which, significantly, rest on the premise of nuclear explosions triggering the mutant monsters taking over the world. More often than not, effective sci-fi on television, like a clutch of episodes from the much beloved series *The Twilight Zone*, was a triumph over limited production budgets.

By far the most successful sci-fi TV series in the history of television – one which, in good fashion, spawned a series of sequels in varied media – was *Star Trek* (1966–1969). Ironically, the show was marginal at best in the ratings during its run but became a huge hit when run in syndication (a term that in a television context refers to individual stations, rather than a TV network, running episodes when the series was no longer in production). In its depiction of a multiplanetary crew presided over by Captain James Kirk (William Shatner), his sidekick Mr. Spock (Leonard Nimoy), and other characters, *Star Trek* offered viewers an optimistic view of a future society in which diversity, reason, and a spirit of adventure prevailed over any number of hostile challenges.

Obstacles to realizing the visual possibilities of SF became increasingly surmountable in the last decades of the twentieth century, when improvements in special-effects technology opened new vistas for simulating new worlds, as well as creating spectacular effects in old ones. In 1982, director Ridley Scott adapted the 1968 Philip K. Dick story "Do Androids Dream of Electric Sheep?" into *Blade Runner*, now regarded as a truly pioneering piece of cinema. Scott also directed the now-classic *Alien* (1979), establishing a name for himself as a quintessential dystopian. A more positive vision of life on other planets was furnished by Steven Spielberg in his films *Close Encounters of the Third Kind* (1977) and *E.T.* (1982), in which benign aliens pay a visit to earth.

By all accounts, however, the towering figure in cinematic SF remains George Lucas. A screenwriter and director of note even before he established a company, Industrial Light & Magic, for special effects, Lucas brought these and other talents to bear in directing *Star Wars* in 1977. It became the basis of five other movies in the next 28 years, in effect creating two sets of trilogies. The Walt Disney Company bought out Lucas's empire in 2012, paving the way for the third trilogy in the series later in the decade.

Science fiction has branched out in other ways as well. Among the most important is the emergence of a series of important female writers in what has long been a male-dominated genre. Among these are Ursula K. LeGuin, whose career began in the early years of the women's movement, and Octavia Butler, an African American writer who has engaged with issues of racism and colonialism in her body of work. Women also made an impact on SF in other ways. One reason why the *Alien* movies are so notable is that they star Sigourney Weaver as Ellen Ripley, a fiercely competent space traveler who battles a terrifying creature (who, it so happens, is also female). Ripley is widely seen as a feminist icon of sci-fi;

women were also important characters in the various iterations of *Star Trek*.

The most recent important cultural innovation in SF rests on a fundamental redirection in collective consciousness from the vastness of space beyond the earth to the vastness of virtual space conjured by computers and, especially, the Internet. A related consciousness, one that has been with us for some time but which has intensified with the spread of computer technology, is the realization that the difference between human beings and machines is far less absolute than was once imagined. The term "cyborg," which refers to such human–machine hybrids, has been augmented by "cyberspace," popularized by the highly regarded William Gibson in his 1984 novel *Neuromancer*, and a whole genre of SF fiction known as "cyberpunk," suggesting a generally countercultural stance that fuses high technology and sometimes alternative, or primitive, lifestyles (drugs and/or altered consciousness is often a part of this mix). The best-known recent example of this sensibility in cinematic culture is *The Matrix* (1999) and its sequels in varied media.

One key question looming over SF in the twenty-first century is how it will evolve given the apparent epochal changes taking place on the globe. In the West, the overall mood is dour and fearful, and dystopias seem more common and realistic than utopias. As technological innovation, cultural prestige, and political and economic power shift toward the East, it's unlikely that science fiction will disappear – one can find antecedents for space and time travel in South as well as East Asian literary traditions – but rather take new forms with new, perhaps more hopeful, accents. The urge to speculate is a deeply human one. It may prove to be a non-human one as well.

Questions to consider

1. Compare science fiction with other genres like the horror or the western. How are they different? What do they have in common? Which matters more?

2. Why has the United States been such an important source of science fiction?

3. What are the advantages and disadvantages of sci-fi for film as opposed to a medium like print? To what degree have modern filmmakers overcome obstacles?

4. Think of some recent major sci-fi works of popular culture. What do they suggest about the United States in the twenty-first century? Do you agree that the national mood is darker now than it was in the twentieth century?

Document Study

The Mercury Theater on the Air: Worlds *war*

Figure 4.3 DRAMATIC GESTURE   Orson Welles at the microphone in his radio heyday. Welles and *The Mercury Theater on the Air*'s 1938 broadcast of their version of Jules Verne's 1898 novel *War of the Worlds* terrified listeners and irritated government authorities forced to deal with the pandemonium that erupted. (Popperfoto/Getty Images)

On October 31st, 1938, a front-page story in *The New York Times* described the widespread panic. In Newark, New Jersey, families fled their homes with wet handkerchiefs and towels over their faces as they ran into the street. In the New York City neighborhood of Harlem, dozens of men and women rushed into a police station asking where they should be evacuated. Students at Brevard College in North Carolina fainted. Residents of Birmingham, Alabama, gathered at a local church to pray. Newspaper offices and radio stations in Chicago and other cities from coast to coast were swamped with phone calls. In Indianapolis, a woman ran into a church yelling, "New York destroyed: it's the end of the world. You might as well go home to die." In Pittsburgh, a man returned home from work to find his wife with a bottle of poison in her hand, screaming, "I'd rather die this way than that."

The reason was Martians. An alien force had landed in the town of Grover's Mill, New Jersey, and was taking over the world. These people knew it was true because they heard it on the radio.

But of course it wasn't true. As Orson Welles, star of *The Mercury Theater on the Air* show broadcast of *War of the Worlds* explained at the end of the broadcast, the show was "a radio version of dressing up in a sheet and jumping out of a bush and saying Boo!" Welles went on to explain, "That grinning, globular invader of your living room is an inhabitant of a pumpkin patch, and if your doorbell rings and nobody's there, that was no Martian ... It's Halloween." Some people were amused, others were scared, and still others were angry at the Mercury Theater's joke. But it was undeniably effective. And to a great degree that's because the show harnessed the unique power of radio.

The origin of *The War of the Worlds* was not in radio, however, but in print. A novel of the same name had been published in 1898 by British writer H.G. Wells, who had first become famous three years earlier with *The Time Machine*, another classic work of science fiction. Wells, a critic of British imperialism and upper-class complacency, used Darwinian logic to imagine a world in which presumed English superiority was turned on its head by alien invaders of superior intelligence who showered destruction on Great Britain the way Britain did in colonial conflicts. In his version of *The War of the Worlds*, a series of cylindrical objects lands in southern England. Fearsome octopus-like creatures emerge from these cylinders, armed with heat rays that incinerate anything in their path and emitting poisonous gas in the form of black smoke. Soon London and its surrounding suburbs are conquered, though the invaders are ultimately destroyed because they lack immunity to ordinary earth microbes. The unnamed narrator of the novel, who works in an observatory, describes events in a matter-of-fact manner, and each of the chapters in the book is titled in the style of newspaper headlines. A hit at the time of its release, *War of the Worlds* remained in widespread circulation in the decades following its publication.

So it's not surprising that the story would become radio fodder. What *was* a little surprising was its production by the Mercury Theater. This highbrow troupe, founded in the 1930s by the prodigiously talented writer-director-actor Orson Welles, specialized in challenging fare that ranged from Shakespeare to avant-garde plays. In addition to mounting stage productions, the company also had a radio show that dramatized literary classics like Alexandre Dumas's *The Count of Monte Cristo* (1844) and Victor Hugo's *Les Misérables* (1862). *The Mercury Theater on the Air* was something of a prestige project for CBS, which supported the show on its own without advertising. But its ratings were not very good, and the effort to boost them with more popular fare led to a decision to adapt *The War of the Worlds*. Welles was already a radio star on the basis of his work on *The Shadow*, a popular crime series that had migrated from pulp magazines to the radio, and welcomed the opportunity to apply his talents to another popular genre.

As with many Mercury Theater projects, this one was produced on a tight deadline under terrific pressure. The script was written by Howard Koch, a talented playwright and screenwriter whose later credits included *Casablanca* (1942), for which he won an Academy Award. But Welles was also a stern taskmaster, distracted for long periods of time with other projects and then incredibly intense when he came on board for revisions. Many of the people who worked on the show feared it would be a bust.

Koch retained many details of the Wells novel, but made a couple of crucial adaptations. The first was to give the story an American setting (he chose the real-life town of Grover's Mill by closing his eyes and bringing a pencil down on a map of New Jersey; he wanted the aliens to land on the outskirts of Greater New York the way they did in Greater London in the novel). The other crucial change involved exploiting the dramatic possibilities in the medium of radio. This emphasis was one Welles had emphasized at the time *The Mercury Theater on the Air* was launched. "The Mercury has no intention of reproducing its stage repertoire in these broadcasts," he explained. "Instead, we plan to bring to radio the experimental techniques that have proven so successful in another medium and to treat radio itself with the intelligence and respect such a beautiful and powerful medium deserves."

The most obvious way of doing this – one that was already long a staple of radio – was sound effects. According to a later documentary about the broadcast, it was suggested that the terrifying moment of a Martian hatch opening was achieved by unscrewing the lid of a pickle jar in a toilet stall. (Ora Daigle Nichols, a rare female in the world of sound engineering, was said to have done this.) One could still hear such techniques put to work on more recent contemporary radio shows like *A Prairie Home Companion*, and occasionally on talk radio.

But the crucial innovation in the radio version of *The War of the Worlds* was taking an already established convention of the medium – the news broadcast – and turning it into an artistic effect. This was achieved by turning the first part of the story into a fake musical program featuring the fictional Ramon Raquello and his orchestra, broadcast live from a New York City hotel ballroom. This "show" was then repeatedly interrupted by "news" bulletins reporting strange, and increasingly ominous, astrological disturbances. They included a reporter's interview with a Princeton astronomer played by Welles, who debunks prevailing theories about Mars, among them an actual one of the time that its surface was covered with canals, presumably those created by living things. This 10-minute piece ends with a return to the New York studio, where we hear an unexplained piano performance, suggesting confusion on the part of the fictive radio producers. The music is then interrupted by a live report from Grover's Mill, where the reporter, still with the previously skeptical professor, has arrived from nearby Princeton. The reporter describes the scene as "something out of a modern Arabian Nights," along with the curious crowd that has gathered to witness it. Their curiosity turns to horror when gigantic machine-like monsters begin emerging from the cylinders, destroying everything in sight. But the most chilling sound amid all the chaos is sudden silence as the transmission gets cut off. An announcer explains that "due to circumstances beyond our control we are unable to continue the broadcast from Grover's Mill." The piano music returns, more unnerving than reassuring.

Eventually listeners hear more reporting from around the country. They learn that the charred body of the reporter has been identified at a local hospital. A cacophony of other voices describe efforts to mobilize militarily against the invaders, who are moving east toward Manhattan. The first machine-like monster is reaching the Hudson as other cylinders land in Buffalo, Chicago, and St. Louis. We hear cryptic signals and someone saying "Isn't there anyone on the air? Isn't there anyone ...?"

The crucial thing to understand amid all of this is that, since *The Mercury Theater on the Air* had no sponsors, the show was never interrupted by commercials that would break the tension. There was supposed to be a station break in the middle of the show, but it ran late, and so the program was more than two-thirds over before a real-life announcer informed listeners they were hearing a simulated apocalypse. The show had been advertised as such in advance, and was described as such at the outset, and an attentive listener would have heard that the events described were those of October 30, 1939, a year into the future. But someone tuning in at any point later along the way wouldn't have known that. Moreover, in a brilliant bending of medium conventions to artistic effect, Welles had edited the script by purposely elongating the musical interludes and chatter as a way of building tension and accentuating the jarring effect of the invasion when it finally did come.

Did Welles and his colleagues know the show would have such an impact? At some level, they could not have known, and indeed had fears it would be a bust. Reports of pandemonium poured in to CBS while the show was still on the air, but Mercury cofounder John Houseman blocked the executive who sought to enter the studio where Welles was speaking. A message that he should ease up on verisimilitude did reach him, and Welles complied. The last 15 minutes or so of the broadcast, narrated by the reflective professor surveying the ruins of civilization – a part of the broadcast that closely followed the novel – was less dramatic.

In the aftermath of the show, there was some talk of criminal charges, which, after an investigation, the Federal Communications Commission declined to file. There were no reports of fatalities, although one man did report that his wife got so excited that she opened a door and fell down a flight of stairs. "Jeez, it was a wonderful broadcast!" he said. But many people also responded with bravery. *The Times* reported that hundreds of nurses, physicians, and city officials volunteered their services, just as, 69 years later, they would do on September 11, 2001, when an all-too-real attack on New York City was reported.

Could something like *War of the Worlds* hysteria happen again? Actually, it did: similar events took place in Portugal in 1958 and Brazil in 1971. But we live in a much more dense media culture than people did then. Moreover, in this post-Photoshop visual civilization, people are less prone to believe what they're seeing, much less hearing. Actually, to a great extent it was the fact that the radio version of *War* was invisible, and thus had to be imagined, that made it all the more powerful. And the fact that it was a shared collective experience, something less likely in a time of podcasts, downloads, and other means of time-shifting.

But there's one other dimension worth considering here. When *War* was broadcast in 1938, a real war – one of unprecedented destructive power – was on the horizon and all too easy to foresee. And it would be under way in less than a year. People were emotionally prepared for the worst; perhaps that, more than anything else, gives such work its power, potential and realized. Consider yourself warned.

Questions to consider

1. What was it about the medium of radio specifically that made *War of the Worlds* so powerful?
2. Though the production is typically associated with Orson Welles, it was in fact a deeply collaborative undertaking. Identify some of the key players in the production and their role in the outcome.
3. *War of the Worlds* was not the first event of its kind (see, for example the hoax of "Moon Men" described in Chapter 1). Would a hoax of this kind be impossible today?

Document Study

Buck Rogers: *Finding time (in space)*

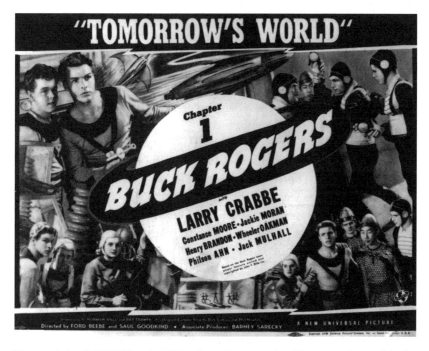

Figure 4.4   IN TIME   A 1939 advertisement for *Tomorrow's World*, the first installment of a Buck Rogers movie serial. The futuristic character, first introduced in 1928 by journalist Philip Francis Nowlan in the famous magazine *Amazing Stories*, was also the basis of a series of radio shows in the 1930s and 1940s. (Archive Photos/Getty Images)

Until recently, science fiction wasn't really a visual genre. To be sure, sci-fi movies are as old as the medium itself – the 1902 Georges Méliès film *A Trip to the Moon* is a landmark of cinema no less than a landmark of the genre. But one's ability to imagine the interplanetary settings and alien characters that typify sci-fi outstripped anything movies or television could offer in their finite budgets and technological limitations. Some of the legendary howlers in film history, among them *Robot Monster* (1953) and *Plan Nine from Outer Space* (1959), are marked by low-rent production values that make them impossible to take seriously. No such problems afflicted print. Radio faced perhaps a little more difficulty, but the evocative possibilities of sound could haunt, frighten, or excite in a unique way, particularly for children at an impressionable age. This may help explain the durable success of the *Buck Rogers* radio program.

Sci-fi was never a major presence on radio – certainly not to the extent of soap operas, for example. But the 1938 broadcast of *War of the Worlds*, based on the 1898 novel by H.G. Wells, was not an isolated case (see "Document Study / *The Mercury Theater on the Air*: *Worlds* war"). Many other famous SF stories became the source of radio broadcasts, among them a 1950 version of Wells's 1895 novel *The Time Machine*. There were also sci-fi shows in a serial format. One of the best-known featured Flash Gordon, a space-traveling hero. The character first appeared in a 1934 comic strip; it was followed by the debut of the (weekly) *Amazing Interplanetary Adventures of Flash Gordon* radio show in 1935, and the (daily) *Further Amazing Interplanetary Adventures of Flash Gordon* in 1936. The character would go on to have a long life in film and television.

On radio, at least, Buck Rogers bested Flash Gordon. Like Gordon, Rogers also has roots in print. But Rogers originated as a work of fiction, and this gave his character a bit more of a backstory. More specifically, Rogers was a child of the pulps. He first appeared in *Amazing Stories*, the monthly magazine published by sci-fi legend Hugo Gernsback. The August 1928 edition of *Amazing Stories* featured a novella entitled *Armegeddon 2419 AD*, by journalist Philip Francis Nowlan.

When the novella begins in 1927, Rogers (here known by the first name of Anthony) is a World War I veteran employed by the American Radioactive Gas Corporation, investigating unusual readings in an abandoned Pennsylvania coal mine. The shaft in which he is working collapses, whereupon he lands in a safe pocket but is knocked unconscious by the rapid accumulation of a mysterious gas.

When the shaft reopens, Rogers returns to consciousness and scampers to the surface, but he is surprised to learn that 492 years have passed. The United States has long since ceased to exist (though places like "Nu-yok" remain), and the world is under the domination of the Han Chinese, decadent rulers who largely regard Americans as beneath attention. Rogers wanders alone in woodland until he discovers what he believes is a young boy floating in the air with the help of a thick belt and a knapsack-like device. When this person is suddenly wounded by an unseen assailant, Rogers lends his assistance and discovers she's a woman named Wilma Deering. He fends off her attackers and befriends her. Wilma takes him to meet her tribe, and before long Rogers is leading the fight against local gangs allied with the Han, a struggle that will eventually culminate in the Second War of Independence.

Nowlan followed *Armegeddon 2419 AD* with *The Airlords of Han*, also published in *Amazing Stories*, in March of 1929. Around the same time, he teamed up with illustrator Richard Calkins to create a comic strip based on the character, whose name was changed from Anthony to Buck. The series was syndicated in hundreds of newspapers across the country and ran until 1967.

The character made his next media conquest in 1932, when *Buck Rogers* hit the airwaves four times weekly on 23 CBS radio stations nationally. The show ran for four years before going on hiatus; it resumed in 1939, 1940, and again in 1946–1947. Though the actors changed, as did the year to which Buck traveled, the storylines were broadly consonant with the comic strip.

In the debut of the 1939 series (episodes of which are widely available online), Buck is awakened from a hypnotic slumber by a scientist and inventor named Dr. Huer, whose assistant is Wilma. Much of their conversation in these shows involves pieces of technology like "electrohypnotic rays," "hypomentalophones," and "gyrocosmic relativators." Buck's adventures, typically 15 minutes in length, are framed by a narrator who explains the situation at the start of each episode and transports the listener with the help of special sound effects (an air-conditioning vent was used to simulate the sound of rockets). These shows were sponsored by Popsicle – the first installment has come to be known as the "Popsicle Episode" – and began with the winner of the "typical American boy" contest, dubbed "Popsicle Pete," excitedly telling listeners about the "gifts" they will receive if they collect bags from Popsicles, Creamsicles, and Fudgsicles. Such marketing efforts clearly indicated the youthful target audience for the show.

Of course *Buck Rogers* was more of a document of the 1930s than it was of the twenty-fifth century. Its breathless excitement about air travel and (cell-phone-like) personal-communication devices reflects a time when such innovations were on the horizon but had not been fully realized. Wilma was more a helpmeet than a partner – in the original novel she has a way of fainting or being conked on the head whenever serious fighting breaks out – and futuristic technologies jostle with much more mundane ones, like the sound of a creaky doorknob that signals when she enters a room. Perhaps the single most challenging aspect of creating credible sci-fi scenarios involves figuring out what new inventions define lives in other times and places while retaining the seemingly timeless dimensions of lived experience.

Even as Buck Rogers thrived on the radio, he continued expanding his presence into new media. A 12-episode film serial – short movies that were included along with longer feature films as part of an afternoon or evening's entertainment – made its debut in 1934. A TV series followed in 1950–1951, as did another in 1979. One measure of Buck's popularity and durability is the Warner Bros. cartoon *Duck Dodgers*, starring Daffy Duck, which first appeared in 1953, with sequels in 1980 and 1996. In 2003, the Cartoon Network ran a *Duck Dodgers* series. The character lives on across the Internet; there has also been talk in recent years of yet another movie.

By now, however, Buck Rogers is less an emblem of the future than a piece of cultural lore from the past. The costumes, especially the helmets, are comic in their cheap, impractical appearance. The radio shows, delivered with formal diction in marked contrast to our more casual and intimate approach to language, are artifacts of a lost world.

Meanwhile, beginning with *Star Wars* in 1977, there seems to be an accelerating capacity for filmmakers to render futuristic or interplanetary worlds in ways that had previously defied imagination. Now sci-fi really *is* a visual genre. And yet it has not entirely lost its hold on radio. It's now possible to download podcasts from a variety of sources, even to acquire a sci-fi radio app. We're still a long way from the twenty-fifth century. But Buck Rogers remains alive and well in the twenty-first.

Questions to consider

1. What can radio do that other media can't in telling a sci-fi story?
2. In what ways is *Buck Rogers* a document of the 1930s? How is a sci-fi show made today likely to reflect contemporary social arrangements? Consider gender arrangements in particular.
3. Is film now the dominant sci-fi medium? Are there imaginative aspects of a sci-fi experience that can't really be captured visually? Like what?

Further Reading

The pioneering historian of radio was Eric Barnouw, whose *A Tower in Babel: A History of Broadcasting in the United States to 1933* (New York: Oxford University Press, 1966) was part of a large body of work that encompassed television and radio. His generational successor, who has also produced a number of works on the subject, is Susan J. Douglas, whose *Listening In: Radio and the American Imagination* (1999; Minneapolis: University of Minnesota Press, 2004) is now the standard work. Other important works of radio history include Robert McChesney, *Telecommunications, Mass Media, and Democracy: The Struggle for Control of U.S. Broadcasting, 1928–35* (New York: Oxford University Press, 1993), and Susan Smulyan, *Selling Radio: The Commercialization of American Broadcasting, 1920–1934* (Washington, DC: Smithsonian Institution Press, 1994).

There are many good studies of science fiction. Good brief ones include Lance Chandler, *A History of Science Fiction: A Brief Introduction to the Genre, the Books, and the Culture that Defines It* (Kindle edition; Anaheim, CA: Minute Help Press, 2010), Thomas M. Disch, *The Stuff Our Dreams Are Made Of: How Science Fiction Conquered the World* (1998; New York: Touchstone, 2000), and Adam Roberts, *The History of Science Fiction* (New York: Palgrave, 2007).

The most comprehensive account of the background, production, and legacy of the *War of the Worlds* broadcast is John Gosling's *Waging War of the Worlds: A History of the 1938 Radio Broadcast and Resulting Panic* (Jefferson, NC: McFarland & Co., 2009). The book includes Howard Koch's original script. See also Joe Bevilacqua, *We Take You Now to Grover's Mill: The Making of the "War of the Worlds Broadcast"* (Newark, NJ: Audible Audio Books, 2011).

Philip Francis Nowlan's Buck Rogers novellas *Armegeddon 2419 AD* and *The Airlords of Han* are widely available for free online. So are 1939 episodes of the *Buck Rogers* radio show. Multiple film and television versions are available from retailers such as Amazon.com; a multivolume collection of Buck Rogers comic strips, now at seven volumes, is being reissued by Hermes Press (2008–).

5

Channels of Opportunity
The Arc of Television Broadcasting

Figure 5.1 JOKERS WILD Dean Martin and Jerry Lewis mugging for
TV cameras, circa 1950. One of the most successful comedy teams of all
time, they were also television pioneers. (The Kobal Collection)

A Short History of the Modern Media, First Edition. Jim Cullen.
© 2014 Jim Cullen. Published 2014 by John Wiley & Sons, Ltd.

Overview

ALL OF THE MEDIA discussed in this book have had a substantial
impact on American life. But none can rival that of television. The
oldest medium, theater, simulates real life with an immediacy that
simply cannot be reproduced. But that's also a problem: literally and
figuratively, you have to be there. The printing press, by contrast,
does something magical in a different way: by taking ideas and
coding them into words on a page, it allows people who have never
met each other – who may not have been alive simultaneously – to
communicate across time and space. But the prerequisite for such
communication is literacy, a skill that has been a minority acquisition
until relatively recently and one that's often not exercised by those
people who have it. Even when we add photography to the picture,
which conquers such language barriers, print is conveyed in physical
objects (books, magazines, newspapers) that must be transported
and acquired.

Radio broadcasting also conquers time and space, and it has the
additional power to transmit information in real time. Moreover, listening to radio does not require literacy – in some circumstances, like
musical performance, not even a shared language is necessary – to be
understood and appreciated. And unlike a print book or newspaper,
radio comes to you (once you have a receiver).

Film goes one step beyond print and radio in that it gives us
sound *and* vision simultaneously. As with print and radio, it records
experience for later access. But while radio is a spectral presence, a
film, like a book, is a material object, a reel of (celluloid) text that gets
"read" (or, as discussed in Chapter 3, neurologically *mis*read) with
the aid of a projector. At least until the digital age, showing a film
was a mechanical process, moving pictures made by moving parts.

Television subsumed all its predecessors: time *and* space, sound
and image, live *and* recorded. Only the stage could rival it as a simu-
lation of lived experience, but television dwarfed all competitors in
the sheer vastness of its reach. And, paradoxically, in its intimacy,
not only in terms of capturing the smallest of gestures, but in its

capacity to deliver them into the most intimate of settings. Even now, it's no mere figure of speech to say that everybody watches television; since the middle of the twentieth century, the medium has virtually defined modern civilization. Its very omnipresence obscures its astounding achievement.

Which is not to say that television has lacked for critics. All new media were widely hailed at the time of their debut, sometimes with claims (like world peace, which is what the famous director D.W. Griffith believed that movies would bring about) that seem ridiculous in retrospect. And all have engendered complaints of fostering immorality, to the point – in the case of theater, for instance – of being banned entirely in some parts of the country for long stretches of time. But no other medium has been subject to the sustained hostility television has. "If the television craze continues with the present level of programs," Boston University President Daniel L. Marsh told the graduating class of 1950, when the medium was in its infancy, "we are destined to have a nation of morons." (Some would say his prediction has come to pass.) A decade later, Federal Communications Director Newton Minow famously described television as "a vast wasteland." In 1978, long after it had been established as the preeminent type of modern media, former advertising executive Jerry Mander wrote a widely cited book called *Four Arguments for the Elimination of Television*. Even as late as 2000, when the Internet had already begun to challenge it for media supremacy, political scientist Robert Putnam described television as the single greatest cause of American civic corrosion in his highly regarded book *Bowling Alone*.

But if television has been criticized for a long time, it was anticipated, with great excitement, for a long time as well – decades, in fact – before most people ever saw it. First used at the turn of the twentieth century, the term "television" (the prefix "tele-," which is Greek in origin, means "distant") referred to the theoretical possibility of moving images to remote locations the way that radio made it possible to move sound. Technologically speaking, television is part of the same genetic line as the telegraph and radio, in that it represents the transmission of coded information. And just as the realization of wired communication with the telegraph launched a quest for wireless that was realized about half a century later in radio, so too did the achievement of radio inaugurate a comparably long quest to supplement sound (audio) with image (video).

But the immediate basis of TV – an abbreviation which first went into circulation in the 1940s – is in film. Like movies, television depends on an illusion whereby our brains perceive movement where none exists. Early attempts at television involved spinning discs studded with punctures through which light was projected. The alternating pattern of light and dark created images comprised of dots shown in rapid succession. At first, these images were little more than shadows. But they got steadily better.

Once it was possible to create images of reasonable clarity, the next step involved sending coded versions of individual images via telephone wire. Such early attempts were akin to facsimile (fax) messages that would later become commonplace. Eventually, technologies were developed to transmit multiple images rapidly in sequence, creating the illusion of motion. Television would adopt a system whereby signals originating in one place – like, say, a television studio – would be sent out to stations connected by a cable. From there, the signals would be projected into the air as a radio signal, whereupon they would be caught by nearby receivers (which is to say television sets) that would project them on a screen.

Much early research and development on television was supported by interlocking interests such as the Radio Corporation of America (RCA), General Electric, and Westinghouse, all of whom were enmeshed in the radio business. But the history of TV is also one of independent inventors making important gains without such corporate support. It was one such Scotsman, John Logie Baird, who first managed to transmit a television image, in the form of a ventriloquist's dummy, in 1925. Though its empire was in decline, Great Britain remained a player in emerging technologies, much in the way the US is in an age of Chinese ascendance.

Even as Baird was refining his invention, however, innovation was proceeding apace on multiple fronts. Of particular importance was the work of Westinghouse engineer Vladmir Zworykin, a Russian immigrant who developed an electronic means of transmitting images involving cathode ray tubes. But it was another independent operator, 21-year-old Philo T. Farnsworth, who in 1927 patented crucial components that complemented Zworykin's. After years of trying to buy him out or shove him aside, RCA was forced to license Farnsworth's work. The result was a system that used a gun-like device to spray electrons on fluorescent glass, creating tiny flashes of light on the screen, which afforded a much greater degree of picture resolution than Baird's work did.

Radio's evolution had been unpredictable: what began at the turn of the twentieth century as a tool to improve merchant shipping became a military asset and a passion for hobbyists before its primary use – broadcasting – finally emerged in the 1920s. There was less uncertainty about television; virtually all the players involved in developing it viewed transmitting sound and pictures as merely the first step in an enterprise that would culminate in lots of people experiencing them at the same time. Such broadcasting would be made possible by established radio networks – the Columbia Broadcasting System (CBS), the National Broadcasting Company (NBC), and, as a result of a government-imposed antimonopoly spin-off of NBC in the 1940s, a new network, the American Broadcasting Company (ABC) – which would dominate television. As with radio, network shows would be paid for via commercial advertising.

Though viewers took commercials for granted, however unhappily, from the start, this economic model was not inevitable (as with radio, Britain financed television programming via taxing TV sets and using the proceeds to pay for programming). It also had significant consequences for what would – and wouldn't – be seen on television. Though it's easy to think that the products broadcasters sell are their shows, this in fact is not the case. Instead, broadcasters sell *people* to *advertisers*. They promise a sponsor a certain number of viewers for a particular price, hoping that the ratings (which, however varied or accurate the methodology, have been a source of obsessive interest from the very beginning) will indicate they delivered on that promise. If not, the broadcaster must make up the difference by any number of complex arrangements. While such a system means that broadcasters have an interest in offering programs viewers will like, they finally answer to the people who actually pay their bills. Whether or not this is the best arrangement is arguable. But private sponsorship has always been the primary basis of American broadcasting, and continues to play a major role in the economics of new media as well.

Still, if broadcasters went into television with a clear game plan, the obstacles to realizing it were considerable. Besides the need for ongoing technological refinement of the medium, there was also the matter of manufacturing television sets at an affordable price. And setting up studios that could broadcast television content. And coming up with sufficiently interesting content to attract viewers. And convincing sponsors that they would. It had taken years for this to happen in the case of radio, and it was understood it wouldn't happen overnight in television, either.

In fact, it took far longer than even the most informed observers anticipated – about 20 years. Partly this was the result of government regulation; having witnessed the free-for-all that had accompanied the rise of radio broadcasting, with competing broadcasters fighting over the same airwaves, the Federal Radio Commission (which after 1933 became the Federal Communications Commission) proceeded more carefully. An added complication was the coming of World War II. Government regulators stopped licensing new television stations, and many of the engineers who had been working on television instead channeled their talents into other innovations, like radar technology.

Despite these obstacles, a critical mass of television sets and television stations was building by the end of World War II. Some stations were individually owned, creating their own programming or contracting with one or more networks for particular shows. But the most stable and successful ones became those that were either owned or affiliated with a single network that could be relied upon for content. Somewhat unexpectedly, the big three networks were joined by an independent upstart, Allen B. DuMont, a television manufacturer who jumped into broadcasting with the help of funding from Paramount Pictures. From 1946 until 1956, DuMont managed to compete with CBS, NBC, and ABC, despite difficulties in expanding stations, being assigned less attractive wavelengths, and lacking the stable of talent NBC and CBS in particular had at their disposal. An attempt to merge with a similarly weak ABC was scotched by Paramount, sealing DuMont's eventual doom.

Whatever their relative strength, the four networks had established television schedules by the end of World War II. But TV shows were only available for a few hours each night in a handful of cities, mostly on the east coast. Given the limited audience in a nation where radio remained dominant, most of the shows that aired were, in one way or another, cheap. News programming relied on the same newsreels shown in movie theaters, for example. Sporting events tended to be limited to events like boxing matches, which required fewer cameras than baseball or football. Game shows, like the successful *You Bet Your Life* hosted by comedian Groucho Marx, relied at least as much on patter with guests than on the structure or outcome of a contest. Many shows were merely 15 minutes long. Reception was often poor.

Still, critical mass was building. One key measure was the migration of established shows and stars from radio. *Meet the Press*, which began as a radio show in 1945, moved to television two years later, and has remained prominent ever since. Arthur Godfrey, known for his informal manner and skill in pitching ads and endorsing products, made the transition from radio to television with ease and became a fixture of the airwaves by hosting a series of variety shows. By the end of the 1940s it was finally clear that, after a long waiting period, television was poised for takeoff.

A key reason why was economic. With the end of World War II – which had come on the heels of the decade-long Great Depression – there was a tremendous pent-up demand for consumer goods in American society. Though there had been initial concern that the end of wartime production would weaken consumer capacity, the US economy began growing rapidly in the late 1940s, an expansion that continued steadily through the next decade. A strong demand for labor put money in consumer pockets, money that was quickly spent on cars, refrigerators, and, especially, televisions.

No single event can be truly considered the turning point, but a series of developments in the early 1950s typically marks the moment in the nation's collective memory when television truly arrived. In 1951, coast-to-coast broadcasting became a reality as stations in dozens of western cities were connected by coaxial cable. (Because the ability to record shows was primitive, most shows were live, creating complications with time zones.) Until this point, fewer than half of US homes had television sets. Within a few years, most did. In 1956, consumers were purchasing 20,000 sets daily. Three years later, 9 in 10 homes had them. One reason why was the growing appeal of particular TV shows, like the wildly popular *I Love Lucy* (1951–1957), which prompted consumers to take the plunge and buy a television set (see "Document Study / Seriously funny: *I Love Lucy*"). *Today*, a multi-hour program of news and conversation, made its debut on NBC in 1952, and has continued its run to this day, as has its companion piece at the other end of the day, *The Tonight Show*, which began in 1954. Both shows were the brainchild of NBC executive Pat Weaver, an early innovator in TV programming. By the mid-1950s, television was not simply a presence, but a bona fide phenomenon.

It was also increasingly a factor in breaking news – and increasingly tangled in politics itself. The early 1950s were a time of high anxiety over the Cold War between the United States and the Soviet Union, and a moment when many politicians addressed – some would say exploited – fears about Communist subversion within the country. As with the film industry, a number of television performers were accused, usually with flimsy evidence, of harboring Communist sympathies. But for the first of a number of times, television also became an instrument for combating false claims. In 1951, the famed radio broadcaster Edward R. Murrow took his radio show *Hear It Now* to television, where it became *See it Now*. Murrow's coverage of the controversial Wisconsin Senator Joseph R. McCarthy did much to expose the nation to his bullying political style, one that was fully unmasked during congressional hearings in 1954, after which public opinion turned decisively against him.

In the decades that followed, the major networks made substantial investments in building a journalism infrastructure. This was not because news was particularly profitable; indeed, most television news divisions lost money. But the federal government owned the airwaves and required television stations to demonstrate they were providing a public service as the price for their often highly profitable licenses. News programs were nevertheless considered important for a number of commercial reasons as well, whether in terms of branding a network – Howard Cronkite of CBS was nicknamed "the most trusted man in America," a key factor in its identity as the "Tiffany" network – or, in the case of local news, in terms of serving as a lead-in for prime-time or late-night programming, since many viewers were not inclined to change channels (at least before the advent of remote controls, the first of which were available in the 1950s but did not become widespread until the late 1970s). Network attitudes toward broadcast journalism began to change in the 1980s, when news divisions were expected to become financially self-sustaining. While this eroded the quality of some news operations and led to increasing reliance on cheaper news stories (like celebrity gossip instead of foreign news reporting), journalism continued to play a prominent role in the medium, particularly in "magazine" shows that consisted of a set of in-depth stories, such as the remarkably durable *60 Minutes*, still going strong since its debut in 1968. News programming was an important part of major television events like presidential elections and the historic first moon landing of 1969.

Culturally speaking, television programming had deep roots in radio, and reflected that heritage long after overtaking it. But TV also tapped other media to sustain its growing momentum. For example, the growth of the medium resulted in a rebirth for the stage genre of vaudeville, resurrected as the television variety show. Many vaudeville stars had continued their careers on radio, but television added a whole new dimension to the experience of comedy, music, and skits that constituted the core of the genre. *Texaco Star Theater* (1948–1956), which had run for many years on radio, became a national sensation with comedian Milton Berle as its host. Ed Sullivan became the premiere master of ceremonies in television with his self-titled variety show, which ran from 1948 to 1971 and introduced the nation to pop icons like Elvis Presley and the Beatles. Sid Caesar led a brilliant array of talent that included Carl Reiner, Mel Brooks, and the very young Woody Allen in *Your Show of Shows* (1950–1954). Despite their avowed iconoclastic style, later staples of television like *Saturday Night Live* (1975–) drew directly from the skit format that runs back through radio into vaudeville.

Traditional drama also experienced a renaissance on television. The early broadcast industry was centered in New York, not Los Angeles, and the cost and technical limitations of the medium put a premium on shows that were relatively easy to stage. One popular format of the time was the so-called anthology, like *Studio One* (1948–1958) and *U.S. Steel Hour* (1953–1963), which featured serious fare that would long be remembered with affection. The classic courtroom drama *Twelve Angry Men* originated on *Studio One* in 1954.

One other stage genre that got a new lease on life was daytime dramas pitched to women, known as soap operas (so named for their sponsors). Soaps, too, had been staples of radio, but came to be considered quintessential television experiences. Though they became less popular as a larger proportion of the female population entered the paid workforce, soaps have shown phenomenal durability; *The Guiding Light* began on radio in 1937 and lasted on television until 2009; *General Hospital* has been on the air since 1963. Soaps have also been a major influence on evening prime-time programming, where budgets, publicity, and audiences were considerably larger. Major hit shows like *Dallas* (1978–1991) and *Melrose Place* (1992–1999) have cultural roots in soaps.

Television also proved to be a hospitable platform for pop-culture genres that had been – and continued to be – vibrant in other media. By the 1950s, for example, westerns were well established on the television airwaves, whether in terms of old classics like *The Lone Ranger* (1949–1957) or the light-hearted TV original *Maverick* (1957–1962). Some of the great all-time works of science fiction, from *Star Trek*

(1966–1969) to the *X-Files* (1993–2002) got their start on television, and branched out into other media from there. Horror has been less prominent, though it was an important component of beloved series such as *The Twilight Zone* (1959–1964), and has been particularly evident in recent years, as suggested by the success of well-regarded shows like *The Walking Dead* (2010–).

Perhaps no genre has proven to be more beloved, and so well suited to television, as the situation comedy, or "sitcom." From the debut of the 15-minute *Mary Kay and Johnny* on the DuMont network in 1947 to that of the far more typical 30-minute (actually, more like 22 minutes after credits and commercials) *How I Met Your Mother* on CBS in 2005, no format has been more instinctively associated with television than sitcoms, in large measure because they're relatively easy to make and allow viewers to bond with particular characters over a long period of time. Sitcoms could also embed themselves deep into the nation's collective unconscious long after new episodes had been produced through the practice of syndication, whereby local stations broadcast old shows, which were cheaper to run than new programming and allowed them to fill their schedules profitably. While other formats often seemed dated in syndication, sitcoms often functioned as a cherished form of nostalgia, which explains why so many can still be seen in reruns today. (See "Genre Study / Screened realities: Situation comedy.")

Another kind of show distinctive to television is the miniseries. These are reminiscent of big Hollywood movie epics, in that they're highly promoted, big-budget extravaganzas, but unique in their ability to command simultaneous audience attention. The first, *Roots* (1977), was a multigenerational saga of slavery and freedom telling the story of Kunta Kinte, an African sold into slavery, and his heirs. It was based on the semi-fictional bestselling book by Alex Haley, and was an enormous television event. Later miniseries like *The Thorn Birds* (1983), a melodrama about an illicit romance between a young woman and a Roman Catholic priest, also drew huge ratings, demonstrating television's unique power to instantly generate vast audiences in the tens of millions.

Miniseries like these were more than milestones in the television industry; they were also indicators of changing social mores. Television's emergence as a mass medium in the 1950s coincided with a moment of relative social conservatism, which was reflected in the tone and content of TV programming. Controversial subjects were studiously avoided. In part, this was an economic imperative as well as a cultural one – advertisers were skittish about sponsoring shows that would offend viewers. With the coming of the 1960s, however, shifting cultural currents, first felt with more reliable youth barometers like pop music, began to assert themselves on television.

Nowhere were these changes more evident than in the portrayal of African Americans. Insofar as black people were seen at all in early television, it was in subservient roles. Even in the rare case of a show featuring a black person – *Beulah*, which ran on radio before going to TV in 1950–1952 with a number of women playing the lead – the character in question was a housekeeper. *Julia* (1968–1971), starring Diahann Carroll as an African American nurse, was widely regarded as more nuanced in its treatment of black life, while comedian Flip Wilson won national prominence for a variety show bearing his name (1970–1974). One reason why *Roots* was such a big deal in the 1970s is that for many it marked the arrival of black Americans into the mainstream of national life. While the portrayal of racial minorities, black or otherwise, would remain a subject for intense discussion for decades to come, few would disagree that times had changed on the airwaves by the 1970s, even if television was no mirror of reality. This was evident in a series of successful sitcoms – *Sanford and Son* (1972–1977), *Good Times* (1974–1979), and *The Jeffersons* (1975–1985) – all of which strived to portray saltier, urban, and working-class accents as part of a more diverse intraracial black culture.

A similar trend could be discerned in the portrayal of women. The transformation of one actor alone – Mary Tyler Moore from her role as a housewife in *The Dick Van Dyke Show* (1961–1966) to a single professional on the *Mary Tyler Moore Show* (1970–1977) – illustrates the change. Gay Americans, by contrast, would have to wait, though they too would have their hour in the sun, whether indicated by the success of stars like Ellen DeGeneres in her show *Ellen* (1994–1998), the gay character-led sitcom successor *Will & Grace* (1998–2006), or yet another miniseries, *Angels in America* (2003).

Yet even as the pacesetting cultural power of network-television broadcasting crested in the 1960s and 1970s, a series of technological and economic forces were reshaping it. At first, such changes only seemed to enhance the medium's power. Color TV, like motion-picture sound, had been technically possible from almost the very beginning. But color posed logistical obstacles, like the need to refit studios as well as adapting or replacing TV sets, which slowed its introduction. When it finally became economically feasible in the mid-1960s, color prompted a new wave of activity in the industry, much in the way compact discs did in the music business or home video did in the movie business in the 1980s.

Actually, video recording also played a major role in television. At first, all TV was live. Within a few years, television stations were able to make crude recordings called kinescopes, which allowed them to stagger national programming by showing a 7 p.m. show three hours later on the west coast, for example. Modern video-taping was possible in the mid-1950s, but was too specialized and expensive a process to be practical for home use. In the early 1980s, the videocassette recorder became the latest must-have electronic gadget, which allowed viewers to watch feature films from the convenience of home, just as TV always did. Such devices also allowed viewers to buy or rent episodes of old TV shows, as well as to view them at a time of their choosing. While both movie and television executives feared that such practices, which allowed viewers to skip over commercials, could hurt their business model, they also created new markets and audiences for their wares.

Other changes in the second half of the twentieth century posed a more direct challenge to the CBS–NBC–ABC axis. One marginal but persistent competitor was public television. One of the pieces of legislation passed as part of President Lyndon Johnson's Great Society in the mid-1960s, the Public Broadcasting System (PBS) offered viewers an alternative to the networks, as well as sparing them intrusive commercials. Some PBS programming, like *Sesame Street*, which began airing in 1969, proved to be educational, popular, and enduring. The network also had a political impact; starved of funds in the early 1970s, it began airing the Watergate hearings in 1973 as an economy measure. The hearings revealed government corruption that proved to be far more fascinating than any crime drama, and prompted other media to pay more attention to the scandal. Public television also became a bastion of documentary programming; the multipart 1990 film *The Civil War*, directed by filmmaker Ken Burns, became a national sensation at the time of its release and remains one of the most admired works in the history of broadcasting.

A more serious threat to the networks was cable television, or TV content delivered by coaxial wire directly into the home rather than relying on the airwaves. Actually, cable had been around since the 1940s; it had first been developed as an alternative for people living in remote rural areas who lacked good reception. The cost was nominal, paid simply to improve the quality of a household picture (as well as for local community programming). The idea that a cable station or network could develop commercial content first took root in the 1960s for athletic events like boxing matches. It got taken one step further when Home Box Office (HBO), founded in 1972, began showing classic and recent movies, unedited and without inter-ruptions, for a monthly subscription fee. It was followed in rapid succession by a companion network, Cinemax, as well as by a host of competitors. Cable also became a source of alternative program-ming that ranged from the Christian Broadcasting Network (CBN), founded by evangelical minister Pat Robertson in 1977, to the Cable News Network (CNN), started by entrepreneur Ted Turner in 1980. As it spread – half of all US households had cable by 1987 – it also specialized in new ways to attract specific audience segments, as evi-denced by Music Television (MTV), whose short-form music videos became wildly popular within a few years of going on the air in 1981.

In the short run, cable television did little to erode the power of CBS, NBC, and ABC, which underwent alternating periods of strength and weakness relative to each other. But, little by little, cable chipped away at their collective control of the airwaves. Nor was cable the only challenger. For the first time since the demise of DuMont in the 1950s, a new network, Fox, was founded by media magnate Rupert Murdoch in 1986. Thanks to smash hits like *The Simpsons* (1989–), Fox became a coequal to the big three by the 1990s, specializing in shows with racial themes like *In Living Color* (1990–1994) that appealed to poorer, non-white audiences without access to cable. Meanwhile, lesser broadcast rivals like Warner Bros. ("the WB") and United Paramount Network (UPN) went on the air in the mid-1990s. Though neither lasted, they signaled a rapidly shifting broadcasting landscape. Other networks would follow in their wake.

The big three networks had achieved their preeminence not only because they had long been the only game in town to deliver programming, but also because they produced it. However, the need for content, whatever its source, made networks willing to broadcast shows of independent creators (of which Desi Arnaz and Lucille Ball's production company, Desilu, the source of *I Love Lucy* and many subsequent hit shows, was the prototype; see "Document Study / Seriously funny: *I Love Lucy*"). This openness was also in part a response to the federal government, which regulated the amount of content the networks could own. In the more lax regulatory environment of the 1980s, those rules were eased; in 1993 they expired altogether. One major reason for this is that there were now so many new outlets for television content that the danger of network monopoly had faded.

Indeed, by the turn of the century cable networks, engorged with cash and able to charge consumers higher prices for premium services, began developing their own shows. Freed from the conventions and censorship regulations of traditional broadcasting, they were able to develop well-funded and innovative programs that effectively inaugurated what could fairly be called a television renaissance. The HBO series *Sex and the City* (1998–2004) was considered pathbreaking in its treatment of female sexuality and independence, while an HBO gangster drama, *The Sopranos* (1999–2007), was widely hailed as among the best-written and acted TV shows of all time. By the second decade of the twenty-first century, even second-tier networks like American Movie Classics (AMC) were broadcasting watercooler fare like *Mad Men* (2007–), which had a national impact on fashion and other dimensions of pop culture.

The twenty-first century has also been notable for the emergence of the reality show as a major genre. These are shows in which ordinary citizens are placed and monitored in unusual situations where unscripted storylines unfold. The reality show is not a new form of programming; forerunners include the widely cited PBS series *An American Family* (1973) and the less high-minded MTV series *The Real World* (1992–). Their name notwithstanding, reality shows are in fact marked by all manner of artifice, beginning from the mere presence of a camera in a room and ending with the editing that takes place before a viewer ever sees the show. Nevertheless, the success of *Survivor* (2000–) and its many variants suggest the ongoing cultural vitality of the genre – and, perhaps, the thinning of a formal barrier between what is considered public and what is seen as private experience.

Television may have been more vibrant by 2010, but it was also more splintered. For all the excitement a single episode or season finale that a show like *Mad Men* generated, it was only seen by a fraction of the number of people who had watched a hit show of the 1950s or 1960s, let alone even a recent monster hit like *Friends* (1994–2004), itself a more modest affair when compared with, say, the *Ed Sullivan Show* in its prime. A successful television program from the 1950s or 1960s could last for generations in reruns – *Star Trek* was considered a flop until it went into syndication – and newer ones did as well. But the more likely way a viewer sees such shows now is on home video, whether recorded, bought, or, eventually, downloaded. In other words, the very basis of television as an industry – broadcasting – has eroded in favor of a much more fragmented, individualistic experience of the medium.

This gradual, yet fundamental, shift was accelerated by the arrival of a new medium that finally supplanted television as the defining one of modern life: the Internet. Like television, the Internet was a long time in coming – it originated with the US Defense Department in the 1960s – and for a long time hardly seemed like a competitor for television. The immediate threat it posed seemed to be for print media like newspapers. But by the turn of the century, the Web was encroaching on prerogatives of professional broadcasting in two ways. First, the dispersion of high-quality, low-cost videocameras and computers – increasingly on the same device – empowered individuals to make and distribute their own content on social networking sites like Facebook, which by the early twenty-first century was soaking up as much teenage time as television ever did. Second, Web sites like YouTube became venues where individuals could upload and stream any manner of TV content, whether or not doing so was sanctioned by networks or program creators. Corporate executives fretted about violations of intellectual property rights, but increasingly got on the bandwagon with sites like Hulu, where shows could be accessed at any time – and commercials effectively became the price of admission. In recent years there has also been a trend toward paying nominal fees to stream TV shows, which may become more common, akin to the way young people buy digital music instead of records or compact discs. The future economic model of the industry is unclear.

In part, that's because the technological model is also unclear. The medium of television took a long-awaited leap forward at the turn of the century with the introduction of high-definition television (HDTV), which dramatically improved picture quality. As with color a generation earlier, HDTV required upgrades by producers, broadcasters, and consumers, which stimulated a new wave of TV-set acquisition. Yet even as this was happening, the future of the medium as it had always been known was in question. For some years now, industry observers have predicted a convergence between the television set and the personal computer, envisioning a time when companies like Google and Apple will become TV brands the way NBC or Fox are. But PCs and TVs alike seem increasingly obsolete in a world of smartphones and tablets. It also remains to be seen whether the Internet will foster its own distinctive kind of programming.

If the history of the mass media tells us anything, though, it's that the Internet will serve as a repository for older ones, much in the way television has. Changing social mores and technological invention have quenched our appetites neither for storytelling nor for some of the familiar forms and genres that have served as vehicles for stories. For those of us old enough to remember when television was king, it still seems odd to think that moment has passed. But TV – as fact, metaphor, memory, and inspiration – will continue to shape our imaginations.

Questions to consider

1. What are some of the ways television has been influenced by other media?
2. Why did it take far longer than originally anticipated for television to become a mass medium? What does the answer suggest about the relationship between technology, economics, and culture?
3. Television became a venue for genres like sci-fi and the western. How did it change them in the process? How and why, for example, is a TV western likely to be different from a film western?
4. For a long time, television was dominated by three major networks. What factors created this dominance? What are some of the reasons it broke down?
5. What is the role of television in modern life? How has it changed in the twenty-first century? What do you imagine will happen by the time you're middle-aged? Why do you think so?

Genre Study

Screened realities: Situation comedy

Figure 5.2 COLORFUL CHARACTERS Peter Griffin and company as the cast of the Fox animated sitcom *Family Guy* (1999–). At the turn of the twenty-first century, animated shows captured everyday life with a candor missing from many live-action sitcoms. (Fox TV/Seth Macfarlane/The Kobal Collection)

One of the defining characteristics of genres as defined in this book is that they jump across media as they emerge: you can find a gangster tale in print, film, or television. This is true even in popular music, which has the most self-contained genres; rock and roll has flourished on TV and online in the form of the music video (and, in recent years in particular, in the form of the Broadway musical).

But even granting this mutability, it's still the case that some forms of cultural expression seem to come so naturally to a particular medium that they come to seem indissolubly linked in the popular imagination. The point is particularly apt in the case of the genre known as the situation comedy – or, as it is commonly abbreviated, the sitcom.

There are a number of reasons why the sitcom works on television which have little to do with audience demand. Indeed, the durability of some kinds of programming (like game shows and talk shows) can be explained by the fact that they're so much cheaper to produce than, say, dramas – even if their ratings are lower, they're still profitable for the networks that broadcast them, which is why they've always been around. Sitcoms tend to be more expensive than a game show, and a successful sitcom can get quite expensive as its stars begin to demand more money to keep acting on long-running productions. But they don't require large casts, exotic settings, or complicated set-ups. Focused on a specific locale like a family home or (especially later) a workplace, sitcoms rely on recurring characters with easily recognizable traits. This sense of intimacy and familiarity is probably why, more than any other kind of TV show, sitcoms tend to last – a good one can survive in reruns for generations.

As its name suggests, the sitcom is about situations – a jury-duty summons arrives, a relative is coming to visit, a wedding ring has been misplaced, and so on. The fun comes from how these particular, recurring characters react to the intruding situation. Initially, all the loose ends got tied up by the end of the episode, which made the show modular: you could start watching at any time and pick up what was going on. Later, running plotlines became more common, particularly as a means of sustaining interest in the show; the tradition of the season finale as a means of keeping audiences engaged from year to year became a staple feature of sitcoms. But the core concept of a set of characters in a specific setting remained central.

The immediate roots of the sitcom are in radio, but not in radio alone. Its lineage also runs back through the stage, in particular to vaudeville. In its approach to entertainment, the essence of vaudeville was variety, within which skit comedy was central. It's no accident that some of the most successful sitcoms in history, among them *The Honeymooners* (1955–1956) and *The Simpsons* (1989–), began as routines that were part of larger variety or anthology shows. (Actually, *The Honeymooners*, which featured Jackie Gleason as a bellowing bus driver, only ran as a sitcom for a single season; much of the large volume of material that subsequently aired derived from specials and skits that were part of later shows.) Vaudeville, in turn, has clear roots in minstrelsy, which may be one reason why some of the most highly rated and controversial sitcoms dealt with racial issues. This is certainly true of what can plausibly be considered the most successful sitcom of all time, *Amos 'n' Andy*, whose roots in minstrelsy were obvious (it also began as a sketch). For most of its long life on the airwaves from the 1920s until the 1950s, the show, which featured white characters in blackface performing racist stereotypes, was a radio phenomenon. It made the transition to television from 1951 to 1953 with black actors and persisted in reruns until the mid-1960s before protests and changing social mores made it too embarrassing and offensive to continue. (For more on *Amos 'n' Andy*, see Chapter 4.)

In the second quarter of the twentieth century, sitcoms were firmly ensconced in radio. They remained there even after television networks began broadcasting in the 1940s, since television budgets were small and the future direction of TV was uncertain. Gradually, with steadily increasing numbers, the biggest radio stars began moving their acts to television. By the end of the decade, the transformation was complete.

One interesting aspect of some popular bi-media sitcoms is their metatextual character – they were often programs about entertainers and their shows. The husband-and-wife team of George Burns and Gracie Allen had appeared on a variety of radio programs before they moved to television for *The George Burns and Gracie Allen Show* (1950–1958), which was about the backstage life of two people who happened to be celebrities. *The Jack Benny Show* (1950–1965), which dealt with the trials and tribulations of the lead character in making a TV program, is regarded by television historians as one of the wittiest shows ever on the air. (Both sitcoms also used the dramatic technique of calling attention to their artifice by breaking the fourth wall, i.e., addressing the audience directly.) Desi Arnaz and Lucille Ball, who had a brief radio career before crossing over to television with *I Love Lucy* (1951–1957), also presented a show about a family in the entertainment business (see "Document Study / Seriously funny: *I Love Lucy*"). The tradition would continue through *The Dick Van Dyke Show* (1961–1966) to *The Larry Sanders Show* (1992–1998) and *30 Rock* (2006–). Though it was famously a show about "nothing," the highly successful *Seinfeld* (1990–1998) featured the title character as a professional comedian.

It must be said, however, that most early sitcoms focused on the traditional family. Here too there were many precedents in radio that crossed over to television. *Mama* (1949–1957), based on a book and film, focused on a Norwegian immigrant family at the turn of the century; *The Goldbergs* (also 1949–1957), featuring the multitalented writer-actor-producer Gertrude Berg, depicted urban Jewish life. These shows were notable for the degree to which they portrayed working-class families, which have tended to be stinted on television, notwithstanding important exceptions like *Roseanne* (1988–1997), a show starring comedian Roseanne Barr about a Midwestern clan struggling to make ends meet. (It's worth noting that *The Goldbergs* and *Roseanne* also featured strong, working-class female leads played by women who were powerful forces offscreen as well.)

Toward the end of the 1950s, many sitcoms effectively relocated to the crabgrass frontier of suburbia. Sometimes, as in the case of *I Love Lucy*, doing so became part of the plot. The change of locale did not change the strongly patriarchal portrayal of family life, however. *Father Knows Best* (1954–1960), *Leave It to Beaver* (1957–1963), *The Adventures of Ozzie and Harriet* (1952–1966): individually and collectively, such shows fostered a stereotypical image of the 1950s as relatively simple and serene, a way of life buttressed by traditional gender roles. In one 1954 episode of *Ozzie and Harriet*, for example, an effort to give Dad a night out on the town is simply disastrous: Harriet can't balance her checkbook, little Ricky can't do his homework, and Ozzie is absolutely miserable over being exiled from home despite his wife's good intentions. Whatever truth there may have been to such portrayals of middle-class life – surely they would not have been savored to the degree they were if they bore *no* relationship to reality – they sidestepped social problems, notably the burgeoning Civil Rights movement, in ways that seem striking in retrospect. But however true or false they were, these sitcoms created an image of the time that has proven durable to champion and critic alike in the decades since.

Sitcoms were not entirely insulated from social change, however, and by the mid-1960s there were signs the genre was registering shifts in American social values. One early indication of this was *That Girl* (1966–1971), which featured Marlo Thomas (daughter of actor and writer Danny Thomas, himself the star of the 1953–1955 sitcom *Make Room for Daddy*, about a frequently absent show-biz father). *That Girl* focused on a young single woman striking out on her own professionally in Manhattan in the swinging sixties. Though she had a fiancé, their relationship was never the defining factor in the plot (it ended with the couple still engaged). Another 1960s sitcom, *Julia* (1968–1971), also featured a single woman (Diahann Carroll) who happened to be African American. While neither show was truly countercultural, both were hailed, and remembered, as pioneering in their time. Marlo Thomas went on to be a prominent liberal feminist known for her work on *Free to Be . . . You and Me*, a 1970s book/record/TV show that challenged gender stereotypes.

The 1970s are considered by many to be the golden age of the sitcom. Three shows in particular stand out in breaking new artistic and ideological ground. *The Mary Tyler Moore Show* (1970–1977) can truly be said to be a feminist show. Mary Tyler Moore was already well-known to television audiences for her role as a suburban housewife on *The Dick Van Dyke Show*, so when she reappeared as a single woman in Minneapolis pursuing a career in TV news, she registered social change at face value. (The plan had originally been for Moore's character to be a divorcee, but network executives feared audiences would assume her divorce was from Van Dyke's character, Rob Petrie.) Not so incidentally, Moore was also cofounder, with husband Grant Tinker, of MTM Enterprises, a production company that would enjoy a string of successes in the 1970s and 1980s, among them sitcoms such as *The Bob Newhart Show* (1972–1978) and *WKRP in Cincinnati* (1978–1982), as well as the critically acclaimed police drama *Hill Street Blues* (1981–1987) and *St. Elsewhere* (1982–1988), a medical drama set in a Boston hospital. *The Mary Tyler Moore Show* also solidified a precedent for intelligent women in the public settings in later shows like *Cheers* (1981–1993), about the crowd at a Boston bar (Shelly Long played a brainy barmaid), and *Murphy Brown* (1988–1998), featuring Candice Bergin as a news anchor, though both showed women subjected to more ridicule than Moore's character had been.

A second important sitcom of the era that really did have a countercultural spirit was *M*A*S*H* (1972–1983), a seriocomic saga based on a 1970 movie about paramedics during the Korean War that effectively functioned as an allegory for the Vietnam War. By the time the show was on the air, the latter had become deeply unpopular with the American public, and the show's mordant wit helped establish a persistent skepticism that affected perceptions of the war long after it ended. Both widely appealing and critically esteemed, the series finale in 1983 was among the most widely watched television shows of all time.

A third important sitcom – among the most adventurous ever made in what is essentially a conservative medium – was *All in the Family* (1971–1983), starring Carroll O'Connor as bigoted dockworker Archie Bunker, and Jean Stapleton as his dim-witted but lovable wife Edith. *All in the Family* grappled with big issues – racism, abortion, marital tension, and generational conflict – in ways that had never really been broached before in the genre. Created by the liberal-Jewish Norman Lear and his partner Bud Yorkin, the show was based on a British sitcom called '*Til Death Do Us Part* (1965–1975). *All in the Family* was broadcast by CBS, a first-place network which was nevertheless looking to retool a schedule filled with old – and old-fashioned – sitcoms like *The Beverly Hillbillies* (1962–1971), a hugely popular fish-out-of-water show about rural folk who strike it rich and head to Hollywood. Characters in *All in the Family* also became the source of a series of Yorkin–Lear spin-offs, among them *Maude* (1972–1978), featuring Archie's salty-tongued cousin (played by Bea Arthur), and *The Jeffersons* (1975–1985), about an upwardly mobile African American family who had been neighbors of the Bunkers.

While relatively edgy shows like these remained popular in the late 1970s and early 1980s, there were also indications that sitcoms were pulling back from social commentary, anticipating the neoconservative mood of the 1980s. Among the most widely watched shows of the time were *Happy Days* (1974–1984) and its even more successful spin-off *Laverne & Shirley* (1976–1983), both of which were set in the 1950s and avowedly nostalgic. Though the sexually suggestive *Three's Company* (1976–1984), about a heterosexual man pretending to be gay and two female roommates, suggested some taboos were being stretched to breaking point, the show was decried as retrograde in its gender politics. Perhaps a better indicator of the changing national mood was *Family Ties* (1982–1989), starring Michael J. Fox as the right-wing son of hippie parents. Originally slated as a minor character, his role grew in response to audience demand, perhaps reflecting the changing times. The conservative temper of the time extended to racial politics in *The Cosby Show* (1984–1992), an extremely popular sitcom about an affluent black family. Supporters argued the show broke stereotypes; critics charged it evaded racial realities.

One of the more striking aspects of sitcoms since the 1990s has been the emergence of a series of animated shows that paradoxically are more realistic than many live-action ones. The sterling example of this subgenre – and the longest-running sitcom of all time – is *The Simpsons*. Having begun as a series of short sketches on *The Tracy Ullman Show* (1987–1990), the series was the brainchild of cartoonist Matt Groening, who managed to pack all kinds of raucous subversion into a show that became the bulwark of the Fox network (a bit ironic given the network's well-known right-wing political orientation, notwithstanding the more varied tenor of its entertainment programming, which has always targeted young audiences). In the eternally dull-witted Homer Simpson, we see the far end of the spectrum of the wise sitcom dads of the 1950s. (About the only modern dad who escaped serious ridicule in recent decades is Bill Cosby, who of course would have been disqualified for patriarchal status on the basis of race in the 1950s.) Other animated sitcoms that mocked traditional authority at the turn of the century include *South Park* (1997–) and *Family Guy* (1999–).

There were some indications at the turn of the twenty-first century that the sitcom had ebbed in its centrality in television broadcasting. This had happened before; in the early 1980s and late 1990s there was also talk that the genre had played out, before shows like *Newhart* (1982–1990) and *Friends* (1994–2004) sparked revivals. In the twenty-first century there has also been talk that the sitcom's contours were shifting, as evidenced by hybrid "dramedies" like *Glee* (2009–). Trends like these can really only be traced in retrospect. However, it seems unlikely that the core elements of the sitcom will undergo fundamental change: they're too adaptable in their simplicity. Indeed, it seems likely that the genre will migrate online as shows disperse virally rather than through traditional broadcast means. However and whenever they appear, sitcoms will still be worth watching.

Questions to consider

1. Name the roots of situation comedy in media older than television. What storytelling problems did the sitcom solve as a genre?
2. What are some of the factors that made situation comedy a genre uniquely well-suited to television?
3. How has the sitcom responded to social changes? Does it tend to lead or follow the culture? Give an example or two of a show that typified its time.
4. Consider some of your favorite sitcoms, whether they're current or old ones you watch as reruns. What do they tend to have in common? What are the qualities you think makes for a good sitcom?

Document Study

Seriously funny: I Love Lucy

Figure 5.3   BALL'S GAME   Publicity still of Lucille Ball and Desi Arnaz from the time of their hit television show *I Love Lucy* (1951–1957). Their artistic and financial collaboration went beyond performing in front of the cameras to decisively shape modern television. (© Moviestore Collection Ltd/Alamy)

The history of popular culture is replete with collaborators whose work together exceeds the sum of its parts. The British duo of W.S. Gilbert and Arthur Sullivan teamed up to create some of the most beloved theatrical works of the nineteenth century. John Lennon and Paul McCartney wrote some of the catchiest pop music of the twentieth. Larry Page and Sergey Brinn generated an algorithm that has powered the most widely used search engine of the twenty-first. Though each of these people was undeniably talented on his own, the synergy they created proved uniquely compelling. The same can be said of the most successful duo in television history: the interracial married couple consisting of Lucille Ball (1911–1989) and Desi Arnaz (1917–1986), creators of the legendary sitcom *I Love Lucy* and the production company – Desilu – that bears their names.

Ball and Arnaz had both enjoyed moderately successful careers in the entertainment business during the 1930s and 1940s. The Cuban-born Arnaz, who came from a privileged family dispossessed by a coup in 1933, arrived in the US as a teenager, establishing himself as an actor and bandleader at a young age. Ball, who was about five years older, came from upstate New York and began her career as a model. In the 1930s she was signed to the RKO studio and nicknamed "Queen of the Bs" for her frequent roles in movies regarded as secondary in Hollywood. Ball and Arnaz fell in love while working together on the 1940 film *Too Many Girls* and married later the same year. They spent much of the 1940s in a long-distance relationship, separated while Arnaz served in the US army during World War II and by their respective careers. By all accounts, the marriage was tempestuous – Ball filed for divorce in 1944 before changing her mind, and Arnaz had a lifelong reputation as a womanizer and drinker – but the bond between the two was passionate and symbiotic. In conscious emulation of married movie stars Douglas Fairbanks and Mary Pickford, who named their lavish home "Pickfair," Arnaz and Ball dubbed theirs "Desilu." Desilu also became the name of the production company they founded, one shaped by the highly enterprising Arnaz.

In 1949, with Ball's status as a starlet foundering on the rocks of middle age, she took a role in a CBS radio program, *My Favorite Husband*, a sitcom about a Midwestern banker played by actor Richard Denning and Ball as his intelligent, but slightly daffy, wife. The show was a surprise hit, prompting CBS to move the show to television. Ball, who still saw herself primarily as a movie star, expressed interest in making the transition to TV, but lobbied for

Arnaz to be cast as her husband, a professional move she believed would have good marital consequences. The network was skeptical audiences would accept a program featuring a Latino married to a white woman. To allay those concerns, Arnaz and Ball organized a vaudeville show starring themselves and took it on a national tour. The show was a smash, and CBS agreed to proceed with the sitcom.

I Love Lucy was hardly the first show to feature a married couple in the leading roles. George Burns and Gracie Allen had experienced sitcom success on both radio and television with their show, as had Ozzie and Harriet Nelson. All four were real-life entertainers who drew on their everyday lives as sources of episodes for their shows. The difference here is that, while Arnaz's character Ricky Ricardo was a bandleader just as he was in reality, his sitcom wife Lucy was not a star but wanted to be – an aspiration her fictive husband decidedly did not endorse in what might be termed the golden age of the housewife. This premise was the foundation of the show's comic tension.

Despite its resemblance to such sitcom forebears, *I Love Lucy* was distinctive in a number of respects. The most obvious was apparent at face value: in a time of widespread racism and ethnic bias, simply having a Latino husband and a red-haired gringa wife was something of a statement, particularly since the show did not treat it as all that strange (some jokes about Ricky's accent and tendency to lapse into Spanish when angry notwithstanding). But perhaps the most important innovations of the show were those behind the cameras. Ball and Arnaz were committed to producing the show in Southern California, where they lived. At that point, however, the locus of the TV business was in New York, not Hollywood. Most of the national viewing audience was on the east coast and saw shows live; those in other time zones sometimes saw kinescopes, a primitive form of video recording. The only way that most viewers could get a good picture would be to shoot the show on film. This was not unprecedented. Nor was Arnaz's decision to use three cameras rather than the customary one, which allowed him to work faster and capture the spontaneity of the actors. What *was* unprecedented was the decision to shoot the show with a live studio audience:

Ball's acting fed on its electricity. What was also unprecedented was the deal Arnaz struck with CBS, which involved a cut in pay to cover the higher production costs – and gave Desilu ownership of the programs. He realized, as few others did, that reruns of the shows would have considerable commercial potential. Arnaz also farsightedly acquired studio facilities in which *I Love Lucy*, among other shows, could be shot. These steps would make him and his wife immensely rich.

But *I Love Lucy* would not have become a television legend without a strong set of collaborators. Principal among them were screenwriters Madelyn Pugh Davis and Bob Carroll, as well as writer-producer Jess Oppenheim. These people generated 181 scripts in which Lucy would scheme and plot her way into a life of showbiz excitement, only to be stymied by any number of unforeseen complications. The cast was rounded out by Vivian Vance and William Frawley, who played Fred and Ethel Mertz, the Ricardos' landlords and friends. Very often their mishaps would have a gendered quality, with the men good-naturedly pitted against the women.

But the core of the show was Ball. She was a comedian of some repute from her various film and stage roles prior to *I Love Lucy*, but the show revealed a range and depth of talent far beyond anything she had previously demonstrated. Ball's face was a marvelously plastic instrument; few other actors in the history of television were able to achieve such expressive effect (one exception was Carroll O'Connor, the bigoted protagonist of *All in the Family*). She also excelled in broad physical comedy; one of the longest laughs in TV history occurred when she danced with her husband in an outfit stuffed with eggs she was trying to hide from him. Though much of the humor of the show seemed spontaneous, the action was usually carefully rehearsed, its execution a reflection of Ball's steely discipline. One of the most memorable examples involved an episode where Lucy connives her way into doing a commercial for "Vitameatavegimin," a so-called patent medicine of the kind that was common in the nineteenth century as a cure for any number of ills but usually consisted of little more than disguised alcohol. Over the course of the shoot Lucy descends into a drunken stupor whose hilarity derives from its brilliant calibration.

I Love Lucy premiered in the fall of 1951 and rapidly became the most popular show on television. A complication occurred in the second (1952–1953) season when Ball became pregnant with her second child. Networks and sponsors considered dealing with such subjects beyond the bounds of propriety – the bedrooms of married couples were shown with two beds well into the 1960s – but Arnaz and Oppenheimer managed to convince CBS and sponsor Philip Morris that it could be handled discreetly (the word "pregnant" was never uttered). Such concerns proved misplaced when the episode on the actual birth of the baby – rich with slapstick, topped by Ricky Ricardo racing to the hospital from the nightclub wearing voodoo makeup and terrifying the hospital staff before fainting himself when presented with his son – proved to be one of the most watched shows in the history of broadcasting, exceeding the inauguration of President Dwight Eisenhower the next day.

Complications of a different kind surfaced in 1953, when, amid the McCarthyite witch hunts of the Cold War, Ball's name surfaced as a possible Communist sympathizer. Arnaz passionately defended his wife on live television. He described her as "my favorite redhead," adding, "that's the only red thing about her, and even *that*'s not legitimate." Philip Morris, the tobacco company that sponsored *I Love Lucy*, stood by her – by this point the show was seen by 50 million people a week, many times more than a hit sitcom today – and the show went on.

Over the course of the next few years, writers would expand the horizons of *I Love Lucy* by having the Ricardos and Mertzes make trips; later, the couples would reflect the social changes in American society by moving from their New York City apartments to houses in Westport, Connecticut. Very often, especially in the later years, celebrity guest stars would appear on the show as themselves. In one episode, for example, Lucy gets into trouble for stealing, and then accidentally destroying, John Wayne's footprints on the Hollywood Walk of Fame. Ricky convinces Wayne to come to their hotel to make a new set, but a series of mishaps forces him to do it again and again (part of the joke is that Wayne knows all about the wacky Lucy Ricardo because of her previous encounters with movie star William Holden). In another episode, Lucy boasts she can get actor George Reeves – star of the hit series *Superman* – for her son's birthday party. When told he can't make it, she dons a costume, intending to play Superman. When the superhero unexpectedly shows up, she hides on the ledge of her apartment building, whereupon her cape gets stuck. (Superman saves the day.)

I Love Lucy ran through the 1957–1958 season. The six-year run was a grueling experience for many of the principals. The pressures of the show were particularly intense for Arnaz, who was also working as a studio executive aggressively adding hit shows to the Desilu stable. The stress contributed to his drinking problem and aggravated marital tensions with Ball. This resulted in attempts to experiment with less demanding formats, ranging from feature films to hour-long episodes that would run occasionally over the course of a television season. Though these often got good ratings, their critical reception was less enthusiastic.

The professional Ball–Arnaz partnership began to fall apart following their divorce in 1960. Desilu sold the *I Love Lucy* series back to CBS, which allowed the couple to finance future acquisitions. Two years later, Arnaz sold his share of the company to Ball, who then became one of the most powerful figures in Hollywood. For much of the 1960s, Desilu enjoyed a string of hits that included sitcoms like *The Andy Griffith Show* (1960–1968), as well as dramas, including *The Untouchables* (1959–1963) and *Star Trek* (1966–1969). In 1967 the company was sold to the Gulf + Western corporation, eventually becoming part of Paramount entertainment holdings.

Despite the collapse of their marriage, Arnaz and Ball remained on friendly terms, and he worked as producer on Ball's subsequent sitcom, *The Lucy Show* (1962–1968). But neither separately nor together could they recapture their magic. Ball went on to perform in a number of movies and plays, and continued to play variations on her Lucy character into the 1980s. Arnaz's alcoholism damaged his standing in the industry, though he continued to work in it until his death in 1986. Ball died three years later.

I Love Lucy remains a television perennial. In the 1960s CBS began showing reruns in its daytime schedule, which imprinted the show on a whole new generation of viewers. Revivals and specials continue to surface regularly, and episodes are widely available online. *Lucy* merchandising has become a big business, and the show has appeared on US stamps. Since the early 1990s, "Lucyfest" has been an annual event in Ball's hometown of Jamestown, New York. The Lucy-Desi Center that grew out of it opened there in 1996; it was augmented by the opening of the Desilu Playhouse museum in 2005.

"We didn't think Desilu Productions would grow so big," Ball said in 1955. "We merely wanted to be together and have two children." As with many cooperative ventures, this one didn't turn out as planned. But amid the disappointments of their individual lives, it's what Ball and Arnaz achieved together on *I Love Lucy* that has lasted long after divorce and death did them part.

Questions to consider

1. What are the elements of a successful collaboration? What kinds of things have to happen for people to work successfully together?
2. What are some of the reasons *I Love Lucy* was such a successful show? Consider aspects of Lucille Ball's artistry, as well as those with whom she worked.
3. Which aspects of *I Love Lucy* persisted in subsequent sitcoms? Which ones were more specific products of the 1950s?

Further Reading

As mentioned in Chapter 4, the pioneering historian of radio was Eric Barnouw. Barnouw is also considered the founding father of television scholarship. His multivolume works on broadcasting have been usefully distilled for the purposes of TV history in *Tube of Plenty: The Evolution of American Television* (2nd rev. ed., New York: Oxford University Press, 1990). His generational successor is Horace Newcomb; see in particular the anthology Newcomb has edited, *Television: The Critical View*, currently in its seventh edition (Oxford: Oxford University Press, 2007). Robert Thompson and David Marc have produced a brief overview in *Television in the Antenna Age: A Concise History* (Malden, MA: Wiley-Blackwell, 2004).

On early television in domestic life, see Cecilia Tichi, *Creating an American Television Culture* (New York: Oxford University Press, 1991), and Lyn Spiegel, *Make Room for TV: Television and the Family Ideal in Postwar America* (Chicago, IL: University of Chicago Press, 1992). Two later takes on TV culture include *Watching Television*, edited by Todd Gitlin (New York: Pantheon, 1986), and Mark Crispin Miller, *Boxed In: The Culture of TV* (Evanston, IL: Northwestern University Press, 1988). See also David Bianculli, *Teleliteracy: Taking Television Seriously* (Syracuse, NY: Syracuse University Press, 2000). For important critiques of television, see Jerry Mander, *Four Arguments for the Elimination of Television* (New York: Morrow, 1978), Neil Postman, *Amusing Ourselves to Death: Public Discourse in the Age of Show Business* (1984; New York: Penguin, 2005), and Robert Putnam, *Bowling Alone: The Collapse and Revival of Community* (New York: Simon & Schuster, 2000).

More recent information about TV can be gleaned online, especially in databases, notably the International Movie Database (IMDb.com). But one very comprehensive and detailed print source is Harry Castleman and Walter J. Podrazik, *Watching TV: Six Decades of American Television* (2nd ed., Syracuse, NY: Syracuse University Press, 2010).

The preeminent scholar of the sitcom is David Marc. See *Demographic Vistas: Television in American Culture* (rev. ed., Philadelphia: University of Pennsylvania Press, 1996) and, especially, *Comic Visions: Television Comedy and American Culture* (2nd ed., Malden,

MA: Wiley-Blackwell, 1997). See also Janet Staiger, *Blockbuster TV: Must-See Sitcoms in the Network Era* (New York: New York University Press, 2000).

The story of *I Love Lucy* has been widely chronicled. A good place to start is Coyne S. Sanders and Tom Gilbert, *Desilu: The Story of Lucille Ball and Desi Arnaz* (2nd ed., New York: It Books, 2011).

6

Sound Investments
The Evolution of Sound Recording

Figure 6.1 RECORD TIME Advertisement for Edison Phonographs, 1901. Originally developed by Thomas Edison as a business application for dictating memos, sound recording eventually became a major mass-entertainment medium. (© North Wind Picture Archives/Alamy)

A Short History of the Modern Media, First Edition. Jim Cullen.
© 2014 Jim Cullen. Published 2014 by John Wiley & Sons, Ltd.

Overview

MUSIC IS AMONG the most complex, moving, and finally mysterious of human experiences. It is also among the oldest: whether using voices or instruments, the intentional creation of alternating patterns of sound and silence is a practice that goes back many thousands of years. Music has long been part of religious ceremonies, civic events, social gatherings, and personal recreation. The nineteenth-century German philosopher Arthur Schopenhauer considered it the greatest of the arts, because it was the only one that didn't take material form: as an expression of pure will, music allowed a sublime interval of self-forgetting, an experience of transcendence like no other.

As such, there was only one way to hear it: live. Any portability and reproducibility music had was in published form, like orchestral scores, which remained inert until read and played by musicians. By Schopenhauer's time, sheet music had become a commercial enterprise, and a fixture of emerging middle-class households, where a piano functioned as a status symbol. Music making was a relatively rare event unless one was a trained performer with access to an instrument. For most of human history, the idea that music not made by oneself could be instantly available was a mere dream.

Radio, which made it possible to transport music over long distances at great speeds, represented one realization of this dream. Live musical performance was central to early radio programming, and major networks maintained large orchestras for this purpose. But here again, a listener could only hope to hear music on a schedule and with a playlist determined by others.

By this point, however, another alternative had emerged, one of historic proportions and dramatic effects: sound recording. Though it was not common in early radio – the quality of such recordings was relatively poor, and legal wrangling often prevented it – by the early twentieth century individually owned records of specific musical performances became an important dimension of popular culture, one that allowed audiences an unprecedented degree of control over what they could hear and when.

The earliest format for sound recording was the eighteenth-century music box: a pocket-sized device that contained perforated metal cylinders or discs. When, powered by a spring mechanism similar to that of a clock, a metal comb passed over those cylinders or discs, a melody was heard. Music boxes got larger and more complex over time; eventually they evolved into player pianos, actual musical instruments that performed songs coded on rolls of paper or metal. In fact, such rolls were the first records. But they were hardly convenient, portable objects. Producing such a technology became a pursuit that got under way in earnest in the late nineteenth century.

But the quest for recording was not necessarily a *musical* one. One key player in this enterprise was Thomas Edison, an inventor whose interests ran in many different directions (see his role in motion pictures in Chapter 3). Edison's goal was to produce a device that would serve a business function: a dictation machine that would allow an executive to record a message a secretary could transcribe later. Building on telephone technology first developed by Alexander Graham Bell, Edison received a patent for his "phonograph" in 1878. Bell, in turn, refined the phonograph in the 1880s. But the breakthrough innovation in sound recording came from a German inventor, Emile Berliner, who replaced the awkward cylinders used by Edison and Bell with flat discs with a spiral groove running around both sides. These grooves contained coded information that could be played back on Berliner's machine, which he called the gramophone. Such devices, whatever their origin, were increasingly described with the generic term of "talking machines." Not much came of the talking machine as a business tool, but by the 1890s it had become a commercial novelty for music in so-called phonograph parlors where one could listen to music much in the way early viewers of movies could peer into kinetoscopes at arcades.

In the early twentieth century an American corporation, the Victrola Talking Machine Company, began manufacturing devices in elegant wood cabinets called Victrolas. By the 1920s, Victrolas became fixtures of middle-class homes, a prized piece of furniture in the living room. A hand-operated crank powered a diamond stylus that pressed on rotating discs, making it possible to listen (and dance) for a few minutes until it became necessary to crank the Victrola again. By the 1920s electrically powered machines removed the need for a crank, allowing for a more seamless experience.

The arrival of the Victrola and competing machines in the first two decades of the twentieth century laid the foundations for an entirely new industry: the record business. Up until this point, sheet music had been the principal means by which music was disseminated. The popularity of any given piece was to a great degree a function of how widely it was heard in hit musicals and other forms of stage entertainment. The paradigmatic example was Charles K. Harris's "After the Ball" (1891), a melancholy waltz that ranks among the biggest pop hits of all time. One important means of marketing such songs was a person known as a song plugger: a musician who performed in stores or on streets to publicize a particular work. Most of the material song pluggers promoted was in the Tin Pan Alley tradition of popular song (see "Genre Study / Notes from the stage: The Broadway musical," in Chapter 2). Composers like Irving Berlin crafted short, catchy, upbeat songs with clever lyrics that were easy to remember. At this point, it was usually the song rather than the performer that was featured. Indeed, Tin Pan Alley is essentially a shorthand term for a shared body of work, sometimes called the "Great American Songbook." The pleasure of listeners to a great degree resided in hearing the way different musicians interpreted a given piece of music; only much later would the notion of a particular song having a definitive version become more widespread.

One reason why Tin Pan Alley was so central to the record business is that the genre played well to the limitations of sound recording, which at this point were considerable. Such songs were short, as was the playing time of a record (a few minutes per side). Playing a symphony, for example, would require one to flip and change a series of discs to hear it from beginning to end. The sound quality of records was also relatively poor, so much so that they were not often played on the radio.

Reluctance to broadcast recordings was not only a matter of technology, however. Record companies, which typically held the copyright on their recordings, were afraid to allow airplay for fear that people would not buy records if they could hear songs for free over the airwaves. In a time when we take hearing music over the radio for granted – indeed, when radio airplay is widely considered a prerequisite for a hit song – it may seem odd that radio and records were rivals and remained so for half a century. Not until the arrival of television did radio programmers, desperate for cheap programming to replace the live shows that migrated to TV, turn to records, at which point the symbiosis between the two industries finally became apparent. In similar fashion, musicians' unions believed for a long time that the record industry would destroy a listener's desire to hear live music. We now know that records actually stimulate people to go to shows. This insight has also been deployed for corrupt purposes, as when programming directors of radio stations secretly accepted payment from record companies to play particular songs, a practice that would come to be known as "payola," a problem that got much attention in the early days of rock and roll, but which was practiced before then and which has remained a chronic issue, in a hazy gray zone of legality, ever since, and is one more illustration of the way popular taste is never simply a matter of audience will or cultural democracy.

While the early record business essentially proceeded on a parallel track to that of radio, both media proved vitally important to the evolution of twentieth-century popular music (a term used here to connote any particular song, in any genre, that was widely heard across multiple media). In effect, radio and records turned music – particularly the music of working-class people, who lacked access to concert halls, conservatories, and the infrastructure of classical music generally – into a mass medium. Before this point, the various varieties of folk music in the United States (black, white, Latino, and so on) were not mediated at all: there were no stages separating performers and audiences. Music was typically a communal experience encountered at church, at work, at parties. The new medium of radio made it possible to conquer distance, and in so doing connected communities that had been largely unknown to each other, catalyzing the emergence of new genres from jazz to hip-hop. And the new medium of recording, like books half a millennium earlier, made it possible for individuals to communicate with each other in a way that conquered not only distance, but time.

So it was that the early records effectively functioned as instant historical documents, capturing musical traditions as they had been known for many generations. This was not necessarily mainstream music, in the sense of being as widely bought or frequently heard as the latest Tin Pan Alley hits (though in many cases such traditions shaped those hits). But over time this folk music – often recorded by small record companies, and distributed to subcultures like African Americans in cities like Chicago – became the seedbed of a fundamentally interracial national culture with international impact.

The foundation of this national musical culture was the black idiom of the blues. A distillation of African and other traditions, the blues emerged as a discrete genre in the post-Civil War decades. More secular and individualistic than black sacred genres like gospel (a more modern and accessible variation on pre-Civil War negro spirituals), the blues rested on a sturdy structure that permitted an endless series of permutations. The genre is built on a folk-musical major scale with flattened third, fifth, and seventh notes to create what is known as a blues scale. Another, perhaps more useful, way of describing the blues is in terms of its reliance on three chords, corresponding to the first, fourth, and fifth notes on a traditional European eight-note scale. The typical blues song consists of three chords and lyrics written in an AAB stanza pattern. It often featured a solitary singer playing a guitar, a distinctly plebian instrument until modern times (and one that would remain marginal in most band settings until amplification techniques made it possible to foreground a sound that was often lost in an arrangement). As its name suggests, the blues is widely considered music of personal despair, and indeed its subject matter is often grim. But it's also a genre marked by humor, psychological depth, and a paradoxically cathartic quality in which expressing pain becomes an at least partial balm for it.

The wandering black southern troubadour became the archetypal image of the bluesman, one that lingered straight through the twentieth century thanks to gifted artists like Robert Johnson, John Lee

Hooker, and B.B. King, who represent succeeding generations of bluesmen who kept the tradition alive through modern times. But to a great degree it was women – Bessie Smith, Ma Rainey, and others – who put the blues on the cultural map, and who emerged as early giants of the record industry. By the 1920s, such blues songs, which were marked by increasingly elaborate arrangements and a more urban sound, reflected the intensifying migration of black southerners into northern cities in the decades following World War I.

It was a time of cultural quickening. Even as older genres like blues and gospel remained popular with black and white audiences alike, both were feeding into the formation of new musical genres. One good example was ragtime, a syncopated style of piano playing that proved wildly popular in the first decade of the twentieth century, thanks to gifted practitioners like composer Scott Joplin. But ragtime was a transitional idiom, separate from the blues and yet instrumental, when blended with it, in creating one of the truly gigantic cultural phenomena of the twentieth century: jazz.

Jazz is a varied and subtle art, one that has spawned a series of subgenres. But for a century it has been sustained by a core tension. On the one hand, it is generally a collaboration between singers and musicians working off a chord progression rooted in the blues. On the other, jazz involves a series of improvisations within that chord progression, in which the various musicians assert a distinctive, yet varying, personality that may never sound the same way twice. This interplay between collective enterprise and individual expression captures the paradox of American identity: out of many, one.

Although there will always be arguments about such things, there is general agreement that jazz emerged in New Orleans, circa 1900. The city had long been a veritable gumbo of cultural diversity, one in which a relatively large proportion of a substantial black middle class had musical training, a tendency aided by the fact that New Orleans was a naval port, and navy bands, which are an important part of military culture generally, tend to create surpluses of instruments. The first jazz combos grew out of marching bands, with a strong emphasis on brass instruments (one novel element was the emergence of the saxophone, which was not widely played until jazz came along). They rapidly became a fixture of club culture not only in New Orleans, but also in Chicago, Kansas City, and New York.

Though jazz was an overwhelmingly black musical culture, the racist underpinnings of national life made it perhaps inevitable that it was a white New Orleans ensemble, the Dixieland Jass Band, that recorded the first jazz songs, "Livery Stable Blues" and "Dixieland Jass One-Step," in New York in 1917. It did not take long, however, for a series of black artists to come to the fore. By the 1920s, cornetist Joseph ("King") Oliver, saxophonist Sidney Bechet, and pianist Ferdinand La Menthe (aka Jelly Roll Morton) established the basic grammar of the genre. Actually, all these men were Creole, which is to say of mixed race, though by the racist logic of the time anyone with the proverbial drop of black blood was considered African American (unless they were light-skinned enough to secretly "pass," if such a person chose to do so). The presence of occasional white innovators like trumpeter Bix Beiderbecke also contributed to the interracial tenor of jazz in terms of performers, just as jazz had always done in terms of audiences.

Perhaps the greatest figure of early jazz history, if not its entire history, was Louis Armstrong. Born in a poor black New Orleans ghetto at the turn of the century, he learned a variety of instruments before settling on the cornet and trumpet. Armstrong started out as a protégé of King Oliver, moving to Chicago in the early 1920s to be part of Oliver's band. Armstrong also began making records at the same time, developing an international reputation that allowed him to form his own ensemble and tour the world tirelessly for half a century. He also emerged as a distinctive singer of note, with a gravelly voice that was nevertheless supremely musical. Though Armstrong sometimes perplexed later jazz artists and critics with his tendency toward popular music and willingness to play (in more ways than one) to white audiences, his reputation as a great American artist is secure.

Another great American artist to emerge from the world of early jazz – at least as much for his songwriting as for his performing – was Edward Kennedy Ellington, affectionately known by his nickname of "Duke" for his taste in couture. The son of a butler who worked at the White House, Ellington rose to fame as the conductor of the house band at the Cotton Club in New York City's Harlem neighborhood, the capital of black America. He also produced an enormous body of work, much of it with fellow composer and arranger Billy Strayhorn. Ellington's career, like Armstrong's, spanned half a century, and at the time of his death in 1974 he was celebrated as one of the greatest composers of the twentieth century in any genre.

By the end of the 1920s, jazz had become the dominant genre in American popular music, its influence as apparent in the work of Tin Pan Alley songwriters like Irving Berlin as it was in the fiction of F. Scott Fitzgerald, who as a young man coined the term "the jazz age" to define the decade. The 1920s and 1930s were the heyday of the famed Cotton Club, where a fabled roster of black performers ranging from Cab Calloway to Lena Horne performed for a white clientele in what remained a segregated social order. Such club venues became an important source of programming content for radio stations, which made these artists famous and helped drive record sales.

As jazz continued to dominate pop music in the 1930s and 1940s, it became a crucial influence even on performers at its periphery, like pop icon Frank Sinatra, and spawned the new subgenre of swing. Loud, flashy, and highly rhythmic, swing was characterized by larger ensembles to permit a fuller sound and more intricacy in arrangements while still leaving room for improvisational solos. Bandleaders like Fletcher Henderson (who pioneered the subgenre) and Tommy Dorsey (in whose band Sinatra rose to fame) generated tremendous excitement that extended into the war years.

Jazz was also an important art form for women. A series of singers, notably Billie Holiday and Ella Fitzgerald, built large and durable followings in the middle decades of the century. Holiday was an innovator in vocal phrasing; Fitzgerald was celebrated for her stunning range and diction. Though subject to double discrimination as African Americans and women – a toll that proved tragically fatal for Holiday, who succumbed to depression-induced addictions – they were nevertheless able to write themselves into musical history.

By the mid-twentieth century, jazz was changing again, one more indication of its vitality and flexibility. By this point, however, the emerging generation of artists – Charlie Parker, Dizzy Gillespie, and other leaders of a subgenre known as bop – were trying to push the boundaries of the form away from the structures and formulas of pop music into an avowedly more experimental direction. Bop attracted passionate devotees who remain as committed as ever in the twenty-first century. But by design, it also moved jazz away from its place at the crossroads of pop music, notwithstanding the efforts of some bop giants, among them Miles Davis and John Coltrane, to tap pop music as a source for their art.

There were, in any case, a number of genres jostling their way toward the center in the first half of the twentieth century. Tin Pan Alley and Broadway show tunes never went away, and singers like Bing Crosby, who rose to fame for his intimate style with a microphone, enjoyed commercial success in a career that largely paralleled the jazz era. Blues, ethnic styles like the polka, and Anglo folk music, typified by the white troubadour Woody Guthrie, were also part of the mix. To some extent, American music still had a strongly regional character, one shaped by the limited range of most radio stations and the record-buying patterns of listeners in cities. Of particular importance were Latin sounds, like samba, a rhythmic style with African accents, and bossa nova, a Brazilian style fusing samba and jazz that emerged in the 1950s.

One genre that has proved to be lasting and truly national is country music – or, as it was called until about the 1960s, "hillbilly music." Its roots are in the South. Contrary to popular perception, much early "country" music was actually urban, recorded in the growing cities of the piedmont South. Like all American music, its essence is anything but pure. But, while jazz is largely a black idiom with white elements, country is a white idiom – more specifically an Anglo-Celtic idiom – with black elements. Among the most important influence is the blues subgenre of the country blues, as practiced by performers such as Sonny Terry and Brownie McGhee. Though country always had a blues component, its twangy guitars, yodeling voices, and a generally more acoustic than electric sound made it distinctive in the wider context of American popular music.

If anyone could claim to have been present at the creation of country music, it would be Jimmie Rodgers. Born in Mississippi in 1897, Rodgers spent much of his youth working on railroads – his nickname was "the singing brakeman" – before striking out on a musical career. He started by touring with minstrel shows before making his first records. Drawing on black musical traditions as well as his distinctive yodeling, he rose to fame with hits like "Waiting on a Train" (1928). Rodgers became a household name in the South in the 1920s and 1930s, touring widely throughout the region. He journeyed to New York to make his last records in 1933, just before his premature death from tuberculosis.

Another pivotal figure in the classic country tradition is Hank Williams. Williams was born in 1923 and grew up in a rural Alabama family. After working as a welder in Mobile shipyards, he began to experience success as a singer; by the late 1940s he had built a national reputation on the strength of songs like "Move It On Over" (1947) and "Cold, Cold Heart" (1951). Williams lived a hard-driving life that involved drugs and alcohol; he died at 29. His posthumous hit, "Your Cheatin' Heart" (1953), is considered among the all-time greatest country songs. Williams's son, Hank Williams Jr., also became a country star, and was known for many years for his music-video intros for *Monday Night Football* broadcasts.

While Rodgers and Williams embodied an itinerant archetype of the solitary wanderer that would become emblematic of country, another strain of the genre emphasized continuity, tradition, and filial ties. The most prominent purveyor of this vision was the Carter Family, a trio consisting of Virginian A.P. Carter, his wife Sara, and her sister Maybelle. (Maybelle married A.P.'s brother Ezra.) The Carter Family recorded hundreds of records in the 1920s and 1930s, and their music was broadcast on radio stations all over the country. Despite the fact that A.P. and Sara divorced in 1933 (the ensemble went through a series of family permutations over multiple generations), the Carters represented a vision of wholesome family values that would be a hallmark of country straight through the Judds in the 1990s and the husband-and-wife dual careers of Tim McGraw and Faith Hill at the turn of the twenty-first century.

The crossroads of country music, both geographically and symbolically, is Nashville, Tennessee: what Hollywood is to movies, Nashville is to country. And the epicenter of Nashville has long been the Grand Ole Opry, a live venue that has represented the apogee of achievement in the business. Radio broadcasts of Grand Ole Opry concerts date back to the 1920s; a live show has been broadcast nationally since 1939. In 1943 the show and broadcasts moved to the city's Ryman Auditorium, where they have been based ever since. No one can truly be said to have made it in country without making an appearance at the Opry.

Like many genres of popular music, country music diversified as it spread. Themes and styles from Louisiana, Texas, Oklahoma, and California entered the mix – hence the "western" in country and western. Honky-tonk, a more fast-tempo subgenre of country that featured percussion, became popular in bars and clubs, also called honky-tonks, where it could rise above the noise of a crowd. Artists such as Bob Wills and His Texas Playboys (known for a sound called western swing), Ernest Tubb, and Kitty Wells became stars in these edgier styles. Further east, bluegrass music, which injected more of a folk sound, became popular, particularly in the music of Bill Monroe.

Because not all honky-tonk bars could afford live musicians, such venues turned to jukeboxes, vending machines for playing music, which emerged in the 1920s. By the start of World War II, there were hundreds of thousands of jukeboxes around the country, each of which held dozens of records. The music business, which had been hurt by the Great Depression, showed signs of strength.

A series of blows, however, set it back in the 1940s. The outbreak of World War II led to a government ban on shellac, the substance used at the time for making records. The 1940 expiration of a contract between the American Society of Composers, Authors and

Publishers (ASCAP) and the National Association of Broadcasters (NAB) led the broadcasters to ban the music of ASCAP members from the airwaves until an agreement was worked out in 1941. Broadcast Music Incorporated (BMI), a company founded to compete with ASCAP, benefited from this feud. While ASCAP had a Tin Pan Alley orientation, BMI was more focused on country. No sooner had the wrangle between publishers and broadcasters been worked out than the American Federation of Musicians union went on strike against the record companies in 1942. This strike meant no records were made by AFM members until the dispute was resolved in 1944, creating an opening for other kinds of pop music (which in turn laid the foundations for rock and roll).

The technology of recorded music was also changing toward the end of the war years. Nazi technological advances in fields like rocketry were eagerly embraced by Germany's rivals, as was Adolf Hitler's tool for simulating "live" broadcasts from multiple locations using a recording format involving magnetic tape, which would go on to have a long life as both a recording method and a playback format. In the late 1940s Columbia Records introduced the "long-playing" or "LP" record made of vinyl. These 12-inch discs were less fragile than shellac, and rotated 33 times per minute instead of the 78 rpm of 10-inch shellac discs. The LP could also hold about 20 minutes per side, compared with about 3 for a 78, which created new artistic possibilities.

Among the first to realize these possibilities was Frank Sinatra, who conceived a suite of thematically related songs whose whole was greater than the sum of its parts, akin to a photographic album of pictures. In a string of records that included *In the Wee Small Hours* (1955), a collection of songs for late at night; *Come Fly with Me* (1957), an album about travel; and *Frank Sinatra Sings for Only the Lonely* (1958), a suite of saloon songs, he pioneered the concept album, an innovation that would be built upon for generations.

The other major technological innovation of the era, which occurred more or less simultaneously with the advent of the LP, was the introduction of the seven-inch 45 rpm record by RCA. These

45s could only hold a single song, but they were ideal for jukeboxes and for radio airplay. The other crucial element in the 45 was the introduction of a record player that could play a stack of 45s in sequence. For much of the second half of the century, the record business was driven by albums (which were more expensive and whose songs tended to get FM airplay) and singles (which were a staple of AM radio). These formats were augmented in the 1970s by eight-track and cassette tapes, which worked well for playing music in cars. Eventually all these formats would be replaced in the 1980s by the compact disc (CD), which played digitized recordings using laser technology. Unlike its predecessors, the CD never wore out, and allowed listeners to program the sequence of songs as well as to play multiple discs.

The rise of new formats in mid-century was accompanied by a shift in the locus of popular music. While jazz became a specialty genre in the postwar era, country music continued to thrive in the arena of multiple genres that constituted pop. To some extent, there was overlap in country-music and rock-and-roll audiences; Elvis Presley, for example, had devotees among country-music fans his whole life, particularly toward the end of it. One of the biggest stars in country music – the "Man in Black," Johnny Cash – made his first recordings on Sun Records, the same label as Presley's. Cash's spare sound and style made him an iconic figure in mid-century; his 1968 album *At Folsom Prison* is a landmark of the genre.

Women also occupied a prominent place in the country landscape in the third quarter of the century. Patsy Cline's rich voice, juxtaposed with the lush arrangements of producer Owen Bradley, led to a string of hits before her untimely death in a plane crash in 1963. Loretta Lynn became a genuine working-class feminist voice on the strength of her 1967 hit "Don't Come Home A Drinkin' (With Lovin' on Your Mind)" and "The Pill" (1975). Dolly Parton emerged as one of the finest songwriters in the history of country music, along with one of the sweetest of voices (and personalities – Parton long reciprocated the affection of her large gay and lesbian audience at a time when such people were considered deviant). Women also featured prominently in a number of married country-music duos, among them George Jones and Tammy Wynette as well as Johnny Cash and June Carter Cash.

In the last quarter of the century, some country musicians rebelled against what they considered an excessively commercial mainstream in the industry typified by performers like Australian singer Olivia Newton-John, whose catchy songs seemed to dissolve the line between country and pop entirely. These rebels developed a more spare sound that reconnected the genre with its roots. Willie Nelson, who began his career as a songwriter – Patsy Cline had a major hit with his 1962 song "Crazy" – broke out on his own as a performer in the 1970s. His 1975 album *Red Headed Stranger* is considered a classic concept album, a relative rarity in country. In 1976 he teamed up with like-minded Waylon Jennings (a big star in his own right), Jessi Colter, and Tompall Glaser for the hugely successful album *Wanted! The Outlaws*. Nelson followed it up with *Stardust* (1978), an album of standards that bridged genres and was again a major commercial and critical success.

In the 1980s, another emerging generation of performers, among them Dwight Yoakum and Steve Earle, revitalized country by drawing upon more of a rock sensibility. Texan Lyle Lovett and Canadian k.d. lang (who were known to tour and record together) were likeminded in their sense of history, one they coupled with a sense of musical range and quirky performing styles that stood in marked contrast to the macho strutting that sometimes seemed to dominate the genre. Roseanne Cash carried her father Johnny's torch, but fused it with a feminist sensibility. At a time when country was sometimes conflated with conservatism, such performers were a welcome reminder that any vibrant pop-culture genre resists easy ideological pigeonholing. This strand of the country tradition was carried into the end of the century with the similarly feminist accents of Mary Chapin-Carpenter and the Dixie Chicks.

Country continued to be a pillar of pop music at the turn of the century. Superstars like Garth Brooks, Shania Twain, and Taylor Swift (see "Document Study / *Speak Now*: The gently assertive voice of Taylor Swift") attained mega-million status that reflected the blockbuster mentality so prominent in pop culture generally. While each had critics who considered their respective styles slick and at times only nominally country, each succeeded in part because their music straddled genres and mastered the pop hooks so central to making hit records. A rock-and-roll sensibility was particularly important in the early twenty-first century, as indicated by the success of hit songs like Eric Church's "Springsteen" (2005), a tribute to the rock legend.

One of the perhaps unfortunate realities of modern pop music, however, is that of racial segregation in the radio and record industries, and nowhere was this more true than in country. Notwithstanding an occasional African American performer like Charlie Pride in the 1970s or Darius Rucker in the 2000s, almost all country performers and musicians have been white. (A few protean artists such as Ray Charles could perform white and black styles, and reach white and black audiences simultaneously.) After initially serving as a bridge between musical cultures at mid-century, rock and roll also became a largely white genre by the 1970s. Insofar as there really was interracial communication, the AM radio dial had been a meeting ground of sorts, a tradition maintained by some Top-40 based FM stations today.

One sometimes overlooked dimension in the history of pop music is the strong influence of Latino traditions, instruments, and songs. In part, this is because it's sometimes hard to distinguish where Latin music ends and black music begins. Similarly, Tex-Mex border sounds, notably conjunto music, combined central European and Central American elements. At different points in the century, specifically Latin sounds such as the tango, mambo, and salsa were popular with a wide range of audiences. And Latin performers like Tito Puente, Ritche Valens, and Carlos Santana became prominent national figures as well as sources of ethnic pride.

Black music in the second half of the twentieth century continued to draw upon blues, jazz, and other traditions. But distinct new genres also emerged. Reggae, a musical form anchored in the Caribbean, became an internationally famous style, thanks in no small part to the music of Bob Marley, a Jamaican singer-songwriter and bandleader who rose to fame in the 1970s before his tragically premature death from cancer in 1981. A popular genre in its own right, reggae influenced a number of others all over the world, including rock (ranging from superstar guitarist Eric Clapton to punk rockers the Clash) and dub, a reggae-influenced variation involving remixing existing records.

Another genre, this one rooted in rhythm and blues or r&b, experienced a remarkably rapid rise and fall in the 1970s: disco. Disco was a highly urban, technology-driven, slickly produced musical form that exploited repetition and elaborate nightclub settings to achieve a hypnotic effect. Disco had strong cultural ties to gay culture, in which overt sexuality was celebrated. Gay audiences were important in making stars of performers like the (heterosexual) Donna Summer, whose erotically charged "Love to Love You Baby" (1976) became a gigantic hit. Latino music and audiences were also important components of disco, as were generous dollops of (synthesizer-based) strings in songs that could go on for as long as fifteen minutes.

Disco went mainstream in the late 1970s with the release of the 1977 movie *Saturday Night Fever* and its soundtrack album featuring the Australian trio the Bee Gees, a 1960s rock group who reinvented themselves for the disco era. Yet even as disco was peaking in popular appeal, racism and homophobia – typified by a rock-burning ceremony held in a Chicago stadium in 1979 – drove a backlash against the genre. Like ragtime, the disco phenomenon proved to be short-lived. But it nevertheless had a deep and enduring influence on popular music, even on rock, which was the source of much of the hostility against it. A disco dimension was unmistakable in the Rolling Stones' 1978 single "Miss You" (released, as many songs of the era were, in an extended disco version) and became a musical pillar in the career of crossover artists like Madonna. Because mixing and arranging was such an important component of any given disco song, it was to a great degree a producer's medium, placing less primacy on the individual musician and more on the mixing and manipulation of recordings and record-playing turntables. These qualities made disco a component of what proved to be the most popular and durable pop-music genre to emerge in the late twentieth century: hip-hop.

Hip-hop marked the latest iteration of a centuries-old black musical tradition that linked Africa, the Caribbean, and North America. This time, however, there was a crucial difference, one encapsulated by hip-hop historian Jeff Chang in *Can't Stop, Won't Stop*: "If blues [and, by extension, black music generally] emerged under conditions of oppressive, forced, labor, hip-hop culture would arise from conditions of no work." By the 1980s, the soaring hopes of the Civil Rights movement had been significantly dashed by economic conditions that were creating a black urban underclass not only in the United States but elsewhere in the world as well, from Jamaica to South Africa. In particular, the New York City neighborhood of the South Bronx had been decimated by urban "renewal" that tore down homes to build a multilane highway, by white flight to the suburbs, and by the destruction of the city's manufacturing base, which led to jobs moving overseas. Gang culture added a toxic element of intraracial violence to a mix already marked by civic neglect. And yet, as had so often happened before, African Americans were able to transform the brutal conditions of their lives into art with global appeal.

It's important to note that early hip-hop – or rap, to use a once more common term – was not only, or even primarily, about making records. Actually, it connoted a larger set of cultural practices that began to emerge in the late 1970s. One was graffiti, a practice of painting public spaces in a personal style that often involved a literal or figurative signature (since graffiti was considered vandalism by public authorities and much of the public, it was typically done in secret). Another was a form of dance known as b-boy, or break dancing, which involved stylish poses and the use of hands to support one's body at least as much as feet. A distinctive style of music often accompanied break dancing, one rooted in dub music of the kind popular in Jamaica at the time. This music, which typically involved long stretches of mixing rhythm tracks, scratching needles on records, and sampling pop-music songs with a pair of turntables, also featured improvisational speech to the beat by an emcee, or MC, who worked alongside the disc jockey, or DJ (sometimes the same person). A key pioneer of this emerging style was the Jamaican-born rapper Kool Herc, who became famous for his work as a DJ at block parties and clubs in the Bronx. Other key figures in this protean moment included Afrika Baambaata and Melle Mel.

Given that hip-hop music was in effect a postmodern pastiche of existing recordings refashioned through rapping for a specific occasion, it was far from clear that it could really become a bona fide pop-music genre. It is thus one of the ironies of the form that the recording many historians consider the first hip-hop record, the Sugar Hill Gang's "Rapper's Delight" (1979), came not out of the Bronx, but out of New Jersey. When entrepreneur Sylvia Robinson, who owned a recording studio, failed to convince prominent Bronx rappers to make a record, her son recruited a trio of unknowns to make a record that drew heavily on Chic's 1979 hit "Good Times" (resulting in the first of many lawsuits that grew out of the hip-hop ethos of sampling). "Rapper's Delight" demonstrated the instant appeal and tremendous potential of hip-hop music. Its power as a source of social commentary also became apparent in the 1982 hit "The Message," by Grandmaster Mel and the Furious Five, featuring Melle Mel.

Over the course of the 1980s, hip-hop evolved rapidly from a fad to the dominant genre in popular music. One key breakthrough occurred in 1986 when the rap duo Run DMC – who hailed from Queens, not the Bronx – made a hip-hop version of the 1975 Aerosmith hit "Walk This Way" that included the original song's vocalist Steven Tyler and guitarist Joe Perry. Released at the height of the MTV era with a video that comically depicted the destruction of a symbolic wall between the acts, Run DMC (whose look was more spare black-and-white, in contrast to the colorful style of early rap) helped overcome the music-television network's resistance to hip-hop, paving the way for its absorption by national as well as international audiences.

But rap, as the music of the late-twentieth-century ghetto, was too powerful and edgy to conquer without controversy. Local scenes emerged in a number of cities, notably Los Angeles, where a glorification of violence, materialism, and machismo met with criticism among white as well as black observers. In 1988, the hip-hop act NWA (Niggaz Wit' Attitude) released the album *Straight Outta Compton*, which contained the notorious hit single "Fuck tha Police," which generated widespread condemnation. Such militancy also characterized the music of Public Enemy, whose anthem "Fight the Power" was featured in the classic 1989 Spike Lee film *Do the Right Thing*. A separate subgenre of gangsta rap, typified by NWA, Ice-T, and the Geto Boys, was characterized by violent imagery and resistance to authority figures. Gangsta was also marked by internecine struggles between west- and east-coast rappers, resulting in the deaths of the hugely talented Tupac Shakur in 1996 and the Notorious B.I.G in 1997. Media caricatures notwithstanding, hip-hop was always more than gangsta (and gangsta at its best was always more than crude celebrations of thug life, something apparent in Tupac recordings like his 1992 signature song "Changes").

Though hip-hop was sometimes assumed to be the province of men, a number of women made a lasting mark on the genre. Rappers MC Lyte and Queen Latifah were among the founding mothers of hip-hop in the 1980s with their albums *Lyte as a Rock* (1988) and *All Hail the Queen* (1989). Salt-n-Pepa enjoyed commercial success with big hits like "Shoop" and "Whatta Man" (both 1993). And Lauryn Hill made one of the most highly regarded concept albums in rap history with *The Miseducation of Lauryn Hill* (1998). All this said, it was never easy for women to get the kind of attention men did in what remained a male-dominated genre.

By the turn of the century, hip-hop had accumulated enough of a sense of tradition for its most skilled practitioners to invoke, allude to, or otherwise rewrite it with historical self-consciousness. Jay-Z invoked the heritage of a 1968 Beatles (white) album in 2003 with *The Black Album*. Kanye West weaved multiple strands of black musical tradition in *The College Dropout* (2004), which included his gospel-infused classic "Jesus Walks." Fellow Chicagoland rapper Common showed a reflective side in his 2005 song "The Corner." Such performers worked alongside more frankly commercial acts like the brash Nicki Minaj, whose colorful couture and playful image made her a media celebrity. The genre also attracted white performers like the Beastie Boys and Eminem, both of whom attained stature among white and black audiences alike.

Hip-hop was now at the center of American musical life. But even as this was happening the record business was undergoing a transformation unlike any in half a century. The technology of the 33-rpm record had been crucial in the emergence of hip-hop culture; even individual songs like "Rapper's Delight" were creatures of the LP format in extended 33-rpm versions. When hip-hop took off as a form of popular music, it migrated to compact disc, at least in terms of consumer sales (as opposed to private parties or nightclubs, where turntables were still used). But by the end of the twentieth century, the CD itself had become increasingly obsolete.

For the first time, music could be made, stored, transmitted, and played without a physical recording like a record or tape. At one time, elaborate stereo systems – big speakers, large receivers, and so on – were the mark of a serious music listener. But in the closing decades of the century, the technology of playing recordings became increasingly miniaturized. The relatively tiny CD itself was an example of this; the introduction of the (cassette-driven) Sony Walkman in the early 1980s made listening more portable and private. As digital files replaced older forms of storage, the computer displaced the stereo system – and computers themselves became smaller as laptops replaced PCs, and hand-held devices replaced laptops.

The issue, and it was a serious one at the turn of the century, was that the ability to move music in the form of electronic documents meant that you didn't have to buy anything to hear it. Record companies were never happy about the way magnetic tape made it possible to copy recordings, but accepted the reality of lost sales (though it was not necessarily the case that much was lost; home taping may well have increased the overall number of record buyers who discovered acts and subsequently bought their recordings). But the ability to move entire record collections virtually instantly via downloads with music-sharing programs like Napster posed a mortal threat to the industry's entire economic model. Legal action against Napster led to its shutdown in 2001. Eventually, commercial operators in the music business harnessed Napster methods to a market model, most notably in the case of Apple, whose iTunes store began selling individual songs for 99 cents, cheap enough to make buying seem easier and safer than illegal methods.

Meanwhile, the whole notion of owning music began to erode with the emergence of yet another model of accessing music by streaming it online via commercial services like Pandora and Spotify, which allowed listeners to choose music with more precision than radio. Some versions of these services allowed listeners free music at the cost of accepting occasional ads; others carried a monthly fee in exchange for ad-free listening. These enterprises were still struggling to make money in the second decade of the twenty-first century – most of their expenses went to paying record companies for the right to play their artists – and there may come a time when a hardware manufacturer offers the buyers of its wares free access to virtually all music, paying record companies as part of the price of their businesses. In any case, it seems likely that the whole notion of collecting records will soon be obsolete, since the entire body of recorded music will routinely be instantly accessible (for a direct or indirect price).

But even before such a transformation is complete, the migration of the music business online – where even radio stations are increasingly heard via streaming rather than broadcasting – is having a profound and ongoing impact on the shape of the industry. Once upon a time musical acts toured as a means to promote the sales of records. Now records are a promotional tool used to beef up the profitability of touring. It's harder than ever to become a star; it's easier than ever to make a record. Amid the ongoing uncertainties of how the radio and record industries will be organized, one fact remains clear: music has always been more than a market. It's also always been more than a way to make a living. At any given time, in any given way, it may be both. But even if it's neither, the desire to make, hear, and share sounds will last as long as human beings do.

Questions to consider

1. Describe the relationship between musical performance and sound recording in the music business as it was understood a century ago. What economic issues arose from the distinction?
2. How did the emergence of sound technology affect American music in the twentieth century? Consider some of the various formats (33- and 45-rpm records, compact discs, and downloads).
3. Describe the relationship between the blues and later genres of popular music, from jazz to hip-hop.
4. One of the core tensions in country music has been between the values of itinerant wanderer and those of the family circle. What are those values? Can you discern such tensions in other genres of pop music?
5. How were the circumstances of the emergence of hip-hop different from those of earlier genres of African American music? How important are those differences in understanding where hip-hop is today?

Genre Study

Joyful blues: The rise and fall of rock and roll

Figure 6.2 KINGLY REGALIA Elvis Presley performing in a $5000 pantsuit, 1973. Widely considered a founding father of rock and roll, Presley was also one of its tragic casualties. (© Pictoral Press Ltd/Alamy)

Of all the paradoxes that lace through the history of popular culture, this is the most profound: that the dominant genre of popular music in the second half of the twentieth century – an era that marked the zenith of US power and affluence – was decisively shaped by the most oppressed and marginalized people in its history: American slaves. The art these people wrought from centuries of misery, art whose influence continues to resonate around the world, was embraced by young people generations later who were in many cases barely aware of their own history, let alone anybody else's. A polyglot nation obsessed with segregation somehow managed to produce an integrated musical culture that remains among its greatest gifts to world civilization.

While a number of genres in slave music were important to the creation of rock and roll – work songs, ring shouts, spirituals – the foundation is a post-Civil War idiom that drew on all of them: the blues. The blues was rock's cornerstone, whether the basis of saying so is musical scales with flattened fifths and sevenths, an AAB lyrical pattern, or the themes of lyrics. Gospel, another postwar idiom, which fused spirituals with Western choral music, was also important, particularly in terms of a call-and-response vocal pattern. And jazz provided a model of improvisation that was widely adopted, particularly by keyboard players and guitarists. Technological innovations like the invention of the electric guitar in the 1930s, so central to rock's development, gave these age-old songs a modern sound.

A series of social and economic factors was also important. The mass migration of African Americans from the South to northern cities, which began to quicken at the turn of the twentieth century, turned into a flood by the time of World War II. This brought black people into new environments that subtly altered their music (the blues, for example, took on an edgier tone with electric guitars, necessary so they could be heard amid the din of nightclubs). It also brought blacks into closer contact with new kinds of ethnic whites and Latinos and *their* cultures. This sense of mixing was intensified by the spread of radio; stations in Chicago, Nashville, and along the Mexican border allowed people in formerly isolated communities to feel part of a broad and diverse national musical culture. (One disc jockey in particular, Alan Freed of Cleveland, is widely credited with midwifing the birth of rock by playing and promoting it on the radio.) The growth of the record industry – and the growing relative affluence among African Americans with disposable income for records – was a part of this mix, especially because the recording business still had a strong regional dimension, creating markets that black audiences could support. Such music was known by the term "race records," reflecting the segregated character of US society at the time.

By the late 1940s and early 1950s the updated blues sound of rhythm and blues – more danceable than traditional blues – made stars of a range of artists, among them Ruth Brown, Lloyd Price, and Hank Ballard and the Midnighters, whose 1954 profane hit song "Work with Me Annie" (followed later the same year by "Annie Had a Baby") is considered a forerunner of rock and roll – a term that was once black slang for sexual intercourse. Meanwhile, a once-parallel country-music culture was converging with rhythm and blues. Jimmie Rodgers had pioneered this convergence back in the 1920s; now Hank Williams and Tennessee Ernie Ford drew on black traditions in forging their own musical styles. Ford's huge 1955 hit "Sixteen Tons," about an indebted coal miner, draws on blues traditions in both its style and its themes.

The locus of country music had long been Nashville, Tennessee. It was a city at the other end of that state, Memphis, on the Mississippi River delta, that provided the seedbed for rock and roll. It was there that Sam Phillips, a native Alabamian and former disc jockey, founded a small record company called Sun Records. Phillips signed a number of Memphis acts to his label, among them a group of prison inmates dubbed the Prisonaires, who had a local 1953 hit with "Just Walkin' in the Rain." Phillips was an exceptionally astute judge of talent. Over the course of the next few years, he signed a series of artists who would go on to have successful careers, among them bluesman Howlin' Wolf, country star Johnny Cash, and rhythm and blues artist Ike Turner, husband of the great singer Tina Turner and writer of "Rocket 88," a song about a car that some historians consider the first rock-and-roll record.

What Phillips really wanted, as the now legendary story goes, was to "find a white boy with the Negro sound and the Negro feel." He found that boy – or, perhaps more accurately, his secretary Marion Keisker found that boy, whom Phillips coached to success over a period of months – in Elvis Presley. The son of a truck driver, Presley, who had been born in 1935 in nearby Tupelo, Mississippi, had grown up poor "white trash," and as such mingled with African Americans more than "respectable" whites of his time did. The family moved to Memphis when Presley was thirteen and lived in welfare housing; after his graduation from high school he got a job as a truck driver who quickly outearned his father (who had spent time in jail for writing bad checks). In 1953, Presley walked into Sun hoping to make a record for his beloved mother, which in effect became his audition. In 1954–1955 he made a string of songs now collectively known as the Sun Sessions, which revolutionized popular music. Presley went to New York in 1956 to begin a career that transformed him into one of the most commercially successful celebrities of all time. Though most observers believe his work gradually declined in quality over the course of the next 20 years, even the late Presley was capable of making records of great power and resonance. His death in 1977 from a drug overdose cut short what had been a truly thrilling career, but his legend has only seemed to grow with time.

Presley was dubbed "the King of Rock and Roll," but he hardly invented it. Western bandleader Bill Haley and his Comets recorded "Rock Around the Clock" in 1954 (it became a hit the following year when included on the soundtrack of *The Blackboard Jungle*, a movie about juvenile delinquency, a subject of much hand-wringing at the time). Presley's fellow Sun-label artist Jerry Lee Lewis had more raw performing talent, and was a spectacular showman. So were many gifted African American songwriters and performers, among them Chuck Berry and Little Richard (Penniman), who could never hope to achieve Presley's stature given the intensity of American racism. But all these people were able to connect with interracial audiences, in part because their appeal was generational: rock was a music by and for young people at a time when young people, with their energy and idealism, were becoming a major force in American life.

Indeed, it's important to remember the immense challenge rock posed to the established cultural order – a challenge that arose at precisely the same moment as the Civil Rights movement was kicking into high gear. (*The New York Times* did its first profile of Martin

Luther King the same week in 1956 as Presley's huge hit "Heartbreak Hotel" was climbing up the pop charts.) In church pulpits, high-school auditoriums, and editorial pages, rock was excoriated as evil incarnate. Rock records were banned, investigations were launched, and protectors of public order warned that such music raised the awful possibility of racial miscegenation. Much of the angst surrounding rock focused on the young, the so-called baby boomers born between 1946 and 1964 who represented an enormous demographic bulge that would soon transform US politics, society, and culture. Baby boomers also transformed the US economy with their disposable income, which they lavished on a variety of products, principal among them newfangled 33- and 45-rpm records they played on their cutting-edge record players, which could now automatically change records.

To some extent, the hoopla surrounding rock receded in the years on either side of 1960. Elvis Presley entered the army in 1958, and was off the scene for two years. Record companies promoted tamer versions of rock stars, like Pat Boone, who smoothed down rock's harder edges and presented it in a more wholesome manner that earned the scorn of critics. Yet these were also years of innovation and excitement. Texan Buddy Holly invented the modern rock band – lead guitar, rhythm guitar, bass, drums – with his group the Crickets, and his songs "Peggy Sue" and "That'll Be the Day" (both 1957, the latter borrowed from the John Ford movie *The Searchers*) helped establish the idea that pop musicians could also be songwriters. Holly died in a plane crash along with two other promising rock stars, fellow Texan the Big Bopper and Chicano sensation Ritchie Valens, in 1959, cutting short promising careers.

Another important locus of musical excitement was Detroit. The so-called Motor City, a magnet for migrating African Americans seeking work in the auto industry, had a thriving music scene by the early 1960s. The man who did more than any other to exploit it was Berry Gordy, a one-time musician who founded Motown Records in 1959. Over the course of the next decade, he signed a series of acts, among them wunderkind Stevie Wonder, the Supremes, Marvin Gaye, and Smokey Robinson and the Miracles, representing one of the greatest concentrations of talent in music history. Berry's great insight was that he could make fabulous pop records on an assembly-line model, using crack studio musicians and cross-pollinating his acts. Songs like the Supremes' "You Can't Hurry Love" (1964), Smokey Robinson and the Miracles' "Tears of a Clown" (1967), and Gaye's "I Heard It Through the Grapevine" (1968) are now at the heart of the pop canon of the 1960s. Berry's acts chafed under his control; eventually, like Wonder, they wrested an element of autonomy that allowed them to do their best work on Motown (like Wonder's 1976 album *Songs in the Key of Life*), or broke with the label to launch solo careers.

Meanwhile, in Memphis, an earthier sound typified by Aretha Franklin, Otis Redding, and Percy Sledge captured the black-is-beautiful ethos of the late 1960s, one first articulated by their dazzling soul forebear, James Brown. The rise of a distinctive Memphis sound corresponded to a more militant phase of the Civil Rights movement, when black artists put more emphasis on affirming their racial identities than pursuing a more integrationist approach to popular music.

If Elvis Presley represented the first great explosion in rock history, the Beatles, four British youths from the working-class city of Liverpool, England, represented the second. As such, they demonstrated the enormous reach of American music in the world at the time, and the way in which US power in the wake of World War II was underwriting European prosperity through the Marshall Plan and other forms of global trade. The great contribution of the Beatles lay in the way they imitated the black idiom they absorbed as teens, crossbred it with traditional British dance-hall music, and in the process created something thrillingly new. Songs like "She Loves You" and "I Wanna Hold Your Hand" (both 1963, released in the US the following year) exploded on AM radios in the mid-1960s. In the years that followed, the Beatles demonstrated an astonishing capacity for experimentation in musical styles, songwriting acumen, and their ability to exploit recording technology, thanks in no small measure to their producer,

George Martin. Their 1967 concept album, *Sgt Pepper's Lonely Hearts Club Band*, is a landmark in the history of popular music, and the album that fully legitimated rock as a form of serious artistic expression. The Beatles' success also triggered a "British invasion" of other acts, among them the Who, the Kinks, and the exceptionally durable Rolling Stones, whose bad-boy image combined with their feel for the blues tradition and made the band among the most widely admired and imitated of the twentieth century.

The third great explosion in rock history came from a different direction: folk music. In the 1940s and 1950s, a folk revival had taken root in some quarters of US society as an expression of leftist politics in the aftermath of the radical movements of the 1930s, captured in the music of Leadbelly, Woody Guthrie, and Burl Ives. By the early 1960s, folk had also emerged (somewhat paradoxically) as a more highbrow expression of the cultural rebelliousness represented by rock, its literary and historical resonances far more self-conscious than rock's rude energy. Joan Baez became a darling of the New York coffee-house circuit on the basis of her earnestness and the purity of her voice. But it was her one-time boyfriend, Bob Dylan, who became the leading figure in folk music on the basis of his distinctive voice and his stunning capacity for wordplay. Early in his career, Dylan was lionized for socially conscious songwriting, epitomized by "Blowin in the Wind" (1962), "Masters of War" (1963), and "The Times They Are a-Changin'" (1964).

But then Dylan did something many of his devotees considered treasonous: he abandoned folk music for rock, a move he ratified in his electric-guitar based performance at the Newport Folk Festival of 1965, in which the hostile reaction he received has become part of rock lore. In the ensuing years Dylan and the Beatles, along with innovators like the California-based Beach Boys, led the movement to take rock music in a decisively new direction, moving it away from the three-minute pop songs housed in 45s to longer, more introspective suites of songs on LP albums. The advent of FM radio in the mid-1960s helped reinforce this development by featuring album tracks not typically played (or designed) for more pop-driven

AM radio. Unlike jazz, however, rock never entirely lost touch with its populist roots, and so remained near the center of pop music for decades to come.

Still, if rock remained at the center, that center was stretching to breaking point. A spirit of experimentation took rock in some striking new directions. New techniques like multitrack recording, sound effects, and other innovations on the part of bands typified albums like the Beach Boys' *Pet Sounds* and the Beatles' *Revolver* (both 1966). To at least some extent, such experiments were the result of drug use, which fostered creativity. At the same time, however, growing drug abuse – from psychedelic drugs such as LSD to more hypnotic ones like heroin – shaped the lives, and in some cases, the deaths, of great performers, among them the magnificent blues-rock singer Janis Joplin and Jimi Hendrix, the songwriter-guitarist who was one of the few virtuosos that rock ever produced. Both Joplin and Hendrix appeared at the Woodstock festival of 1969, in which hundreds of thousands of young people gathered to hear some remarkable music (amid some remarkable squalor) in upstate New York, creating a symbol for the utopian aspirations of the 1960s. However, the grinding and increasingly violent and disillusioning course of the Civil Rights movement and Vietnam War dashed this hopeful mood. Its spirit was replaced by that of the Altamont Festival in northern California in 1970, a violent event featuring the Rolling Stones, during which four people died.

By the early 1970s, rock fractured into divergent streams. One was represented by the increasingly hard-edged (and macho) blues sound typified by Led Zeppelin, distinctive for the controlled use of distortion with electric guitars common to the "heavy metal" sub-genre. Another was a quieter, more folkish strain represented by a new generation of artists typified by James Taylor, Joni Mitchell, and Carole King, who had begun her career writing catchy pop tunes before striking with the feminist-minded album *Tapestry* (1971). These were also years in which rock, whose initial energies had been rooted in racial integration, in effect resegregated, notwithstanding important exceptions like the interracial Sly and the Family Stone, whose 1971 hit "Everyday People" kept alive the receding hopes of the 1960s. To some extent, black artists and audiences made a detour into disco (see "Overview"). One man who tried, with uneven success, to extend the old integrationist spirit with fidelity to the music of the early 1960s was Bruce Springsteen, whose 1975 album *Born to Run* has become the quintessential expression of rock neoclassicism. Springsteen's early music, which included black musicians and a jazz-influenced style, grew increasingly spare over the course of the 1970s and 1980s as he reconnected with rock's folk roots. His overwhelmingly white audience is piquant testimony to how even the best-intentioned musicians have had trouble unifying audiences in an age which, Civil Rights successes notwithstanding, has been marked by de facto polarization, racial and otherwise.

Black musicians also tried to bridge the gap. One of the most prodigiously talented of the era was Prince, a writer-producer-singer-guitarist who made some of the most exciting records of the time, among them his 1984 album *Purple Rain*, the basis of a film of the same name. Another pivotally important figure was Michael Jackson, a former member of the Motown-based Jackson 5, whose 1979 album *Off the Wall* and, especially, his monster hit *Thriller* (1982) united American audiences in a way no artist has since. (See "Document Study / "Beat It": The integration of Michael Jackson.")

Rock also showed some capacity for revitalization in the late 1970s and early 1980s with the punk rock explosion. Punk was an Anglo-American phenomenon. In Britain, the dominant emotion was rage, expressed most forcefully and thrillingly by the Sex Pistols, whose sole album, *Nevermind the Bollocks Here's the Sex Pistols* (1977) reinvented rock by contemptuously mocking the idea of convention, artistry, and the encrusted weight of pretense that had come to characterize much of the rock world by the mid-1970s in so-called "progressive" rock bands like Pink Floyd, Yes, Jethro Tull, and their baroque imitators. The Sex Pistols could barely play their instruments, but songs like "Anarchy in the UK" and "God Save the Queen" (which was banned by the British Broadcasting Corporation) embodied the rage of a Britain in the throes of economic decline. The band's torch was carried forward by the Clash, a more ambitious and focused punk rock band that had a lasting impact on rock history on the basis of *London Calling*, released in Britain in 1979 and the US in 1980. A lingering punk spirit also enlivened the music of the Irish band U2, which would go on to have an unusually long and productive career.

In the US, by contrast, punk often had a more playful spirit, along with the harder-edged sound apparent in west-coast bands such as X, fronted by the charismatic Exene Cervenka. But the US movement was centered in downtown New York, where bands such as the Ramones made loud, fast, and short songs whose simplicity was irresistible. Other groups, like the Talking Heads and Blondie, had more interest in musical sophistication and reaching a broad audience, which they did. (Blondie dabbled in a number of genres, among them disco and hip-hop.) But they retained the subversive spirit of punk's energy and helped give rock and roll a new lease on life.

Rock got two more injections of vitality in the early 1980s. The first was the arrival of Music Television (MTV), which generated a new wave of excitement in the form of music videos, particularly those of Michael Jackson, which MTV initially resisted broadcasting out of a misplaced fear that white audiences would not be interested. The cultural ramifications of MTV were widespread and profound, ranging from a new wave of British imports (British acts had been making videos for TV shows in the UK for years), a new emphasis on hit singles (Bruce Springsteen's 1984 album *Born in the U.S.A.* spawned a string of them), and a proliferation of rapid editing and other visual techniques that influenced media style for years to come. The era was also generally marked by brighter, more slickly produced music, in which synthesizers and other computer-generated sounds were evident. The second big development of the decade was the introduction of the compact disc (CD), which among other things called attention to a rich history as older recordings were re-released in the new format and buoyed a record industry still confident in its powers.

By the end of the decade, however, there were signs that rock was finally losing steam as the dominant genre in pop music. Hip-hop, which emerged as a competitor on the airwaves and on MTV in the mid-1980s, had more obvious vitality. And the baby boomers, whose youthfulness had done so much to drive rock music's commercial appeal, were now solidly middle-aged. Local scenes like that of Seattle spawned the subgenre of grunge, popularized by the critically acclaimed band Nirvana, whose 1991 album *Nevermind* managed to be catchy and hard-edged at the same time.

Rock music hardly disappeared after 1990. Bands such as Green Day – which enjoyed enormous success with its latter-day punk album *American Idiot* (2004), which became the basis of a Broadway musical that opened five years later – had a high profile, and there remained vibrant local scenes and any number of subgenres that flourished, largely under the mainstream radar. But hip-hop, not rock, was the defining musical genre of the turn of this century. Rock increasingly seemed to be headed for a fate like that of jazz: admired, beloved, and still capable of attracting young devotees and practitioners. But its day, like that of the American Century that underwrote it, seems to be over.

God, it was fun.

Questions to consider

1. What were some of the historical forces shaping the emergence of rock and roll? Consider the legacy of slavery, class consciousness, mass migration, and technological innovation, among others.
2. Describe the role of racism in the response to rock and roll and its subsequent development.
3. Which performers in rock history do you consider the most innovative? What do you regard as the basis of their accomplishment?
4. To what degree would you say rock is a male genre? Would you say rock is more male than other genres of music (or popular culture generally)? Which women performers do you regard as important?

Document Study

"Beat It": The integration of Michael Jackson

Figure 6.3 STARTIN' SOMETHIN' Michael Jackson, the self-titled "King of Pop," at Wembley Stadium, London, during the *Bad* concert tour, 1987. Jackson leveraged the emerging genre of music video to showcase his prodigious performing talents. (© Trinity Mirror/Mirrorpix/Alamy)

There are two seemingly paradoxical truisms in the history of rock and roll in the United States. The first is that rock is a decisively black musical idiom – polyglot for sure, as all American culture is, but with the blues as its cornerstone. The second is that in the popular imagination rock is a white (and male) genre, as reflected in generational icons such as Elvis Presley, the Beatles, and Bruce Springsteen. The dominant African American figures in pop music in the last 75 years, from Ray Charles to Beyoncé, have tended to congregate in other genres, among them rhythm and blues, disco, and hip-hop.

In fact, however, there have always been black musicians who fall squarely into the rock tradition. Ike Turner wrote and performed "Rocket 88" in 1951 – a landmark in the history of the genre – and his wife, Tina Turner, was a bona fide rock star straight into the twenty-first century. Chuck Berry has long been lionized as among rock's greatest songwriters and guitarists. Jimi Hendrix virtually reinvented the guitar during his own all too brief career, which also included a memorable body of his own songs as well as dazzling interpretations of others, from his 1968 version of Bob Dylan's "All Along the Watchtower" (1967) to "The Star Spangled Banner" (1814). In the late 1970s and early 1980s, Prince traversed the line between rock and r&b as the last major star before hip-hop took center stage in pop music.

The late Michael Jackson was not a rock musician. But he was an astoundingly versatile man: songwriter, singer, and dancer, among other talents. When he was at his commercial and artistic height, Jackson tried his (gloved) hand at the genre as part of his landmark album *Thriller*. The result is one of the truly great rock songs of all time: "Beat It."

When *Thriller* was released in the fall of 1982, Jackson was only 24 years old. But he had already enjoyed a career of distinction. Born into a highly musical family in Gary, Indiana, in 1958, the eighth of 10 children, Jackson was tutored by his stern (and abusive) father, who forged him and his four brothers into the Jackson 5. From an early age, Michael stood out, an instinctive prodigy of a vocalist who modeled his early performing style on masters such as James Brown and Jackie Wilson.

The historical context for Jackson's rise is important: he was a child of the Civil Rights movement. Jackson grew up in an age of integration, and while his music rarely betrayed any direct political message, pivotal historical figures like Martin Luther King Jr. and legislative landmarks like the passage of the 1964 Civil Rights Act and 1965 Voting Rights Act were the backdrop of his life.

In 1968, the Jackson 5 were signed to Motown Records, the fabled label owned by Detroit entrepreneur Berry Gordy, who made a career out of recording and packaging black music in ways that captured the imaginations of interracial audiences. By this point Gordy had already launched the careers of a panoply of stars, among them Diana Ross and the Supremes, Marvin Gaye, and Stevie Wonder. The Jacksons represented the last great flowering of Gordy's genius for developing new talent. By 1970 the group began enjoying a string of hits that included "I Want You Back," "ABC," and "I'll Be There." Like many Motown acts, however, the Jackson 5 became increasingly restless with the strictures of Gordy's management, and left the label in 1975. Michael, meanwhile, was increasingly restless performing as part of a family act. He had cut a solo single as early as 1971, and had a chart-topping hit with "Ben," a song about a pet rat from the horror movie *Ben* (1972). But he struck out on his own for good with the release of his 1979 album *Off the Wall*, which became a smash, featuring the hit singles "Don't Stop 'Til You Get Enough" and "Rock with You." Arriving at the tail end of the disco era, the album became one of the great dance albums of the time, signaling the arrival of Jackson as a major pop artist.

Off the Wall marked a significant artistic juncture for Jackson, because he teamed up with producer Quincy Jones, one of the more important figures in modern popular music. Jones, who had composed, arranged, and conducted music for acts ranging from Duke Ellington to Frank Sinatra, helped give Jackson's music a newfound sense of maturity as well as a spare, elegant, and distinctive sound. The two continued to work together; from the spring into the fall of 1982, Jackson, Jones, a stable of songwriters, and a set of veteran studio musicians collaborated in crafting a set of nine songs that would come to be known as *Thriller*.

Jackson was a ferociously ambitious figure – he followed in the footsteps of his role model, Brown, lionized as "the hardest-working man in show business" – and conceived *Thriller* as an album that would stake his place at the center of pop culture. The leadoff single, an otherwise forgettable "The Girl Is Mine," was a duet with former Beatle Paul McCartney, who had befriended Jackson (though the two would later have a falling-out when Jackson bought the publishing rights to the Beatles catalog that McCartney had hoped to acquire). The title track, "Thriller," paid homage to scary movies with specially recorded dialogue by horror-movie legend Vincent Price. The song became the soundtrack for an almost 14-minute-long 1983 music video – a short film, in fact, unprecedented in its scale – that attracted worldwide attention.

But Jackson's ambitions were also more purely musical. He affirmed his African heritage with the polyrhythmically percussive "Wanna Be Startin' Somethin'," one of four songs he wrote for the album, which included modified music and lyrics from the 1972 disco song "Soul Makossa" by Cameroonian saxophonist Manu Dibango (who sued Jackson for a copyright violation; the case was settled out of court). And in the marvelously sinuous "Billie Jean," another song he wrote, Jackson tells the story of an anxious, and not entirely credible, man who denies paternity of a child by the title character as a bass line snakes behind him.

It was Jones, however, who nudged Jackson to include a bona fide rock song on the album. "I had been thinking I wanted to write the type of rock song that I would go out and buy, but something totally different from the rock music I was hearing on Top 40 radio at the time," Jackson later wrote in his 1988 autobiography, *Moonwalk*. The piece he wrote was an angry denunciation of street gangs: "To me, true bravery is settling differences without a fight and having the wisdom to make that solution possible." Verbally sketching a series of scenarios in which a character imagines demonstrating his toughness, the singer emphatically replies, "Just beat it."

The initial demo of "Beat It" did not really have a rock flavor, however – there was no guitar part, for example. Jackson and Jones bent it in that direction though by using a crack team of musicians that included guitarist Steve Luthaker, who laid down the famous riff that would be repeated throughout the song. Luthaker had been a member of the successful rock band Toto, but Jackson and Jones wanted a really big-name star to provide a solo that would give the song street cred. So they turned to Eddie Van Halen, guitarist for the hard-rock band Van Halen, which was in the middle of its commercial heyday with lead singer David Roth (there would be others later). Van Halen was by most accounts the best rock guitarist of his day.

Jackson almost didn't get him. Jones kept calling Van Halen, whose phone wasn't working properly – he couldn't hear a voice on the other end of the line. After multiple attempts by Jones, an irritated Van Halen finally asked, "What the fuck do you want, you asshole?" Jones finally was able to make himself heard; once he did, Van Halen readily agreed to play. A decade later the guitarist told a British journalist that his bandmates didn't like it when he made such extracurricular excursions. But, he said,

> Who's going to know that I played on a black guy's record? Michael said, "I love that high fast stuff you do." So I played two solos over it and said, "You guys pick the one you want." It was 20 minutes out of my day. I did it for free and later everybody was telling me, you could have got a royalty point out of that record. But it didn't matter because Quincy wrote me a letter thanking me, and he signed it 'The Asshole'. I framed it. Classic.

"Beat It" followed "The Girl Is Mine" and "Billie Jean" as the third single from *Thriller* in March of 1983, and spent three weeks at number 1 on the *Billboard* pop chart. But in an important sense, this was only the beginning of its career in the bloodstream of American popular culture.

The next major iteration of "Beat It" was as a music video, the new cultural hybrid that was exploding into national consciousness in the early 1980s. A new network, MTV, hit the airwaves in 1981, and quickly established itself as a powerful force and a tastemaker in the pop-music industry. There was a conspicuous absence from MTV's air, however: African American artists. Jackson's label, Epic Records, was outraged by the network's policies – MTV claimed audiences would not accept black music on what was largely a white rock playlist – and its parent company, the CBS Records, threatened to withdraw providing (free) videos entirely from the network, which depended on record-company-supplied content. Though there continue to be disputes around how the conflict was resolved – network executives insist they did not cave in to such pressure – Jackson videos finally entered MTV playlists in early 1983, by which time the album had already established itself as a major hit.

A key turning point came in March. Early that month, Jackson performed "Billie Jean" live as part of a celebration of Motown Records' 25th anniversary celebration, and the subsequent broadcast of his dance moves – the now legendary "moonwalk" – became a classic moment in television history. It was also in March that the "Billie Jean" video went into heavy rotation. Though relatively primitive by later standards, it became a major hit. It was also in March of 1983 that Jackson unveiled the video of "Beat It." Like "Billie Jean," it was shot by British director Bob Giraldi, who had made a name for himself shooting commercials. "Beat It" boasted visibly more sophisticated production values than just about any video of the time, and a large cast that included professional dancers as well as members of Los Angeles street gangs ("they were a nice bunch of guys," he would later write without irony). The video was highly choreographed, climaxing with Jackson, wearing a red leather jacket, arriving on the scene of a multiracial knife fight set against Van Halen's solo. Jackson breaks it up, whereupon the former combatants follow his balletic dance moves. Hokey, and yet riveting. I can vividly remember standing around the den of a friend's house, a group of us waiting for every fourth hour when "Beat It" could be seen again. The song brought people together in a way few works of popular culture ever do.

"Beat It" has had a long life in subsequent American culture as well. The song has been covered, sampled, or alluded to many times. Weird Al Yankovic's parody, "Eat It," was actually a *Billboard* Top-20 single in the spring of 1984. The neopunk band Fall Out Boy performed a similar feat with their version of the song in 2007, which featured a Van Halenesque solo by John Mayer. Generations of college students whose knowledge of the 1980s might otherwise be sketchy nevertheless know the song.

In retrospect, *Thriller* marked the apex of Michael Jackson's career. His next album, *Bad*, was comparably successful (and featured another rock song, "Dirty Diana," which also had a howling guitar solo, provided by Stuart Stevens, who played in the band of British punk artist Billy Idol). But Jackson, who crowned himself the "King of Pop" and was briefly married to Elvis Presley's daughter Lisa Marie, gradually lost his place at the center of American pop culture. This was probably inevitable – generational icons almost by definition must give way – but Jackson's reputation took a series of blows that made subsequent comeback efforts more difficult. His painful childhood appears to have cast long shadows; persistent rumors and accusations that Jackson was a pedophile lingered for the rest of his life but were never proven (he settled one case out of court). Rumors surrounded the reason for the evident lightening of his skin apparent by the late 1980s, which was publicly ascribed to vitiligo, a condition that causes depigmentation, but which was also suspected to be the result of plastic surgery (obvious in the case of the reconstruction of his nose), dismaying fans who suspected Jackson of repudiating his African American identity. Video footage of Jackson cavalierly holding his son by his second wife in front of a Berlin hotel balcony in 2002 shocked many viewers, and solidified a perception of him as someone out of touch with normal human behavior. In public appearances Jackson could seem a pained, even pathetic, figure. Few close observers were surprised, if still saddened, to learn of a death that resulted from the use of illegally administered sleep medication in 2009.

But as is the case with so many artists, it's the work, not the life, which remains to be cherished. For Jackson, performing was a haven from the demons that haunted him. Those of us who have heard his music, forged on the anvil of racism, partake of a fallible greatness. So it is that we experience a sense of artistic integration, in the fullest meaning of that term, which so often eludes us in life.

Questions to consider

1. How did the history of race in America shape the career of Michael Jackson?
2. In what ways could he be considered an integrationist? Consider the term in racial as well as other senses.

3. To what degree should the circumstances of Jackson's personal life affect our estimation of his art? Are the two entirely separate? Is it legitimate to honor an artist if we *believe* he was a criminal? What if we *knew* he was a criminal?

4. How would you describe Michael Jackson's place in contemporary media culture? In what ways is he seen as a man of his time? Are there any ways in which he transcends it?

Document Study

Speak now: The gently assertive voice of Taylor Swift

Figure 6.4   SWIFT CURRENT   Taylor Swift performing at the Country Music Association (CMA) music festival in Nashville, June 13, 2010. Though she first emerged as a country artist, Swift proved herself a master of a series of pop genres, among them rock and roll. (© ZUMA Wire Service/Alamy)

"It's my party and I'll cry if I want to," pop singer Leslie Gore asserted in her 1963 hit single "It's My Party" (followed later that year with its sequel, "Judy's Turn to Cry"). Ever since, generations of young women – Janis Ian, Debbie Gibson, Alanis Morissette, Avril Lavigne, among others – have given voice to the hopes and fears of adolescent females in pop music. As such, Taylor Swift is part of a long tradition. But in the space of a few years, she has staked a claim to cultural history that may well prove to be broader and deeper than most.

Some careers in pop music are the product of private turmoil and professional struggle. Youthful adversity has shaped legends ranging from Elvis Presley to Shania Twain. Swift's background, by contrast, is one of comfort and security. She was born on December 13, 1989 in eastern Pennsylvania, the eldest of two children. Both her parents were in the financial-services industry at the time of her birth – her mother left the profession to become a full-time mom – and the family had a Christmas-tree business on the side. Music figures strongly in her heritage; Swift's maternal grandmother was a professional opera singer, and both her paternal grandparents were musicians. She was named after singer-songwriter James Taylor (a notable fact considering the trajectory of her evolution in the music business). Swift demonstrated a penchant for performing very early in life, appearing frequently in local stage productions and entering karaoke contests. She was inspired by the career of child-sensation Leann Rimes, who influenced Swift's orientation toward country music. She was a child herself when her mother began taking her down to Nashville in a quest to get the attention of record-company executives. While lightning didn't strike immediately, Swift got sufficient encouragement in the form of development deals (which paid some recording costs in exchange for a future option to sign) and the family decided to relocate to Hendersonville, Tennessee, a suburb of Nashville, when she was 14 years old.

Between 2004 and 2006 Swift's career took shape as she began collaborating with professional songwriters, as well as forming a professional relationship with producer Nathan Chapman and executive Scott Borchetta, who was in the process of founding his own label, Big Machine Records. In 2006 Swift released her first single, "Tim McGraw," named after the country star she later befriended. The song, in which she expresses the hope that a former boyfriend will think of her whenever he hears a particular McGraw song, combines an aching sense of loss with a subtle sense of retribution, two qualities that would characterize Swift's work in years to come. A string of subsequent hits from her 2006 self-titled debut album followed, including "Teardrops on My Guitar" and "Our Song."

For an adolescent, Swift showed an unusually mature degree of discipline as a songwriter and recording artist, and extended it to other aspects of her career: relentless touring (generally expected of a country-music star) and assiduous attention to detail in terms of managing her career in arenas like social media (which was not). She was really the first country-music star of the digital age, selling millions of downloads in an industry only gradually making the transition from compact disc, and one who demonstrated a desire to connect with her fans reminiscent of the young Bruce Springsteen, an artist Swift is said to admire. (She is also a fan of a favorite of her mother's, the rock band Def Leppard, with whom she has performed.) These qualities, combined with skillful promotion, made her second album *Fearless* (2008) one of the most successful of the decade, spawning a whole new series of hit singles, among them "Love Story," "You Belong with Me," and the title track, which describes the hope and anxiety of a high-school freshman on the first day of school with disarming directness.

Swift was richly rewarded for her talents, not only in terms of phenomenal sales, but also in the bevy of awards she won for her work, among them a series of prestigious Country Music Awards (CMAs). But her career took an unusual turn in September of 2009 when she won a Video Music Award (VMA) from MTV for Best Female Video. Swift had just begun her speech acknowledging the honor when she was interrupted by rapper Kanye West, who took the microphone she was using away and congratulated her but opined that his friend Beyoncé really deserved the honor for her song "Single Ladies (Put a Ring on It)." Swift was stunned into silence and left the stage. When "Single Ladies" ultimately took the award for Video of the Year, a gracious Beyoncé coaxed Swift back to finish her remarks. Amid the widespread condemnation of West – President Barack Obama called him a "jackass" – Swift received sympathy and a new wave of attention.

In the fall of 2010, just as she was turning 21, Swift released her third album, *Speak Now*. In the liner notes, she described it as a concept album whose songs "are made up of words I didn't say when the moment was right in front of me. These songs are open letters. Each is written with a specific person in mind, telling them what I meant to tell them in person." Though her subjects are never identified explicitly, it's not hard to guess to whom they're directed. So, for example, the song "Innocent" seems addressed to West, expressing sympathy for his well-known inner turbulence and forgiving him for his excess. Another, less charitable, song, "Dear John," is addressed to former paramour John Mayer – the bluesy style of guitar playing alone is a dead giveaway. In one way or another, Swift's well-chronicled romantic life had always been the source of most of her music, and this album is no exception.

That said, *Speak Now* represented an important developmental leap forward. One reason is that Swift wrote all the songs on the album herself (though she no doubt got input from Chapman, among others). Another is that the record marked a bold foray in a new musical direction: *Speak Now* is at heart a rock record. To be sure, Swift's country heritage continued to be evident, nowhere more so than on the hit single "Mean," which was marked by bluegrass elements. (The song, a cheerfully acidic rant, was directed toward a critic who complained that she couldn't sing.) But a bona fide heavy-metal element was evident on a number of tracks, in particular the catty "Better than Revenge," in which she scalds a rival for stealing her boyfriend. But the best showcase for Swift's command of a rock idiom is the shimmering title track, echoing the early Beatles in its catchy hook and hand-clapping. The song, almost cinematic, is reminiscent of the 1967 movie *The Graduate*, except that this time it's the girl, not the guy, who rescues her true love from the altar of matrimonial disaster.

Perhaps the most important dimension of Swift's growth in *Speak Now* is a new sophistication in her songwriting. The great appeal of her early records was their emotional simplicity (albeit a deceptive one in that such an effect was achieved through a strong sense of songcraft, something that often involves subtraction rather than addition). Swift's previous hit "You Belong with Me" is a schoolgirl's lament that she can't compete with a cheerleader for the heart of a boy; the cliché-riddled "Love Story" works not so much because the imagery is original but rather because you believe that the adolescent who invokes Romeo and Juliet is living a romantic drama for the first time. In *Speak Now*, however, the conflicts are more recognizably adult ones. In the album's opening track, "Mine," the narrator tells her boyfriend, "you made a rebel of a careless man's careful daughter," a line that manages to encapsulate a lonely childhood and suggest how liberating having a partner can be. The very exultant intensity of "Mine" seems to derive from how close a call, how truly unexpected, such an outcome was – and is. "Do you believe it?" she asks toward the end of the song, the joy in her voice mingling with surprise.

In "The Story of Us," the surprise is that a love story ends not happily ever after, but miserably. The narrator, who believed she was part of a blessed union, instead finds herself locked in a stubborn struggle with a man who defies her script about the way a relationship should work. Another song marked by hard-driving guitars, "The Story of Us" derives much of its power from the exasperation in Swift's voice – and the abrupt way the song severs at the end.

Speak Now was another triumph for Swift, selling over a million copies in the first week of its release in October of 2010, and 4 million copies by year's end. In the five years following the release of her first album she sold over 20 million records – this at a time when record sales have dropped sharply amid a global recession and the upheaval caused by digital music – and was cited by the *Guinness Book of World Records* for scoring 11 consecutive singles on the *Billboard* pop charts. If one were to assume she never made another hit record, her place in the annals of pop music history would be secure.

Swift followed *Speak Now* in the fall of 2012 with *Red*, another successful album (it too sold over a million copies in the first week of its release). *Red* showed her continuing to move decisively away from country toward rock – and, above all, staking out a place at the center of pop music with hook-laden songs like "We Are Never Ever Getting Back Together." The clanging guitars and soaring vocals of

"State of Grace" seem far closer to the Ireland of U2 and the Cranberries than the Nashville of Tim McGraw; "Trouble" owes more to Rihanna than to Faith Hill. Though a mandolin showed up here and there (and is likely to remain part of her musical palette for the rest of her career), Swift has come of age as a rocker. Musical style aside, the promise and peril of romance continued to be the central theme of her work; one of the curiosities of Swift's career is that her musical development seems to outstrip the thematic dimensions of her songs.

Indeed, there are those who wonder how much staying power she has. Certainly, the history of pop singers, female and otherwise, is littered with sensations whose youthful work remained memorable but whose later work has, rightly or wrongly, largely been forgotten. But she has also shown herself to be an apt pupil in the ways of pop music, and made the transition to adulthood with relative grace. Perhaps her fate will be closer to that of Joni Mitchell, the singer-songwriter she expressed an interest in portraying in a forthcoming movie, whose body of work has won her generations of admirers. At the moment, at least, there are plenty of people who are eager to grow old Swiftly.

Questions to consider

1. How did Taylor Swift's personal background shape her career?
2. What elements make *Speak Now* a rock album? To what extent do you regard it as a departure? What do you see as her place on the contemporary music scene?
3. How do you view her prospects? Consider the careers of other artists who enjoyed early success, from Michael Jackson to Justin Bieber, in evaluating them.

Further Reading

For an overview of how the record industry emerged, an excellent place to begin is David L. Morton, *Sound Recording: The Life History of a Technology* (Baltimore, MD: The Johns Hopkins University Press, 2006). Histories of popular music tend to be organized by genre. For a general overview, see Larry Starr and Christopher Waterman, *American Popular Music: From Minstrelsy to MP3* (3rd ed., New York: Oxford University Press, 2009).

On the Tin Pan Alley tradition, see Philip Furia, *The Poets of Tin Pan Alley: A History of America's Great Lyricists* (New York: Oxford University Press, 1992). Furia is also the author, with Michael Lasser, of *America's Songs: The Stories Behind the Songs of Broadway, Hollywood and the Tin Pan Alley* (New York: Routledge, 2006).

The classic study of blues in the United States is a book by LeRoi Jones (Amiri Baraka): *Blues People: Negro Music in White America* (1965; New York: Harper Perennial, 1999). Lawrence Levine provides some excellent analysis in his chapter on the blues in *Black Culture and Consciousness: Afro-American Folk Thought in Slavery and Freedom* (1977; New York: Oxford University Press, 2007). On gospel, see *We'll Understand It By and By: Pioneering African American Gospel Composers*, edited by Bernice Johnson Reagon (Washington, DC: Smithsonian Institution Press, 1992).

Good histories of jazz include Ted Gioia, *The History of Jazz* (2nd ed., New York: Oxford University Press, 2011). For a primer on how to appreciate the genre, see John Szwed, *Jazz 101: A Complete Guide to Learning and Loving Jazz* (New York: Hyperion, 2000). On country music, the standard history has long been Bill Malone, *Country Music U.S.A.* (3rd ed., 1968; Austin: University of Texas Press, 2010). For the role of cities in the birth of the genre, see Patrick Huber, *Linthead Stomp: The Creation of Country Music in the Piedmont South* (Chapel Hill: University of North Carolina Press, 2008). On disco, see Alice Echols, *Hot Stuff: Disco and the Remaking of American Culture* (New York: Norton, 2010). The best history, hands down, of rap music and culture is Jeff Chang, *Can't Stop, Won't Stop: A History of the Hip-Hop Generation* (New York: Picador, 2005). See also Tricia Rose, *Black Noise: Rap Music and Black Culture in Contemporary America* (Middletown, CT: Wesleyan University Press, 1994), and *The Hip-Hop Wars: What We Talk about When We Talk About Hip-Hop – and Why It Matters* (New York: Basic Books, 2008).

African American studies scholar Michael Eric Dyson has also written extensively about hip-hop; see in particular *You Know What I Mean? Reflections on Hip-Hop* (New York: Basic Books, 2010).

Though now dated, the various books on rock music published by *Rolling Stone* magazine contain some of the best writing on the emergence of the genre. See in particular *The Rolling Stone Illustrated History of Rock & Roll*, edited by Anthony DeCurtis, James Henke, and Holly George-Warren (1977; 3rd ed., New York: Random House, 1992), and Ed Ward, Geoffrey Stokes, and Ken Tucker, *Rock of Ages: The Rolling Stone History of Rock & Roll* (New York: Summit, 1986). Glenn Altschuler gives a good rendition of the emergence of rock from a social-history perspective in *All Shook Up: How Rock 'n' Roll Changed America* (New York: Oxford University Press, 2003). For more on this angle, see Michael T. Bertrand, *Race, Rock and Elvis* (Urbana: University of Illinois Press, 2004).

Michael Jackson has been one of the most commented upon figures in media history, though the overall tenor of the discourse is not particularly incisive. His autobiography *Moonwalk* (New York: Doubleday, 1988) is probably the most authoritative point of departure, though it's not a particularly revealing self-portrait. Nelson George's *Thriller: The Musical Life of Michael Jackson* (New York: Da Capo Press, 2010) was rushed into print at the time of Jackson's death, and it shows. But there are nuggets of insight in the book, which focuses on the making of the album.

Taylor Swift's life and work is still largely in the realm of journalism. Probably the best available account currently available is music journalist Andrew Vaughn's *Taylor Swift* (New York: Sterling, 2011).

7

Weaving the Web
The Emergence of the Internet

Figure 7.1 CALCULATED ORDER Inventors J. Presper Eckert and J.W. Mauchly work on the Electronic Numerical Integrator and Computer (ENIAC), January 1946. The foundations of the modern digital world have their roots in government-sponsored research during World War II. (© Bettmann Archives/Corbis)

A Short History of the Modern Media, First Edition. Jim Cullen.
© 2014 Jim Cullen. Published 2014 by John Wiley & Sons, Ltd.

Overview

THOUGH WE can't know how the past will be seen in the future, it's hard to believe that the period between the late nineteenth and late twentieth centuries will not widely be viewed as a crucible – perhaps *the* crucible – in the formation of the modern media. Sound recording, film projection, radio and television broadcasting: these were experienced as revolutionary developments for the people who witnessed their emergence, and each continued to play a vibrant role in the nation's cultural life even as they were elbowed out of the limelight by the next, much in the way that print culture and the theater managed to survive, even flourish, as old-fashioned sources of a good time. To some extent, new media swallowed aspects of the old in the process of their own formation; radio journalism, for instance, built upon the practices of newspapers while capitalizing on radio's ability to deliver information over the airwaves. Television captured the simultaneous appeal of sound and image the way film did, but fostered a new sense of intimacy and convenience that led to genres like the sitcom (refurbished from radio). This cycle – perhaps more accurately, this spiral – characterized the interplay between culture and technology between the 1890s and the 1990s.

In some crucial respects, the pattern I'm describing here holds for the emergence of the most recent and most powerful media innovation in American history: that complex set of technical conventions we know by the shorthand of "the Internet." Like other once-new media, the Internet was a creature of what came before it. More specifically, its trajectory proceeded down tracks first laid by radio, particularly in terms of its military applications and gradual commercialization. The Internet was also like its predecessors in the way its most attractive features absorbed much of what came before: today we use it to read books, listen to radio programs, watch movies and television shows, or play music from a record collection.

In at least one crucial respect, however, the Internet represents a departure from its media predecessors. The general tendency in the twentieth century for the production and dissemination of media content was centralization. Many of the most distinctive cultural phenomena of modern times – minstrelsy, jazz, westerns – typically originated on the literal or figurative edges of American life. They only became popular culture once they were filtered through concentrated power centers like New York, Hollywood, or Nashville, whose publishing houses, studios, or stations had the power, whether in terms of manufacturing, distribution, or publicity, to pipeline content across the country through a tightly controlled commercial infrastructure.

Though its uniqueness is sometimes exaggerated, the Internet was in some respects subtly but crucially different in this regard: transmission is less often a matter of *broadcasting* from a single point of transmission than chains of *dispersion* across decentralized communication channels. Sometimes this information is appealing to highly specific audiences, albeit global ones, such as Web sites devoted to arcane subjects or dead celebrities. One also sees it in "the long tail" whereby retailers can profit in their ability to deliver a large and varied stock through modern methods of distribution (e.g., Amazon.com's ability to sell just about any book in print). At the same time, the dispersal of information can also work another way, in that it achieves a kind of gradual mass that may well exceed that of broadcasting – to use a perhaps unfortunate disease metaphor, information goes "viral."

As we've seen, radio was also a highly decentralized affair in the early decades of its existence. The fact that radio communication was eventually concentrated in relatively few hands – a tendency that has only intensified in the twenty-first century – should serve as a reminder that there's no natural law to prevent this from happening to the Internet, either. In fact, some observers believe that it already has. Information may want to be free, as the fondest champions of its decentralized, non-commercial origins like to say. But that doesn't mean it always will be. But before we can imagine, much less shape, the future, it's best to review the tracks of the past.

We sometimes think of the Internet as a virtual reality, especially because so many of its products seem to exist nowhere but on a screen. In some sense this is true, the acres of server farms of a Google or a facebook stationed around the globe notwithstanding. But the origins of the medium rest on the arrival of a long-imagined piece of hardware that finally became a reality in the first half of the twentieth century: the electronically powered computer. Though we now think of computers as ubiquitous objects, so pervasive that we barely notice them – or so small that we can't see them – the first computers were anything but virtual. They were gigantic machines whose presence was a source of awe.

But before that, computers were not things: they were people. The term referred to individuals, many of them women, who did the math of everyday commercial life. Managing weekly payrolls, calculating monthly premiums, drawing up annual budgets: this was the work of "computers."

The dream of replacing people with machines had begun long before that, however. It can be dated all the way back to the invention of the abacus in ancient Mesopotamia. In the early seventeenth century Scottish mathematician John Napier developed a device known as the Napier Rod (popularly known as Napier's Bones), which simplified the work of performing complex calculations. In the mid-seventeenth century the French mathematician and philosopher Blaise Pascal invented the first adding machine. Later refinements of this idea culminated in devices that used wheels and keys to keep track of numbers, and helped bring about the related technological invention of the cash register, which was developed by American mechanic James Ritty in 1879 and led to the creation of the National Cash Register Corporation (NCR), which remains a corporate colossus to this day. Adding machines became standard operating equipment in many nineteenth-century businesses. They were also important for organizations like railroads, which collected and processed vast amounts of information to manage train travel, and the US government, which collected census data.

One especially significant figure in the evolution of modern computing is the American statistician Herman Hollerith. Hollerith developed a system of punch cards to perform calculations at the end of the nineteenth century, variations on which would be used

244 THE EMERGENCE OF THE INTERNET

well into the twentieth. One crucial aspect of Hollerith's work involved the transmission of electrical signals, part of a larger transition from machine-assisted manual calculations to truly automated information processing that came to be known as analog computing.

By the early twentieth century, then, computers were becoming facts of life in American commerce. A series of corporate mergers, acquisitions, and executive machinations among adding-machine and analog-computing companies resulted in the 1924 creation of International Business Machines (IBM), which under the leadership of executive Thomas J. Watson became one of the great success stories of corporate capitalism. Over the course of the next generation, IBM led the way in the development of increasingly elaborate machines that could perform ever more complex calculations. Moreover, they could increasingly perform multiple calculations at a time – the pivotal innovation of parallel processing at the heart of what it means for a machine to be a modern computer. These early computers were often enormous pieces of engineering, with lots of sensitive moving parts that occupied large rooms and required delicate management.

As important as it was in the development of modern computing, corporate capitalism didn't really give the world the Internet, however. The United States government did, drawing heavily on academic expertise. The government did so not as a civilian enterprise, but rather as part of war-making machinery. Computers were vital to the processes of code-making and -breaking, for example. They had other uses as well. During World War II, the US government financed the work of University of Pennsylvania team J. Presper Eckert and John W. Mauchly, who developed the Electrical Numerical Integrator and Computer (ENIAC), for the purpose of performing ballistics calculations for artillery, among other tasks. Work on the ENIAC was not completed until the war was over; Presper and Mauchly capitalized on their creation to found a company that developed the Universal Automatic Computer, or UNIVAC, which represented an important milestone because this machine could not only perform calculations, but also store information.

One significant step in expanding information-storage capacity was the development of digital computing, which involved translating a particular piece of information into a string of numbers composed of ones and zeroes. This new method, in contrast to traditional analog computing, which required much more precision, allowed for a vast expansion of computing power. The importance of this new approach is suggested by the way we sometimes refer to modern life as "the digital age," which has shaped the way we watch movies, listen to music, and do a great many other things.

The digital age emerged in the shadow of a more ominous one: the atomic age. Wartime use of computer technology was an important part of the Manhattan Project, which led to the creation of the two nuclear bombs dropped on Japan in 1945. But it was the implications of atomic warfare even more than the bombs themselves that proved instrumental in the creation of the Internet, and the pivotal figure here was Massachusetts Institute of Technology engineer Vannevar Bush. Bush invented a machine called the differential analyzer, an important landmark in computer development back in the 1920s. He did a good deal of theoretical speculation on how information might be stored and accessed quickly to assist government policymakers in wartime, and the organizational framework he developed would be referred to, and built upon, frequently in the second half of the twentieth century by the designers of the Internet.

Of particular concern to Bush and other planners was the US government's ability to act decisively and responsibly in the event of a nuclear war, a threat that became all too real after the Soviet Union acquired atomic weaponry in 1949. In 1946, the US government created the Research and Development (RAND) Corporation, which grappled with such problems. It was followed in 1958 by the Advanced Research Projects Agency, or ARPA. (The agency was renamed the Defense Advanced Research Projects Agency, or DARPA, in 1969.) In the early 1960s a government researcher named Paul Baran focused on how computers might coordinate activities with each other amid the likely communications breakdown that would accompany a nuclear strike. Working with other researchers,

Baran developed a method that came to be known as "packet switching," in which messages sent between two destinations in a connected series of computers – a web, as it were – would be broken up into small pieces upon their departure and sent through different routes before being reassembled at their destination. This networked approach reduced the risk that the destruction of any one channel of communication would sever military planners' access to information.

Though there were many intermediate steps in the process, the concept of packet switching between circuits of inter-network connected computers – abbreviated as the "Internet" – would be central to the development of one of the most important innovations of the last half-century: electronic mail, or e-mail. Like the traditional US post office (now known as "snail" mail for its relatively glacial pace), electronic mail is a delivery service. Somebody writes a message and transmits it via packet-switching to an electronic storage queue known as a "mailbox." In 1982 ARPA developed a simple mail-transfer protocol (SMTP) to simplify the process, which included the use of the "at symbol" – @ – to route messages. Later refinements to this system of communication would lead to instant messaging and chat rooms, in which exchanges are virtually simultaneous. E-mail is perhaps less central than it used to be, but, like the US mail, continues to have vital uses.

Baran's work with other technologists, among them another network theorist, J.C.R. Licklider, demonstrated the power of the US government as a source of technological and social innovation in the mid-twentieth century. Their work had significant civilian applications, particularly in the corporate sector. Computing remained big, in every sense of the term. The machines were too large and complex to be widely owned and used; indeed, most businesses that used computers rented them for short periods of time to solve specific problems. The next chapter in the evolution of the Internet involved shrinking computers down to a manageable size – and cost – so that they could be mass-distributed. The crucial invention was the transistor.

A transistor is a device consisting of a tiny piece of material, initially germanium but later silicon – as in Silicon Valley, the region in greater San Francisco where many are designed – in which a series of electrical connections can be made, like a toy brick that can be used to build a larger structure. Depending on how they're manipulated, these transistor connections may facilitate or impede an electrical current; hence their name "semiconductors." Transistors were first developed to replace the liquid-filled tubes on televisions and radios. Just as a group of semiconductors makes a transistor, a group of transistors is known as an integrated circuit (IC), or "chip." The IC was first patented by coinventors Jack Kilby and Robert Noyce of Texas Instruments in 1958. (Kilby is also the inventor of the hand-held electronic calculator.) In the half-century that followed, transistors increased in power even as they decreased in size, to the point that some today are microscopic. This, in turn, allowed computers to become smaller and cheaper – to make them, in fact, household devices that could be owned and operated by an individual.

And it's here that we find an important shift in the dynamics of this story. For much of the twentieth century, the development of computers and information transmission was conducted on a large institutional basis, whether the institution in question was that of government or business. With the advent of transistors, however, the game changed: now it was individuals and small groups of people, often operating outside conventional academic or business channels, who became the locus of innovation. Like the radio hams of the early twentieth century, these often geeky people, known collectively as hackers, made computers – and communication between computers – literally a matter of fun and games. Perusing technical manuals, magazines like *Popular Mechanics*, and conversing with each other, hackers began building improvised computers out of transistors, sharing their insights and building on word-of-mouth innovations. Chip manufacturers like Intel, and companies like Radio Shack, began selling plans, components, or relatively simple computers on a retail basis that could be manipulated or recombined for any number of purposes. These machines, like the widely hailed Mark-8 or Altair computers, did not resemble those we see today – they lacked keyboards and screens for example, because their primary function remained mathematical. But they were evolving quickly.

Among the most creative of these hackers were a pair of men known as "the two Steves": Steve Wozniak and Steve Jobs, who founded a company in a Silicon Valley garage they dubbed Apple. One of their early creations, the Apple II – which *did* have a keyboard and a screen – represented a great leap forward. Apple and its competitors also began including simple word-processing programs in their machines, which initiated the process of transforming a computer from a tool whose primary functions were mathematical to one that could be used in any number of domains in everyday life.

Recognizing the vast appeal of the personal computer – and the threat it posed to its traditional business model – IBM rushed its own model, the PC, into the market in 1981. In ways it couldn't fully anticipate, IBM's entry into what was now a technology race had significant ramifications. Because it wished to tap the entrepreneurial energy of hacker culture and achieve acceptance in this influential demographic, the IBM PC used an open architecture that could be replicated or adapted by other designers, like COMPAQ or Dell, whose machines were known as "clones."

Ironically, it was around this time that Apple computers, whose design and features were always widely admired – many of which were first developed by Xerox at its Palo Alto Research Center before that company decided to get out of the computer business – became increasingly proprietary. Apple leapfrogged to the front of the pack in 1984 with the premier of its Macintosh computer, which deployed graphic interfaces such as folders, trashcans, and windows to make what in fact were highly complex operations seem as simple as working on a literal desktop. Apple's Macintosh became for computers at the end of the twentieth century what Ford's Model T had been for cars at the beginning of that century: not necessarily the cheapest or most advanced machine, but one which proved versatile, beloved, and vastly influential for millions of users who adopted it with real affection. One feature of the Macintosh was an elegant piece of programming for connecting data known as HyperCard; though Apple didn't do much with it, HyperCard proved to be a bridge to a similar program known as hypertext, a building block for the World Wide Web (see below).

Yet even as IBM and Apple were fighting for control of the personal-computer business, the nature of the industry was changing. Somewhat unwittingly, it was IBM that pointed the way. In its haste to get the PC to market, the company licensed the work of a Harvard dropout named Bill Gates and his partner Paul Allen, whose company, Microsoft, created a piece of software known as an operating system to run IBM machines. (Eventually, Microsoft would imitate Apple's Xerox imitation in creating the system we know as Windows.) Significantly, Microsoft's terms with IBM left the company free to offer its operating system to clone manufacturers, which by the early 1990s made Microsoft the dominant power in the entire computer businesses. Like film pioneers such as Thomas Edison, who paid far more attention to film projection than to the content of the movies themselves (which is where the real money proved to be), it was ground-level hackers, not corporate-minded chieftains, who proved to be the hinge of history. Software, not hardware, was king.

It was at this point that the game shifted once again. As computers became household objects – as, indeed, transistors made it possible to pack tiny computers into cars, appliances, and any number of gadgets, particularly cell phones – the individual machines themselves became less important than the connections between them. As we've seen, connectivity was at the heart of computer innovation as early as World War II. Over the course of ensuing decades, DARPA's computer network became increasingly large and more complex, drawing more people into its web of communication. Universities, many of which had defense ties, represented an important segment of this traffic, which began to go in other directions than military or strictly scientific use. Until the late 1970s, the scope of this Internet was relatively narrow, not only because of technical difficulties, but also because Bell Telephone, which held a monopoly, made it difficult, if not impossible, to connect computers via phone lines, the most obvious means to expand the domain of data transmission. A series of antitrust decisions, however, broke Bell's power, decentralizing the phone business in the 1980s. Meanwhile, the diffusion of DARPA's transmission-control protocol and Internet protocol (TCP/IP) accelerated, along with the development of so-called local area network (LAN) systems for smaller, more geographically centered clusters of computers, like those of private companies. In the early 1990s, the government eased restrictions on commercial Internet activity. The nation as a whole was gaining exposure to what was becoming a vast communications infrastructure – in other words, a new mass medium.

The fact that such a medium existed, however, didn't mean people could easily access it. A key link in bridging individuals to the Internet involved the dissemination of devices known as modems, which connected computers with phone lines, allowing data to travel in a relatively conventional manner. Modems had been around a long time before they became household devices; once they did, connectivity to the Internet exploded.

If data was the passenger, and the modem was the car, there was still the question of the roads by which to reach the new information superhighway. E-mail was one, and to this day remains an important component of all Internet traffic. File-transfer protocol (FTP), a system by which bodies of data could be moved between machines, was another. But such thoroughfares worked best for those who had good travel directions and knew exactly where they were going. Maps were hard to come by. One source of help were Internet service providers (ISPs). Among the best-known were Prodigy (a joint venture between IBM and Sears) and America Online (AOL), which assisted users by offering a portal with lots of signage through which they could find presorted channels of information like news, weather, and shopping.

But the best-paved road to the Internet came from British computer scientist Tim Berners-Lee, based at the European Organization for Nuclear Research (CERN) in Geneva. Berners-Lee developed a system of instructions, written in hypertext markup language (HTML), to link an individual computer and a source of information. This link took the form of a hypertext transfer protocol (HTTP) that included a "universal resource locator" (URL). The first part of a URL, the letters "www," is an abbreviated reference to the overarching system in which a hypertext transfer protocol operates: what Berners-Lee called "the World Wide Web." It was now possible for a relative novice to locate information on the Internet with a relatively simple address and domain (such as .edu for educational institutions, or .com for commercial ones), rather than a complicated string of numbers or instructions that required technical literacy. So for example, in the URL http://www.ecfs.org, the "http" is the hypertext transfer protocol, the "www" refers to the Web, the "ecfs" identifies the address (the school where I teach), and the .org indicates that the domain is a (non-profit) institution. Rather than rely on America Online or some such ISP, you could find your way to a destination on your own once you knew the URL.

Being able to find what you were looking for was one thing – a big thing, but only one thing. There was also the issue of how to navigate one's way through a growing ocean of data available when you *didn't* – a practice we have come to know as "surfing." One tool that made this possible (the surf*board*, if you will) was a type of computer program we have come to know as the search engine. Among the first search engines was one developed at the University of Minnesota known as Gopher, named in honor of the school's mascot (it was also widely regarded as a form of shorthand for "go for"). Gopher was popular among hackers in the early 1990s, but was quickly outpaced by a series of competitors like Lynx and Yahoo! The reigning champion of search engines is Google, founded in 1998 by a pair of Stanford undergraduates, Sergey Brin and Larry Page. So pervasive has been their success that the term "google" has entered common parlance as a verb to denote Internet-searching, much in the way "kleenex" has become synonymous with paper tissues.

The other great innovation in Web surfing was the development of the browser, a computer application we typically experience as a box at the top of a screen in which we can type or paste a URL. The breakthrough here was provided by Marc Andreeson, a 21-year-old undergraduate at the University of Illinois (one more illustration of the way the computer revolution was wrought by kids), who in 1992 developed a program called Mosaic that allowed users to browse through lists of data on a particular subject. Andreeson commercialized his invention the following year as Netscape, which for a while was the most popular browser on the Internet. Netscape's supremacy was contested by Microsoft, which, having missed the Internet boat, tried to recover its dominance by installing its own browser, the Internet Explorer, as part of every operating system it sold, using strong-armed tactics with computer manufacturers and retailers that were later declared illegal. By the early twenty-first century, however, browsers like Firefox (an open-source tool developed by the Mozilla foundation/corporation), Safari (an Apple product), and Chrome (Google's entry into the sweepstakes) had become about as widespread.

The last major piece in the emergence of a recognizably modern Internet experience was the replacement of traditional telephone lines as the primary source of computer connections with better alternatives. Though relatively cheap, phone lines were slow and highly limited in terms of the volume and type of information they could carry. Phone service was increasingly replaced by integrated service digital network (ISDN) lines, typically offered by phone companies; digital subscriber lines (DSL), typically offered by cable companies; and wireless communication networks, typically offered by both. Until this point, most Internet traffic took the form of text and graphics, which were almost too cheap to meter. Now, however, music, photographs, and video, all of which took up more volume in traveling across space, could be moved efficiently.

Up until now, my discussion of the Internet has been almost wholly conducted in terms of technology. As such, that makes this chapter a little different from its predecessors, which are at least as attentive to the cultural effects of a new medium as they are to technological ones. To a great extent, this reflects the fact that, relatively speaking, the Internet is still new. Movies, radio, and television all experienced decades of technical experimentation, innovation, and adaptation before they assumed forms that we recognize as stable and modern. (About 35 years lapsed between the first kinetoscopes in the 1890s and sound movies in the 1920s, and it would be another decade before color became common.) When viewed in this light, the Internet is still in its relative infancy – or, at any rate, adolescence. The full force of its cultural impact may well be largely ahead of us.

And yet that impact was discernible from the start. Perhaps the most subtle, yet striking, way the Internet has affected collective consciousness is the spatial metaphors we use to describe our interactions with it: geographic ones. We speak of "visiting" or "going" to "locations" in trips that take place without doing more than lifting a finger. Many media have been prized for the way they have conquered time and space. But no medium has been more powerful in this regard than the Internet has; the "World Wide" part of the Web is no mere hyperbole.

At first, though, the Internet seemed most potent in the way it provided new ways of doing familiar things. One of the most obvious examples is shopping. The Internet in effect recreated the mail-order firm, in which people could order items from a catalog and have them delivered by snail mail. One of the most important – and, eventually, hugely successful – exemplars of e-commerce is Amazon.com, founded in 1995 as an online bookstore that has since become the greatest retailer in American history since the rise of Sears & Roebuck in the nineteenth century. While online shopping appeared to have some initial advantages over traditional retailing, particularly in sparing merchants the tremendous overhead costs of operating an actual brick-and-mortar building, it took a while for consumers to get acculturated to practices like giving their credit-card numbers online, accepting the delayed gratification (and costs) involved in shipping, and other considerations. Such factors continue to give traditional merchants important advantages that keep them in business. But wider selection, lower prices, improved shipping options, and 24-hour convenience have established e-commerce as a major factor in the US economy.

The Internet also provided a new means of delivering journalism. The emphasis here needs to be on *delivering*; like early radio, the online world was not so much a *source* of news reporting as it was an *outlet* for it. From a fairly early stage, the nation's newspapers established an online presence, typically free, whereby readers could access news stories. This has begun to change, gradually, as more and more people get their news from other means than paper, with important ramifications for the future of news organizations generally. In one way or another, users of the Internet for news are going to have to start paying for reporting to survive. A news outlet like the *Huffington Post*, which was launched in 2005 largely as an aggregator of news from other sources, has gradually dipped into generating its own content. So have the Web-based side of major news organizations like the Cable News Network (CNN) and MSNBC, a joint enterprise started by Microsoft and the National Broadcasting Company (NBC) that launched in 1996 (it became solely owned and operated by NBC in 2012).

While the Internet was allowing people another means to access traditional media, it was also subtly changing those media in the process. In the case of journalism, for example, individual stories became the coin of the realm in the news business rather than a particular publication or TV network. Connections to stories were distributed far beyond their original source, since computer files are more portable than the traditional newspaper clipping or TV or radio news story. Another example of such portability can be found in the music business. The advent of digital downloads has shifted the business away from albums, or even particular artists, in favor of individual songs. Still another example is the publishing business, where the Internet is effectively destroying the once-profitable genre of reference books like dictionaries, encyclopedias, and travel guides by making information immediately available and regularly updated in ways that bound books simply can't match. (See "Document Study / Wikipedia: The wisdom of crowds.") E-books have also revitalized the market for certain genres of print, like short stories and essay-length non-fiction, which could not be profitably published in hard-copy form. Over the course of the next few decades, the face of the book business may well undergo a transformation greater than any since the invention of moveable type in the fifteenth century.

These are the ways in which the Internet is reshaping that which we consider familiar. But it was also apparent from the start that the Internet would look – and, increasingly, sound – a little different from anything that came before it. The most obvious manifestation of this is that distinctively Internet-centric phenomenon we know as the Web site. Strictly speaking, this is something I should have mentioned or described long before now in this chapter, probably around the time I was talking about search engines and browsers, since the end result of using such tools would typically be to arrive at a Web site. I've deferred that particular discussion until now because I wanted to cover the technology before I got to the culture, but also to make the point that I could get away with such an omission: unlike a minstrel show or a radio serial, a Web site is so familiar to you that it needs no introduction or explanation. Indeed, you probably imagined or saw a Web site as I described the goal of a Google or Netscape search without actually ever realizing I was avoiding using the term. So it is that we come to understand some things without ever formally being told what they are.

Web sites are distinctive, and uniquely adaptive, formats for the presentation and organization of information online. At the most basic level, a Web site is little more than a database – a discrete body of information that a person can access at will (or upon entering a password). The question has always been a matter of how to organize that information. The answer goes back to the hypertext (originally HyperCard) part of the HTML language. In effect, Web sites make information three-dimensional, in that "behind" selected pieces of data like text or a photo, one can "click" on a particular "link" which in turn leads to other Web sites in ways that can branch out in multiple directions. In this regard, a Web site is a more horizontal experience than print, which is typically read from top to bottom. The print analogy nevertheless holds firm: one speaks of a particular desktop presentation of a Web site as a "page."

In the opening decade of the twenty-first century, Internet Web sites became more dynamic: rather than a fixed body of information to be accessed at any given time, they were updated with increasing frequency. They also became more interactive, developing the capacity to foster discourse among visitors. Creating, refining, and developing Web sites has increasingly become a specialty in its own right, one that can be done by individuals with relatively little formal training, as well as those with substantial professional experience.

But Web sites were never the sole feature of the Web. Another much beloved activity is game-playing. The origins of home computer games date back to the Atari Corporation's 1970s game "Pong," a form of computer table tennis played by hooking up a console to a television, which would be regarded as laughably primitive today. Over the course of the 1980s, computer games, like Pac-Man, increasingly approximated the experience of stand-alone arcade games of the kind found in amusement-park, restaurant, hotel, and other lobbies. Early personal computers could not store all the data necessary to play such games. Instead, the information was stored in a variety of formats, eventually that of a compact disc similar to that used for recorded music. But the proliferation of ISDN lines, coupled with the growing storage capacity for new personal computers, allowed gaming to migrate online, where it has become increasingly elaborate in its ability to resemble real life (sometimes, to critics who lament their violent sounds and imagery, regrettably so). Much more than traditional games, online gaming allows for a degree of interactivity – and design – that has made it an important form of popular culture in its own right. It has also become a gratifyingly collective experience, in which multiple players can participate at one time from multiple locations, and in which communities of shared passions thrive. Today new games are premiered, reviewed, updated, and discussed with a level of engagement and sophistication one associates with movies or publishing. Which perhaps isn't surprising, since the revenues games generate now exceed those of the movie business.

To a great degree, the success of particular Web sites (like that of Cable News Network) or games (like those of the Electronic Arts Corporation) reflect the degree to which the Internet had become commodified by the start of the twenty-first century. Hacker culture had been resistant – at times downright hostile – to the idea of the Web as a commercial enterprise. A similar ethos had marked early radio; as with radio, however, corporate forces became ascendant. Like radio and television, the Web increasingly relied on advertising as a source of revenue. Indeed, a company like Google, which most users think of as a search engine, in essence sells eyeballs to advertisers, promising them highly tailored audiences based on the information it gathers every time a person makes a search. Such companies justify their actions to consumers by emphasizing "personalization," which allows them to filter and tailor information based on past usage and demographic information.

Actually, the fact that such information is often freely given by users, or unwittingly captured every time a user visits a Web destination (thanks to pieces of software called "cookies"), has given rise to increased privacy concerns. For the moment, however, corporate interests have managed to prevent systematic consumer protections from taking root in the United States, unlike in Europe, where privacy, not exploitation, is the default setting in determining whether or not information can be used for commercial or government purposes. Such issues are particularly pronounced in the case of social networks, and are likely to remain so for some time. (See "Genre Study / Shared exchanges: Social media.")

Anxiety about the Internet goes far beyond privacy concerns. Stories about unscrupulous hackers posting plans on how to build bombs, criminals stealing identities and committing financial fraud, and terrorists coordinating surprise attacks have become proverbial. It seems likely that the next major war will have a significant Internet component, as combatants seek to disrupt their enemy governments' military as well as civilian infrastructures. Programmed drones will take the place of human soldiers (as indeed they already do in places like Afghanistan), and casualties are likely to include vanished savings accounts as well as shattered limbs.

Such concerns notwithstanding, there was a growing perception in the first decade of the twenty-first century that the intensification of user engagement with the Internet – now globally measured in billions – and its capacity to handle more traffic were moving the medium into a more pervasive phase of its existence. The ability to send and receive such data wirelessly using cell-phone technology was particularly important in the advent of newer "smartphones" that allowed users to do many more things than place calls or send text. In effect, the Web was migrating beyond the mainframe, personal, or laptop computer into new domains, among them tablets, e-readers, and other devices. This series of changes has come be known collectively, if a bit vaguely, as "Web 2.0."

The pervasiveness factor was one dimension of Web 2.0. Another was the latest chapter in the struggle between the entrepreneurial individual and the large institution that has long marked the history of the mass media. As we've seen, the success of products like the IBM PC was to a great degree a function of their open architecture, which allowed tinkerers of various kinds to carve out new gadgets and applications of their own. A company like Apple, long marked by a penchant for control, nevertheless tapped such energies as it developed products like its fabled iPhone® and iPad®, allowing entrepreneurs to sell discrete applications for their products through its online store. Another manifestation of this do-it-yourself ethos was the proliferation of Web logs, or blogs, in which individuals or groups maintained a running record or commentary. Perhaps the most powerful – certainly the most commented upon – manifestation of the Web 2.0 was the advent of social networking, represented paradigmatically by facebook. (See "Genre Study / Shared exchanges: Social media.")

Meanwhile, even as the current Internet grows and diversifies, work on its successor – known as Internet2 – has been under way since 1996. A non-profit consortium consisting of dozens of government and hundreds of educational institutions is literally and figuratively laying the groundwork for our communications future.

Not even its architects can be certain exactly what it will mean. Computers inside our bodies? Our lives recorded as we live them? Something else we can scarcely imagine?

One thing's for sure: the future is virtually here.

Questions to consider

1. How does the Internet resemble earlier media in the way it emerged, and in what it does? How is it unique?
2. Describe some of the important milestones in the evolution of the computer. Pay particular attention to the role of the government, and what it suggests about its relationship with the private sector.
3. Why were hackers so important in the development of computers and the Internet? What did they need to flourish? What did they contribute that institutions could not?
4. Assess the role of the Internet primarily in terms of the way it allows people to do things they've always done (shop, read, etc.) in new ways, or in terms of the way it's fostered entirely new experiences (like social networking). Which strikes you as more important?
5. How significant do you regard the distinction between Web 1.0 and Web 2.0? Where do you imagine the Internet2 is headed?

Genre Study

Shared exchanges: Social media

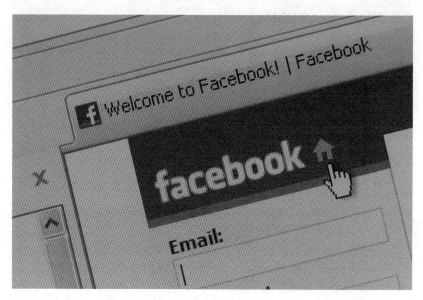

Figure 7.2   SHARED SCREENS   Screenshot of facebook. The social-media network was part of a broad set of Internet transformations in the early twenty-first century collectively known as Web 2.0. (© Gary Lucken/Alamy)

In an important sense, all media are social. By definition, a medium is something that's between people – plural. A book doesn't come to life until a writer connects with a specific reader (hopefully more than one). A big part of the appeal of radio broadcasting is the way in which it creates instant communities of listeners; half the fun of watching a TV show is talking about it with friends the next day.

But if all media are social, direct communication tends to move in one direction: between producer and consumer. To be sure, there are feedback loops like sales figures or public commentary that in effect talk back to the originators of a message, which in turn may lead them to update, improve, or otherwise renew contact. But the relationship between sender and receiver is rarely equal in terms of power, whether measured in terms of talent, technological access, or publicity.

Such an imbalance of power has not been quite as evident on the Internet. To be sure, powerful people and institutions have disproportionate influence on content and the ways it gets produced and disseminated. But individual pluck has always been a part of the story; indeed, some of the great innovations of our time, from Google to YouTube, would have been impossible without it. What may be even more striking about the Internet, however, is not who *invents* what, but who *uses* what – and the unusually high degree to which individuals have been unencumbered by private, regulatory, or other impediments beyond the mechanics of the medium itself.

This relative freedom has characterized the Internet from the very start. But its sharp increase in volume and variety at the turn of the century led to the emergence of a specific term to describe this kind of traffic: "social media," which, according to Merriam-Webster online, first entered common parlance in 2004. The dictionary defines the term as electronic communication "through which users create online communities to share information, ideas, personal messages, and other content."

One could argue that a community gets created any time two people exchange e-mail, something that began happening back when the Internet was part of the US government's Advanced Research Projects Agency (ARPA) about half a century ago. But for the purposes of this discussion, we'll define "community" as a set of more than two people – not necessarily more than two people actually commenting, but more than two people privy to an exchange. Even by this standard, social media started very early. Despite the fact that Defense Department employees understood the Internet as a tool of the workplace, it was nevertheless used for more informal kinds of exchanges.

The operative metaphor for early social-media exchanges as they evolved in the 1970s was the bulletin board: a shared virtual place where individuals could make announcements or seek information – whether jobs sought or available, cars to be bought or sold, or similar kinds of messages. Extending the metaphor further, such messages were known as "posts," as if they had been tacked onto cork. In the late 1970s a Chicago hacker named Ward Christensen invented a computerized bulletin-board system (CBBS), an important step in the movement of the concept to the private sector. In 1979, a pair of Duke University students created another system, the user network, or Usenet, that became one of the most popular bulletin boards before the advent of the World Wide Web in the 1990s.

Once Web browsers became commonplace in the mid-1990s, the bulletin-board concept could move to a whole new level. In 1995 an entrepreneur named Craig Newmark, who published an e-mail newsletter listing events in San Francisco, started craigslist, a Web site for classified advertisements. It rapidly became, and remains, one of the most popular destinations on the Internet. A big part of the reason why is that the site is decisively user-driven, whether in terms of community norms of policing content, procedures for expansion to new cities, and, in the words of the site, the "relatively non-commercial nature, public service mission, and non-corporate culture of craigslist."

Another important form of social network was the chat room, which, like a bulletin board, offered opportunities for exchanging information in real time. As their name suggests, chat rooms are also more conversational in nature. One variation on the concept is a type of site known as a multiple-user domain (MUD), some of which take the form of games. At many of these sites, users invent anonymous or fictive identities, which can become quite elaborate. Some of these identities have entire backstories; when given a visual presentation, such characters are known as avatars.

Other forms of social media were more avowedly commercial. Match.com, a dating site, was launched in 1994. The following year, Classmates.com, a site to promote connections about school alumni, went online. Both were fee-based; while they and others like them may have free features, their economic model rests on paid memberships, as well as advertising and collecting information about users that can then be rented, sold, or otherwise distributed for profit.

The most robust social networks continued to be free ones. Among the most fabled – and controversial – was Napster, a music-sharing service started in 1999 in which users could exchange entire record collections online. Napster was non-commercial; in some important sense it was *anti*-commercial, threatening the entire economic model of a recorded-music industry that depended on selling music. Legal action resulted in the shutdown of Napster in 2001. But it played an important role in shifting the music business away from material recordings to digital downloads, and a major reorganization of the industry. Once upon a time, musicians generated interest in selling records; now records are increasingly used as promotional tools to drive touring revenue.

None of these examples probably fit your notion of the paradigmatic social medium: facebook. But they share with facebook a user-driven, personalized, (initially) non-commercial character in which participants experience the company of others, often while they're actually alone. One important forerunner of facebook was sixdegrees.com, a New-York based Web site that started in 1997. Two important aspects of sixdegrees were a requirement for participants to use their actual identities, and that membership was limited to those who received an invitation from an existing member. The site never quite developed critical mass, and was defunct by 2001. It was succeeded by Friendster, a site that launched in 2003 and managed to gain several million users. Most of its current membership is in Asia, however, and it continues today principally as a gaming site.

Perhaps the most important social network of the twenty-first century prior to facebook was MySpace. The site was founded in 2003 by a cluster of programmers that included Tom Anderson, an avid Friendster user. MySpace had a more indulgent stance on authentic identity than other sites did; much of its appeal rested on the way it allowed users to fashion identities for themselves on individually created pages with lots of bells and whistles of various kinds. The site also made it exceptionally easy to set up a profile, with no prior programming knowledge required. By mid-decade MySpace had tens of millions of users, and its potential profitability was deemed so great that the Fox communications empire bought the site for over half a billion dollars. The hope was that it could generate tremendous ad revenue, one that proved to be a bust. MySpace had less cachet than some of its competitors, in part because its audience was skewed toward adolescents. The site is known today principally as a venue for musicians to showcase their work.

One variant on these models that specialized at the outset was LinkedIn, a social-networking site for professionals that was founded in 2003. Unlike other social networks, LinkedIn did not emphasize personal pleasure as the basis of its existence. It has instead prospered as a source of professional networking. LinkedIn has also stoked participation by playing the role of aggregator, fostering discussion groups, news groups, and other forms of intra-member communication.

So by the time facebook emerged in 2004, social networking already had a real history. Indeed, to a great extent the site succeeded by benefiting from the example of previous experience. As you probably know – indeed, much of the story has become a form of modern folklore, mythologized in the 2010 hit movie *The Social Network* – facebook began as a social-networking site for Harvard University students. The first attempt to organize undergraduates as the basis of a social-networking site was at Stanford in 2001. A standard rite of passage for all college students is the directory known by various names (pigbook, facebook, and so on) by which they can size each other up. A number of Ivy League students were pressing administrators to publish such directories online, but no school had done so before Mark Zuckerberg took the initiative and built one at Harvard that he called thefacebook. Zuckerberg had already gotten himself into trouble for hacking his way into university servers to fashion a crass site by which users could compare classmates by their looks; thefacebook was notable for its simplicity and the voluntary basis of membership, and it caught on quickly. (There was also some controversy in this enterprise, in that Zuckerberg was accused of pirating the idea of classmates; that dispute was settled out of court.) Within months Zuckerberg had relocated to Palo Alto, where he and his collaborators refined and expanded their reach to an ever growing number of colleges and universities, dispatching competitors via a "surrounding strategy" that involved adding schools nearby and thus encircling them. In 2006, the refashioned and now officially commercial site, by this time simply called facebook, became available to anyone over the age of 13. In 2012, the site added its one billionth user.

To a great extent, facebook was a beneficiary of what is known as the network effect, in which the sheer number of people involved in an enterprise becomes a source of value its own right. Moreover, the amount of time involved in building and maintaining a profile becomes an asset users are reluctant to relinquish or move. Facebook's simplicity made it attractive, not only in terms of its clean user interface, but also because one could literally make friends at a click. Some observers have questioned the meaning or validity of the term "friendship" to characterize such a relationship, though these so-called weak ties can be of considerable value in terms of searching for advice, self-promotion, or other purposes.

Facebook's elite origins and sleek design gave the site a sense of cache from the start, one Zuckerberg reinforced by abjuring the kitchen-sink approach of MySpace. But over time his team judiciously added features that have enhanced its appeal. Among the most important is photography, whose effect is enhanced by a tagging feature that identifies subjects in ways that are widely regarded as helpful. Facebook has also become a destination of choice for game-playing and other apps of the kind associated with Apple, a company that in recent years has been seen as a competitor, particularly given reports that facebook plans to move into Apple's hardware turf.

Like Apple, facebook has been a target of suspicion and criticism. Some of this can be attributed to rapid sentimental attachment: just about any tweaking of the site results in widespread squawking by users. But even more than Apple applications or popular Web sites, facebook is a vacuum that sucks up user information, deploying it in ways that are little understood. The company has repeatedly affirmed that users can control privacy settings, though critics regard them as difficult to find and manipulate. After many years of waiting, Zuckerberg took his creation public by offering stock to anyone who wished to buy it in 2012, putting facebook in the corporate limelight. At least initially, the attention proved awkward; the company's stock price dropped quickly, in part because of doubts that the site could monetize its obvious appeal by selling ads, particularly since so much of that appeal rests on the anti-commercial tilt in much of the social-media world. Facebook is likely to remain a lightning rod for criticism for the foreseeable future.

For all its global power, facebook remains only one prominent feature of the contemporary social-media landscape. Twitter, a so-called microblogging site launched in 2006, also generated considerable excitement. Twitter is a means for individuals to publicize their ideas or actions. Its requirement that all postings take up no more than 140 characters gives them a haiku-like quality, one well-suited to the demands of mobile computing of the kind found on smartphones. Many observers believe that the long-term viability of facebook will rest on whether or not it will be able to migrate to mobile devices as thoroughly as Twitter has.

Social networking of a more expansive kind emerged in 2005 with the arrival of YouTube, a site that allowed users to upload videos – and for viewers of those videos to post comments. Not all the content that has ended up on YouTube is user-created; indeed, the site has become a de facto repository for popular culture of the last century, dating back to silent movies. As with Napster, YouTube, which was acquired by Google for $1.65 billion in 2006, became a locus of scrutiny for copyright violations, which has partially restricted the availability of content. But it appears to have a promising future as a source of programming that can compete with (displace?) traditional television, evident in the growing panoply of "channels" it offers viewers.

By the second decade of the twenty-first century social networking had emerged as a genuinely democratic locus of popular culture in the United States, offering individuals the opportunity to interact on a basis of relative equality that was unequaled in American history. And yet that sense of democracy was fragile, limited – if not besieged – by larger forces that sought to check if not destroy it. Though they were often created in a hacker ethos of experimentation and openness, social media have resulted in a level of personal surveillance that, if revealed, would probably shock many of those who readily disclosed details of their lives wittingly and unwittingly over a period of years. Advertising, which initially had little traction in the online world, has become increasingly intrusive, inserting itself between user and content. As in so many aspects of the non-virtual world, it makes sense on the Internet to listen, and speak, selectively.

Questions to consider

1. How would you define "a social network"? What examples would you give prior to sites like facebook? Which sites today to you think best illustrate the concept?
2. Consider the way cultural forces like social class have shaped the success, and failure, of social networks.
3. How serious are the privacy concerns you sometimes hear raised about social networks? Are you personally worried about how your information is being used? Why or why not? What changes do you advocate? How easy would it be to implement them?
4. How permanent do you think facebook will be? What challengers do you see on the horizon?

Document Study

Wikipedia: The wisdom of crowds

Figure 7.3 COLLECTIVE WISDOM Home-page screenshot of Wikipedia. The crowd-sourced encyclopedia represents one of the great ongoing experiments in democratic education. (© TomBham/Alamy)

In an age of Twitter, Tumblr, and Instagram, a free online encyclopedia may not be the first thing that comes to mind when imagining a quintessential example of social media. But if, as Merriam-Webster defines it, such a site is one where "users create online communities to share information, ideas, personal messages, and other content," then Wikipedia, a site launched in 2001, falls squarely into that category. The difference is that, while many social-media sites have an educational or civic dimension, Wikipedia has had a uniquely clear – and uniquely effective – mission in serving the public good.

Having all the available knowledge of the world at one's fingertips is among the oldest of human aspirations. The ancient Greeks had a word with the general idea: "enkylios paideia," or "rounded education," a term that translates to "encyclopedia." Ever since, great world civilizations have undertaken projects to compile, edit, and publish collections of books, whether as scrolls or as bound volumes.

It was a Roman, Pliny the Elder, who presided over what has survived as the earliest known example of the genre. His *Naturalis Historia*, published in 77 CE, was a 37-volume set that attempted to cover the whole world, from art to zoology. The massive Chinese Yongle encyclopedia was even more ambitious, using thousands of scholars who coordinated their activities between 1403 and 1407. Unfortunately, much of that text perished in a fire, and surviving fragments are scattered across libraries and private collections. Perhaps the most famous modern example of an encyclopedia is the *Encyclopédie* of Denis Diderot and Jean Le Rond d'Alembert, published in France between 1751 and 1772, widely regarded as the quintessential expression of the eighteenth-century Enlightenment. In response, researchers in France's great rival, Great Britain, produced the more traditional *Encyclopædia Britannica*, first published in Scotland between 1768 and 1771. *Britannica* remains the gold standard of encyclopedias to this day.

Encyclopedia publishing proliferated in the twentieth century, particularly in the United States, where a strong emphasis on education made works like the *World Book* a staple of mid-century middle-class homes and small-town libraries. Updates and ancillary materials like yearbooks made it a lucrative corner of the publishing business.

But few aspects of the publishing industry – few aspects of any industry – were more severely upended by the arrival of personal computers and then the Internet. The first big challenge to bound encyclopedias came from Microsoft, which, newly enriched by the runaway success of its operating-system software, began branching out in different directions, encyclopedias among them. Rather than a work of dozens of volumes, Microsoft's Encarta encyclopedia stored information on disks that could be popped into a desktop computer. First unveiled in 1993 as part of a bundled package included with Microsoft Windows software, Encarta improved and became a stand-alone product by the turn of the century. Encarta was not only more compact and cheaper, but in some ways inherently better than its print competitors, particularly in regard to features like video.

Encarta's triumph proved short-lived. The proliferation of Internet access made the disks obsolete, not only because information could be accessed instantly without advance purchase, but also because online data could be updated continuously. Britannica partially recovered its economic foundation by developing an online presence – the company ceased publishing a print version in 2012 – and charging subscription fees. So did Encarta; both also generated revenue from online advertising. Encarta, however, became defunct in 2009.

The Internet was important not only in the way it purveyed knowledge, but also in the way it subverted traditional notions of intellectual property and the commodification of information. The hacker ethos of the 1970s asserted that "information wants to be free," and to that end many of the most creative minds of the era devoted themselves to developing open-source products for the common good. One of the most important figures in this movement was Richard Stallman, a computer programmer who in the 1980s helped pioneer the concept of "copyleft": work explicitly premised on rejecting private profit implicit in the term "copyright." Stallman crafted a "general public license" (GPL) to allow free access to such works and prevent them from being copyrighted by unscrupulous individuals who might try to claim ownership of works in the public domain.

For most of the early Internet era, copyleft was focused on programming. But there were people who were also interested in the content side of the equation. Among the most important was a Portland programmer named Ward Cunningham, who was intrigued by an Apple note-organizing program called HyperCard, which he thought had tremendous potential. (Apple, more focused on hardware, never did that much with it.) In the mid-1990s Cunningham used HyperCard principles, as well as those of Internet pioneer Vannevar Bush, to fashion a new software program he named "WikiWikiWeb." (Wiki is a Hawaiian word for "quick"; it was also the name of a Honolulu shuttle bus that inspired Cunningham.) The program made it exceptionally easy for users to create, augment, or revise a database of material.

In the late 1990s, a pair of entrepreneurs named Jimmy Wales and Larry Sanger had formed a company to create Nupedia, a free encyclopedia with articles written by recognized experts in their respective fields. But the process was going slowly. To speed it along, the pair decided to use wikis, or less authoritative pieces, from volunteers as an intermediary step in building Nupedia. But the level of wiki activity was so rapid and strong that the tail soon began wagging the dog. In 2001, the two launched Wikipedia, an open-source encyclopedia whose content and maintenance relied on self-appointed volunteers. Almost immediately, Wikipedia became one of the great success stories of the Internet, and to this day remains among the most frequently accessed Web sites in the world.

The idea of a major reference work to which anybody can contribute may seem strange, even counterintuitive – Sanger stepped aside in 2002, uneasy about the decentralized shape Wikipedia was taking – but it is not unprecedented. Work on the great *Oxford English Dictionary* began in 1859 with an open call to the public to provide definitions and meanings for words, which resulted in 1000 contributions a day during the peak of the process. Of course the *OED* had editors and intermediaries of various kinds. One might plausibly think that a publication to which anyone can contribute by registering to the site would be a recipe for chaos; indeed, even the creators of the site did not believe it could be self-regulating, which is why they initially viewed it as ancillary to Nupedia. But Wikipedia quickly demonstrated a phenomenon known as "the wisdom of the crowd," in which the biases or quirks of individual opinion tend to cancel each other out over time, yielding collective discernment. If an unwitting or malicious falsehood surfaces in a particular entry, it's typically only a matter of time before it gets corrected by another writer or a site administrator, and a running set of revisions is preserved for every article. This belief has a name among Wikepedians: "eventualism." No human enterprise is perfect, and, as I'll discuss momentarily, this one isn't, either. (Actually, not all the contributions to the site *are* by humans – administrators allow some automated programs, otherwise known as "bots," to update or add data like census records.) But Wikipedia has been extraordinarily successful in leveraging the good will and intelligence of a vast number of people, who volunteer their skills and time for a cause larger than themselves.

Over time, and under Wales's low-key leadership, Wikipedia has evolved some basic principles, five of which are central:

1. Wikipedia is an encyclopedia (i.e., not a source of original research).
2. Wikipedia is written from a neutral point of view.
3. Wikipedia is free content that anyone can edit, use, modify, or distribute.
4. Editors should interact with each other in a respectful and civil manner.
5. Wikipedia does not have firm rules.

These policies are part of a broader code of conduct that governs the site, which includes protocols on how disputes are to be handled. Site administrators are nominated and elected by Wikipedians themselves. The overall ethos encourages participation; one of the most important mottoes of the site is "be bold."

To be sure, there are problems. Coverage of topics on Wikipedia can be uneven; articles on popular culture, perhaps unsurprisingly, tend to be more detailed than those on other kinds of topics. Errors of fact do slip in, though perhaps not as many as some might expect; an oft-cited 2005 study by *Nature* magazine found an average of four errors in each Wikipedia article, compared with three in Britannica.

More problematic are practical jokes and malicious entries. Former White House aide John Seigenthaler was not amused in 2005 when his anonymously written Wikipedia profile falsely suggested that he was involved in the murder of his former boss, 1968 presidential candidate Robert F. Kennedy. An investigation by Daniel Brandt, founder of the site Wikipedia Watch, tracked down the offender, who ultimately apologized (the site banned anonymous entries and implemented new rules governing entries on living persons as a result of the scandal). Other pranksters wrote an entry about an apparently fictitious organization, the Gay Niggers Association, which was eventually removed. Other times, entries become a little too contentious. The Wikipedia article on "George W. Bush" was subject to so many conflicting edits during his presidency that the article had to be frozen for a time. However laudable it might be, neutrality may not always be possible.

There's a general perception that Wikipedia has gotten better with time – more complete and better sourced, with links that can take you to those sources directly – but the site continues to have its skeptics. Even those teachers who consider it reasonably accurate worry that the site is too convenient, a first resort for students who should be researching their work more thoroughly, and an all too tempting source of plagiarism. In 2007, Middlebury College grabbed national headlines when the school's history department banned Wikipedia as an acceptable citation for student essays. It nevertheless seems safe to say that the site continued to be consulted, however secretly or silently.

I'll come clean: Wikipedia was a valuable resource in the writing of this book. My policy in drafting it was to fact-check any assertion I based on the site with at least one outside source, though I can't recall a case where I was unable to verify something at Wikipedia that I considered relevant to my research. Actually, the site was less important to me as a source of information in its own right than as an example of how to distill information I had already collected, or simply to review the facts as I had learned them elsewhere. I salute this quintessential expression of the Internet's democratic culture, which continues to survive, even thrive, at a time when democracy seems to be in decay in so many precincts of our national life.

Questions to consider

1. What are some of the ways encyclopedias have been created? What purposes do they serve?
2. What mades Wikipedia better than its competitors? In what ways is it vulnerable to abuse?
3. How does Wikipedia figure in your own academic life? What are its limits?

Further Reading

The best recent introduction to modern computing culture is Johnny Ryan's *A History of the Internet and the Digital Future* (London: Reaktion Books, 2010). Paul Ceruzzi offers a more comprehensive account in *A History of Modern Computing* (2nd ed., Cambridge, MA: Massachusetts Institute of Technology Press, 2003). See also Martin Campbell-Kelly and William Aspray, *Computer: A History of the Information Age Machine* (2nd ed., Boulder, CO: Westview Press, 2004).

On transistors and the birth of Silicon Valley, see David A. Kaplan, *The Silicon Boys and Their Valley of Dreams* (New York: HarperCollins, 2000). Katie Hafner and Matthew Lyons capture hacker culture in their now classic *Where Wizards Stay Up Late: The Origins of the Internet* (New York: Touchstone, 1998). See also Stephen Segaller, *Nerds 2.0.1: A Brief History of the Internet* (New York: TV Books, 1998). Walter Isaacson renders the definitive version of Steve Jobs's life in his biography of the same name (New York: Simon & Schuster, 2011). Tim Berners-Lee recounts his pivotal work in *Weaving the Web: The Original Design and Ultimate Destiny of the World Wide Web* (New York: HarperBusiness, 2000).

Important books on the emergence of Web 2.0 include Ken Auletta, *Googled: The End of the World as We Know It* (New York: Penguin, 2010), David Kirkpatrick, *The Facebook Effect: The Inside Story of the Company that Is Connecting the World* (New York: Simon & Schuster, 2011), and Andrew Lih, *The Wikipedia Revolution: How a*

Bunch of Nobodies Created the World's Greatest Encyclopedia (New York: Hyperion, 2009).

Perhaps the most thoughtful analyst of the impact of digital media on everyday life is MIT sociologist Sherry Turkle. See her noted trilogy, *The Second Self: Computers and the Human Spirit* (1985; Cambridge, MA: MIT Press, 2005), *Life on the Screen: Identity in the Age of the Internet* (New York: Simon & Schuster, 1995), and *Alone Together: Why We Expect More from Technology and Less from Each Other* (New York: Basic Books, 2011).

Index

Note: page numbers in *italics* refer to figures.

A Short History of the Modern Media, First Edition. Jim Cullen.
© 2014 Jim Cullen. Published 2014 by John Wiley & Sons, Ltd.